FAMILY POLICY AND DISABILITY

This book explores the status and scope of family policies related to households of children with disability, providing an in-depth, evidence-based review of legal, programmatic issues. It includes a discussion of the gaps between family needs and contemporary family policies in the United States and European countries, as demonstrated in these households' surveys. In addition, the volume offers a comparative analysis of cash benefits, tax credits and deductions, and in-kind provisions between the United States and select European countries (UK, France and Sweden).

Most importantly, this book identifies and continues the discussion regarding the critical role of family-centered policies, as expressed in the United Nations Convention on the Rights of Persons with Disabilities (CRPD), as well as the future of family policy toward families of children with disability at a time of economic crisis.

Arie Rimmerman is Richard Crossman Professor of Social Welfare and Social Planning, founding Dean of Social Welfare and Health Sciences, and head of the School of Social Work at the University of Haifa, Israel. He is the author of *Social Inclusion of People with Disabilities* (2012). Aside from his academic work he has served as an adviser to ministers of labor and welfare in Israel and to public committees on disability policies in Israel, Europe and the United States.

CAMBRIDGE DISABILITY LAW AND POLICY SERIES

Edited by Peter Blanck and Robin Paul Malloy

The Disability Law and Policy series examines these topics in interdisciplinary and comparative terms. The books in the series reflect the diversity of definitions, causes, and consequences of discrimination against persons with disability while illuminating fundamental themes that unite countries in their pursuit of human rights laws and policies to improve the social and economic status of persons with disability. The series contains historical, contemporary and comparative scholarship crucial to identifying individual, organizational, cultural, attitudinal and legal themes necessary for the advancement of disability law and policy.

The book topics covered in the series also are reflective of the new moral and political commitment by countries throughout the world toward equal opportunity for persons with disability in such areas as employment, housing, transportation, rehabilitation and individual human rights. The series will thus play a significant role in informing policymakers, researchers and citizens of issues central to disability rights and disability antidiscrimination policies. The series grounds the future of disability law and policy as a vehicle for ensuring that those living with disability participate as equal citizens of the world.

Books in the Series

Ruth Colker, *When is separate unequal? A disability perspective*, 2009

Larry M. Logue and Peter Blanck, *Race, ethnicity, and disability: veterans and benefits in post–Civil War America*, 2010

Lisa Vanhala, *Making rights a reality? Disability rights activists and legal mobilization*, 2010

Alicia Ouellette, *Bioethics and disability: toward a disability-conscious bioethics*, 2011

Eilionoir Flynn, *From rhetoric to action: implementing the UN Convention on the Rights of Persons with Disabilities*, 2011

Isabel Karpin and Kristin Savell, *Perfecting pregnancy: law, disability, and the future of reproduction*, 2012

Arie Rimmerman, *Social inclusion of people with disabilities: national and international perspectives*, 2012

Andrew Power, Janet E. Lord and Allison S. deFranco, *Active citizenship & disability: implementing the personalisation of support for persons with disabilities*, 2012

Lisa Schur, Douglas Kruse and Peter Blanck, *People with disabilities: sidelined or mainstreamed?*, 2013

Eliza Varney, *Disability and information technology: a comparative study in media regulation*, 2013

Peter Blanck, *eQuality: The struggle for Web accessibility by persons with cognitive disabilities*, 2014

Arie Rimmerman, *Family policy and disability*, 2015

Family Policy and Disability

Arie Rimmerman
University of Haifa

CAMBRIDGE
UNIVERSITY PRESS

CAMBRIDGE
UNIVERSITY PRESS

32 Avenue of the Americas, New York, NY 10013-2473, USA

Cambridge University Press is part of the University of Cambridge.

It furthers the University's mission by disseminating knowledge in the pursuit of education, learning and research at the highest international levels of excellence.

www.cambridge.org
Information on this title: www.cambridge.org/9781107049178

First published 2015

A catalog record for this publication is available from the British Library.

ISBN 978-1-107-04917-8 Hardback

CONTENTS

Preface . . . . *page* ix
Acknowledgments xii

1. **Introduction** 1
2. **Family policy: a conceptual base** 8
3. **Families of children with disability: core needs** 34
4. **Family policies related to children and youth with disability in the United States** 62
5. **Family policies and disability in selected European countries** 92
6. **Assessment of family disability policies** 128
7. **Comparative family policies of the United States and European countries** 148
8. **The UN Convention of the Rights of Persons with Disabilities (CRPD) and family policies** 175
9. **Closing remarks** 196

Index 205

PREFACE

In the postscript of my recent book, *Social inclusion of people with disabilities: national and international perspectives*,[1] I highlighted the central role that the family plays in providing socialization, support, stability and opportunities for social inclusion. This is a particular challenge for a family of a child with severe disability, which requires coping with extra demands in order to provide the care needed. There is no doubt that this responsibility takes its toll on personal and marital life, is a financial burden and curtails employment opportunities. In my earlier book, I noted that government policies are primarily aimed toward individuals with disability, with those targeting family protection or support being the exception.

I have been interested in studying families of children with disability throughout my academic career in social work research and social policy. I have written about the intentions of families to seek out-of-home placement in the late 1980s and early 1990s.[2] The overwhelming belief then was that the main reason was personal, and that the inability of families, primarily parents, to cope with ongoing stress induced them to apply for placement. Critical resources include financial and professional assistance for associated medical problems and family social support.[3] I do believe today that one of the main reasons that

[1] Arie Rimmerman, *Social inclusion of people with disabilities: National and international perspectives*. (Cambridge: Cambridge University Press, 2012).

[2] See Arie Rimmerman, "Alternatives to institutions and family support." In *The human rights of persons with intellectual disabilities: Different but equal*. Edited by Stanley S. Herr, Lawrence O. Gostin and Harold Hongju Koh (Oxford: Oxford University Press, 2003), 415–28.

[3] Gwynnyth Llewellyn et al., "Out-of-home placement of school-age children with disabilities and high support needs," *Journal of Applied Research in Intellectual Disabilities* 18 (2005),

parents apply for out-of-home placement is the lack of family-support policies that would help parents to balance the demands of caring for the child with disability and the needs of other family members, sharing workload and responsibility, and integrating the child into the everyday world.

The introduction of disability rights legislation in the early 1990s, and particularly the social model, shifts the attention of social scientists to the range of inequalities that families with children with disability experience as compared to those without disability.[4] One of the outcomes of my involvement in family policy research was a joint study with Susan L. Parish, Michal Grinstein-Weiss and others, analyzing participants of the 2001 *Survey of Income and Program Participation* (SIPP) to determine the extent of disability-based net worth and income gap among US households.[5] The findings demonstrated that households with a member with disability had substantially reduced net worth and income compared to households without adults with disability, regardless of family structure. This involvement did not end there; I have been asked by Israeli Central Statistical Bureau to lead the first Israeli household study on disability, as well as by Ministry of Welfare and Social Affairs, to survey support needs of families of children with intellectual disability.

Two recent events inspired me while writing this book – the first was a conference held by advocacy organization KESHER to promote new legislation of behalf of Israeli families of children and adults with disability, and the second was a conference on the implementation of the UN Convention of the Rights of Persons with Disabilities (CRPD) in Israel, held at the University of Haifa.[6] The KESHER conference

1–6. In this particular study, the researchers explored the relationship between family life variables and out-of-home placement tendency for families of school-age children with disabilities and high support needs. Out-of-home placement tendency was associated with three interrelated family life variables: (i) difficulty balancing the demands of caring and the needs of other family members; (ii) sharing workload and responsibility; and (iii) integrating the child into the everyday world.

4 Monica Dowling and Linda Dolan, "Families with children with disability – inequalities and the social model," *Disability and Society* 16 (2001), 21–35.

5 Susan L. Parish et al., "Assets and income: Disability-based disparities in the US," *Social Work Research* 34 (2010), 71–82.

6 KESHER is an advocacy organization that aims to strengthen the status of parents and families with a disabled child, promoting their rights and the utilization of these rights, and developing further services that will benefit and empower them. This NGO provides a range

debated the need to enact new legislation for families, to supplement unmet needs in the current social protection legislation and to modify tax regulations. My lecture, which discussed current European comparative support policies aimed at families of children with disability, was based on this book's Chapter 7, "Comparative family policies of the United States and European countries," while Chapter 8, "The UN Convention of the Rights of Persons with Disabilities (CRPD) and family policies," is based on my presentation at the University of Haifa on the CRPD. The thoughtful discussion afterwards convinced me to add a closing section on the future of family policy and disability in times of economic crisis.

I hope that the book will provide a comprehensive and insightful understanding of governments' response to families of children with disability and, in particular, present the family policies provided in Western countries to respond to their needs and concerns.

Arie Rimmerman
Haifa, Israel

of services for special families, including a center for information, guidance and advocacy, groups offering support and parental guidance, as well as groups for additional family members (siblings), and demographics. Their conference, held on January 30, 2014, in Kiryat Ono, discussed the need for supplemental legislation for families. The one-day International Conference on Implementation of the UN Convention of the Rights of Persons with Disabilities (CRPD) was held at the University of Haifa on February 4, 2014.

ACKNOWLEDGMENTS

This book was made possible by the generous and consistent support of my research staff at the Richard Crossman Chair of Social Welfare and Social Planning at the University of Haifa. I am grateful to colleagues and graduate students who share with me my thoughts about the book and have offered their comments and suggestions. I have been fortunate to learn a great deal from my recent contacts with KESHER regarding their efforts to advocate for new family-support legislation.

Special thanks to Susan Parish and Michal Grinstein-Weiss, then at the University of North Carolina at Chapel Hill, for involving me in their secondary analysis of the 2001 Survey of Income and Program Participation (SIPP) to determine the extent of disability-based net worth and income gap among US households.[1] The end result was not only a joint article but a recognition of the importance of assets and income status among families with members with disability. I am thankful to Gerard Quinn for his insightful thoughts about the CRPD, and particularly Articles 12 and 19, which were helpful in the writing of Chapter 8. I would like to thank my colleagues with whom I informally discussed some of the ideas examined in the book. Finally, I am grateful to my family for facilitating this important project, and in particular my wife Shula for her tremendous support.

[1] Susan L. Parish et al., "Assets and income: Disability-based disparities in the US," *Social Work Research* 34 (2010), 71–82.

1 INTRODUCTION

Over the past three decades, there have been a number of attempts to encourage a family perspective in policymaking.[1] Despite these endeavors, there has been no sustained effort to analyze policy from such a perspective, and few groups consistently represent family interests. There is no doubt that the social status of people with disabilities has changed since the early nineties, as traditional medical and social welfare approaches have been replaced by social-functional and human rights perspectives. One of the core questions is whether this transition has incorporated responses to concerns raised by families of children and adolescents with disability. Family policy addresses families of children younger than eighteen years or those whose offspring are enrolled in full-time education, not having left the parental household or not being married or in a relationship.[2] Kamerman and Kahn defined it broadly – "everything that government does to and for the family."[3] These policies encompass four explicit functions: family formation, economic support, child-rearing and caregiving.[4] Despite the pivotal

1 See, for example, Thomas Bahle, "Family policy patterns in the enlarged EU," Jens Alber, Tony Fahey and Chiara Saraceno (eds.), *Handbook of quality of life in the enlarged European Union* (London: Routledge, 2007), 47–73; Linda Hantrais, *Family policy matters: responding to family change in Europe* (Bristol: Policy, 2004).

2 Theodora Ooms, "Families and government: implementing a family perspective in public policy," *Social Thought* 16 (1990), 61–78.

3 Sheila B. Kamerman and Alfred J. Kahn, "Families and the idea of family policy," Sheila B. Kamerman and Alfred J. Kahn (eds.), *Family policy: government and families in fourteen countries* (New York: Columbia University Press, 1978) 3.

4 David Blankenhorn, "American family dilemmas," David Blankenhorn, Steven Bayme and Jean Bethke Elshtain (eds.), *Rebuilding the nest: A new commitment to the American family* (Milwaukee, WI: Family Service America, 1990) 3–25.

role of families in our society, policymakers tend to make decisions through individual lenses rather than from the perspective of families in which most individuals reside.[5] A similar reality is seen in the disability area, with most of the policies aimed toward children or adults with a specific impairment, responding primarily to their medical and social welfare needs. Although families efficiently perform several important functions within society in ways that no other institution can either do or do as well, governments tend to view them as secondary to their policy decisions and allocation of resources.

This book aims to explore the status and scope of family policies related to households with disabled children and to provide an in-depth review of legal and programmatic aspects of these policies at the national level. In addition, the book presents and discusses conceptual, legal and evidence-based differences in family-centered policies between the United States and European countries, particularly the United Kingdom, France and Sweden. Europe has two different models, France and Sweden with generous policies, and the United Kingdom with a piecemeal approach. Finally, the book continues the discussion regarding the critical role of family-centered policies as expressed in the Convention on the Rights of Persons with Disabilities (CRPD). This important international treaty challenges current domestic policies and requires countries to apply practices and entitlements related to families of disabled children.

Chapter 1 provides the reader with the guidelines and structure of the book. Chapter 2 introduces the conceptual base of family policy and demonstrates and discusses US and European core family policies. If the first part of the chapter intends to provide conceptual base, the second introduces US and selected European family policies and discusses major differences between the two. The chapter also presents the diversity of family policies within Europe, as with France and Sweden, which have probably the most progressive explicit family policies, and the United Kingdom with more conservative and regulated implicit policies in the middle. The chapter ends with reference to family

[5] Linda L. Hass and Steven K. Wisensale (eds.), *Families and social policy: National and international perspectives* (Binghamton, NY: Haworth, 2006).

disability policy and raises two core questions: does family policy intend to cover all families, including those with children with disability, and is there a need for a specific family disability policy or can it be added as a supplement? These questions will be responded to in the next chapters in discussing US and European family policies toward families of children with disability.

Chapter 3 introduces the needs of families of children with disability and their personal, marital and financial challenges. The focus here is on the financial burden; because childhood disabilities have direct and indirect economic costs on the family and society, the burden is strongly linked to type and severity of disability. Chapter 3 demonstrates ways of measuring direct monetary costs as well as indirect or out-of-pocket costs. The chapter also discusses both the difficulties in estimating reductions in parents' ability to sustain paid employment and the cost of the unavailability of adequate childcare. These estimates vary from one country to another and greatly depend on explicit and implicit policies. Aside from the financial burden on families, the chapter reviews core surveys on families' met and unmet needs. Finally, there is an extensive review of the demonstrated needs of parents of children with autistic spectrum disorder (ASD), medical complexities (CMC) and mental illness and their vulnerability to considering out-of-home placement.

Chapter 4 characterizes US family policy and describes the in-kind benefits with modest and inconsistent cash benefits to some low-income families and the tax benefits to the middle and upper classes. There is an extensive review of these services, primarily Supplemental Security Income (SSI) and Medicaid, as well as the Individuals with Disabilities Education Act (IDEA), formerly called P.L. 94–142 or the Education for All Handicapped Children Act of 1975.

The chapter discusses three themes that reflect family policies in this area. The first introduces the division between families with middle-high to high income regarding provisions for their children with disability. The second theme addresses the Americans with Disability Act (ADA) and the rights of children with disability and their parents' to accessibility and inclusion in society. Finally, the chapter discusses the progressive legislation of IDEA and the right of parents to be informed and participate in the educational decision-making process.

Chapter 5 reviews and discusses family disability policy in three European countries – the United Kingdom, France and Sweden – based on the Esping-Andersen's Comparative Macro-Sociology of Welfare States. The United Kingdom represents the liberal and social democratic approaches of welfare state; French policy is a mixture of liberal and conservative corporatist principles, while Sweden is a typical social democratic welfare state.[6] The chapter discusses the United Kingdom's mixed family policy and its ambitious plans such as its Aiming High for Disabled Children policy, with particular focus on cash benefit policies and special provisions for children with disability and their families.[7] French social insurance policy and comprehensive childcare system is discussed with respect to the gradual transition from universal to tailor-made family policy. The chapter ends with Sweden's comprehensive social insurance coverage for families of young children including means-tested supplements for those with disabled children (maintenance support and housing allowance, and care allowance for disabled children).[8] Sweden still looks like a family policy leader with an impressive array of benefits to children with disability and families, though less so than in the past.

Chapter 6 introduces assessment instruments used to examine family policies provisions and family disability policy in particular. It presents four types of assessment including recipients' profiles, government entitlements and their costs, access and utilization, and impact of certain entitlements or social rights on recipients. Unfortunately, there are few studies on families of children with disability or entitlements and issues of access, utilization and impact. Most of the studies try to establish common and standard disability measures for children's disability and characterize socioeconomic needs of their parents. The

[6] Esping-Andersen's "typology of welfare state" is presented in Gøsta Esping-Andersen, *Three worlds of welfare capitalism* (Princeton, NJ: Princeton University Press, 1990).

[7] Patricia Sloper, Bryony Beresford and Parvaneh Rabiee, "Every Child Matters outcomes: what do they mean for disabled children and young people?" *Children in Society* 23 (2009), 265–78.

[8] There are two general allowances: *Barnbidrag or* child allowance and *Tillfällig föräldrapenning id vård av barn,* which provides parental benefit, temporary parental benefit, pregnancy benefit, child pension and pension rights for childcare years. In addition, there are three universal pieces of legislation, the Social Services Act (1982), the Health and Medical Services Act (1983) and Sweden's Education Act 1985.

chapter reviews efforts made by the Organisation for Economic Co-operation and Development (OECD), as well as other international bodies, to compare countries and states with respect to selected entitlements or social rights, particularly regarding their cost. The same applies to studies that assess the impact of certain policies on families of children with disability or assess accessibility and utilization issues.

The most common comparison presented is cross-country family policies by entitlements or social rights. It provides insightful information demonstrating differences between the United States and European countries and within those countries. Secondary are accessibility and utilization studies examining implementation of certain entitlements or UK and US provisions. Finally, the chapter discusses the quantitative and qualitative impacts of certain social entitlements on children with disability and their families. Most of these studies used secondary data and tended to track changes in household measures such as household income and employment, rather than children's progress or well-being.

Chapter 7 analyzes US and European policies toward families of children with disability as reflected by comparative analyses of their cash benefits, tax credits and deductions and the in-kind provisions of the United States, the United Kingdom, France and Sweden. The chapter introduces an interesting comparison between two central cash benefits schemes, the US Supplemental Security Income (SSI) and the UK Disability Living Allowance (DLA), which provides insights on the substantial differences between the two countries. Both programs are intended to assist with the extra cost of caring for their children with disability. However, the SSI is means tested and geared toward low-income families, whereas the DLA is non–means tested and is provided based on severity and mobility elements. There are additional comparisons related to tax credits and deduction and in-kind provisions, demonstrating that Sweden and France provide marginal tax credits and deductions, the United Kingdom moderate tax credits or deductions, while the United States provides more tax deduction opportunities than the rest of the countries. Finally, the chapter demonstrates the differences in services infrastructure among these countries and explains the linkage between cash benefits and tax credit and deduction with in-kind provisions.

Chapter 8 presents and discusses the place of the family in the CRPD, examining whether this treaty supports family rights or regards them just as a supplement to members with disability in the family. This debate parallels the discussion about the centrality of family policy in most of the developed countries and those between conservatives and liberals regarding the role of the state in providing rights and services. The first section provides an overview of five explicit articles concerning the family (8, 16, 22, 23, 28) and eleven articles (5, 6, 7, 9, 12, 18, 19, 24, 25, 30, 33) implicitly requiring a mainstreaming of the family dimension in order to ensure effective implementation. The second part is basically an analysis of gaps and conflicts between the CRPD's explicit and implicit articles related to family policy and US, UK and European countries' domestic legislation. Obviously, the most fascinating debate has been around ratification of the Convention in the United States, where conservative advocacy groups raised concerns that US ratification may give governments, and not US parents, the right to make educational and treatment-related decisions for their disabled children. On the other hand, the Obama administration defused these concerns, stating that current US legislation supports parents' rights and that there will not be any major change. At the center of the debate is Article 7(2) concerning the debate about protecting the best interests of the child with disability and the fear of homeschooling advocates that the Convention would undermine their parental right to educate their children.

The chapter also discusses the approach of European countries to the Convention, which is basically favorable, with the European Union (EU) ratifying the CRPD just weeks after the European Commission (EC) published the European Disability Strategy 2010–2020.

In "Closing remarks" (Chapter 9), the author shares with the reader five themes that reflect his insights and a future projection of family policy and disability. The first theme discusses the conceptual basis of family policy, particularly the differentiation between explicit and implicit policies and their relevance to families of children with disability. The second theme identifies the gaps between family needs as demonstrated in surveys of households and contemporary family policies. The third theme provides insights into the differences between the policies of the United States and three European countries toward families of children with disability and within European countries. The fourth theme discusses the CRPD, in particular articles that touch upon family issues and family policies. Finally, the author discusses the future of family policy toward families of children with disability in times of economic crisis.

2 FAMILY POLICY: A CONCEPTUAL BASE

In the past fifty years, the family has undergone significant transformation. In many Western countries, the extended family has almost disappeared, and the traditional two-parent family has become much less widespread. Families have seen more significant changes in the labor market, and as a consequence more mothers are employed. These changes, including in education, longevity and lifestyle, have had remarkable impacts on housing, pensions, health care and childcare. Regardless of these changes, families are central to our existence and play a valuable role in society by promoting socialization, economic productivity, social competence and, indirectly, additional merits.[1] Interestingly, they are considered to be an important political asset by local and national politicians and endorsed by all political parties regardless of their ideological platform.[2]

There are, primarily, different ways of looking at families, most of them relating to structural or functional features. The structural approach views the family according to the composition of its membership as related to blood, marriage or legal bond, such as adoption or sharing a household. Structural definitions of family also focus on the relationships that create social bonds between members. Important bonds are created by communication, power and affection, as well as

[1] For comprehensive coverage of the role of families in society, see Karen Bogenschneider and Thomas J. Corbett, "Building enduring policies in the 21st century: the past as prologue," Marilyn Coleman and Lawrence H. Ganong (eds.), *Handbook of contemporary families: Considering the past, contemplating the future* (Thousand Oaks, CA: Sage, 2004), 451–68.

[2] Karen Bogenschneider, *Family policy matters: how policymaking affects families and what professionals can do* (New York: Taylor & Francis, 2002), 24.

the daily work and leisure of family members. Families may be structured by such characteristics as gender, age and generation, as well as by their connections to the outside world. These structures are also useful for distinguishing families from other kinds of social groups and organizations. A second way to look at families is on the basis of functional elements, centering on the importance of human reproduction and nurturing dependent children, including those with disabilities, for a relatively long period of time. The functional approach tends to understand the relationship within the family and to identify dysfunctional types.

It is evident that these types of definitions have their own limitations. For example, the structural definition excludes homosexual partners and cohabitating couples who are not related by birth, marriage or adoption but who nevertheless fulfill family-like functions. Therefore, there is no consensus on a single definition or whether both structural and functional definitions are needed.[3] A close look at the US Constitution shows the family is not mentioned or recognized as a legal institution, just the individual.[4]

The most desirable approach is to define families according to the particular issue involved.[5] Aside from the difficulty in defining family, Theodora Ooms claims that "Families are everyone's concern, but nobody's responsibility."[6] According to Patricia Strach, the family plays an important role in American politics, particularly in campaigns and slogans, but is often viewed as part of the private realm.[7] A similar view is commonly held in the United Kingdom and other European countries, where the family is seen as a private entity and separate from public life.

[3] See Karen Bogenschneider, *Family policy matters: how policymaking affects families and what professionals can do*, 3rd ed. (New York: Routledge, 2014).

[4] Theodora Ooms, *Toward more perfect unions: putting marriage on the public agenda* (Washington, DC: Family Impact Seminar, 1998).

[5] Phyllis Moen and Alvin L. Schorr, "Families and social policy," Marvin B. Sussman and Suzanne K. Steinmetz (eds.), *Handbook of marriage and the family* (New York: Plenum, 1987), 795–813.

[6] See Theodora Ooms, "Families and government: implementing a family perspective in public policy," *Social Thought* 15 (1990), 77.

[7] Patricia Strach, *All in the family: the private roots of American public policy* (Stanford: Stanford University Press, 2007), 1–17.

The twentieth century saw significant changes in the demography of Europe and the United States associated with the need to redefine roles and the structure of families. Among the notable changes were increased longevity, deferred age of marriage, lower fertility, increased divorce and declining existence of extended families. The early twenty-first century is characterized by even greater family diversity; the "traditional" breadwinner/homemaker family no longer constitutes the main family form or the only normative environment in which children are born and raised.[8] Instead, single parenthood, one-person households, unmarried and same-sex cohabitation and remarried families have become more prevalent and are increasingly recognized as suitable living arrangements.

Family-related regulations and provisions existed in civil law and in many social policies long before explicit family policies were formulated. Nevertheless, there is an impression that policies toward families, in particular in Europe, have been changed over time in response to changing concerns about family life.[9] Early family policies focused on the provision of children's allowances and benefits to increase fertility rates and reduce the costs of child-rearing. The increasing rates of divorce, cohabitation and single parenthood have weakened the traditional bonds of family life, requiring different government responses. The role of the state has expanded in helping to address these issues by offering a wide range of public measures, which are reflected in the growth of social welfare provisions for cash and in-kind benefits, including family allowances, household help, parental leave, lone-parent cash benefits and payments for childcare.

There is disagreement among scholars as to whether family policies are restricted to families and children or also include adults and aging populations. However, it appears that most of those policies aimed toward adults and aging populations are family-support policies. Children may be distinguished from other groups of the population

[8] See Bahira Sherif Trask, *Globalization and families: accelerated systemic social change* (New York: Springer, 2010). The book argues that globalization has had profound implications for understanding social life and in particular gender ideologies, work-family relationships and conceptualizations of children and youth. Therefore, there is a need to make the interplay between globalization and families a primary focus.

[9] See Neil Gilbert, "Motherhood, work, and family policy," Jill Berrick and Neil Gilbert (eds.), *Raising children: emerging need, modern risks and social responses* (New York: Oxford University Press, 2008), 98–115.

using an age criterion (for example, younger than 18 years) or other criteria, such as participating in full-time education, remaining in the parental household or not being married or in a relationship.

DEFINITIONS

In spite of growing recognition of family matters, there is lack of agreement as to how to define "family policy." It is evident that this term is at the center of controversies over family values, and in particular the tension between individualism and communitarianism ("familism"), particularly in the United States and the United Kingdom. A search of the literature reveals that there are different definitions varying in their scope, source, aim and content.[10]

In terms of scope, Kamerman and Kahn offer a very broad definition – "everything that government does to and for the family."[11] However, their definition is too inclusive and fails to set clear boundaries for the term. In addition, the definition fails to differentiate between policies that are aimed at families and those that touch on them. Phyllis Moen and Alvin L. Schorr phrase family policy as "a widely agreed-on set of objectives for families, toward the realization of which the state (and other major social institutions) deliberately shapes programs and policies."[12] Interestingly, their definition has been perceived as too narrow and unacceptable by stockholders regarding a piece of legislation or policy.[13]

The other dilemmas concerning family policy are whether to focus only on government bodies or to also include those issues related to employers and nonprofit organizations, and whether family policy

[10] Joan Aldous and Wilfried Dumon, "Family policy in the 1980s: controversy and consensus," *Journal of Marriage and the Family* 52 (1990), 1136–51; Karen Bogenschneider, *Family policy matters: how policymaking affects families and what professionals can do*, 2nd ed. (Mahwah, NJ: Lawrence Elbaum 2006), 21–2.

[11] Sheila B. Kamerman and Alfred J. Kahn, "Trends, issues, and possible lessons," Sheila B. Kamerman and Alfred J. Kahn (eds.), *Child Care, parental leave, and the under 3s: Policy innovation in Europe* (New York: Auburn House, 1991), 3.

[12] Moen and Schorr, "Families and social policy."

[13] Eileen Trzcinski, "An ecological perspective on family policy: a conceptual and philosophical framework. Special issue: Dimensions of family policy: research, education and application," *Journal of Family and Economic Issues* 16 (1995), 7–33.

should be restricted to economic aspects, to functioning, including child-rearing and caregiving, or both.

A pragmatic approach has been offered by Sheila B. Kamerman: a differentiation between explicit and implicit family policies.[14] Although this distinction between explicit and implicit policy has not been embraced by all, it is more widely accepted than other definitions. Explicit family policy views family as a whole and aims at protecting, promoting and strengthening families.[15] It touches on family income security policies, employment-related benefits for working parents, maternal and child health policies and childcare policies. On the other hand, implicit family policies are not geared primarily toward families but may have important consequences for children and their families as well. Therefore, implicit policies can refer to families as a criterion for determining benefits or service, a means for achieving other policy goals or as an instrument to administer eligibility for benefits or specific provisions.[16] Based on this distinction, it is probably feasible to compare countries on the basis of their explicit and implicit family policies. However, this distinction seems much more complicated when comparing countries with mixed approaches, those that are in transition from implicit to explicit family policy or those transitioning from explicit to implicit policies. Another aspect that requires reference is whether family policies address the family as a unit or focus on the needs of individual family members and only indirectly affect the family as such.[17]

THE DIMENSIONS OF FAMILY POLICY

Family policy is seen as a *domain*, covering four core family functions[18]: (a) family creation policy aimed toward marriage, divorce, adoption

[14] See Sheila B. Kamerman, "Families and family policies: developing a holistic family policy agenda," *Hong Kong Journal of Pediatrics* 14 (2009), 115–21.

[15] Strach, *All in the family*.

[16] The provision of financial aid to students based on the economic status of their parents or to promote employee productivity by providing family-friendly childcare arrangements.

[17] Chiara Saraceno, "Family policies: concepts, goals and instruments" (Carlo Alberto Notebooks, No. 230, December 2011), 3–5. Accessed 11/10/2013 at http://www.carloalberto.org/assets/working-papers/no.230.pdf.

[18] Karen Bogenschneider, "Family policy: why we need it and how to communicate its value" (paper prepared for the United Nations Expert Group Meeting, "Assessing family policies: Confronting family poverty and social exclusion & ensuring work family balance," New

and foster care are important in facilitating development of human capital and not necessarily consumption[19]; (b) the provision of basic economic support and infrastructure enabling families to take care of their members; (c) supporting families to secure attachment relationships, supports that are crucial in raising caring and committed citizens; (d) means of promoting positive child and youth development.

A similar view of the family policy domain, according to four societal contributions, was offered recently by Karen Bogenschneider.[20] Family policy is aimed at promoting productive workers, rearing caring future citizens, investing in societal goals and contributing to child and youth development.

Family policy has to reward families for being the primary engine of the economy and developing human capital and the labor force. Second, policy has to secure families so that they are able to develop caring, committed citizens who are responsive to society. Third, government has to invest in families because it cannot afford to fully replace the functions families perform for the benefit of their members and the good of society. Finally, policy has to invest in children and youth development because this is the best way to create a healthy society. In sum, family policies are essential in providing economic stability, social stability, continuity and caring for children and for those who cannot always care for themselves, among them the ill and the disabled. Therefore, they are politically popular and perceived as more acceptable than policies aimed toward individuals.[21] *Family perspective* analyzes the consequences of any public or social policy and refers broadly to examining what the consequences are of any policy or program on family well-being and as a means to accomplishing other policy ends.[22] However, it is often misused in social welfare to portray families without mentioning the role or benefit to fathers or other family members.[23]

York, June 2011). Accessed 6/10/2013 at http://social.un.org/index/LinkClick.aspx?fileticket=UmDEKVA4giU%3d&tabid=1555.

19 See Philip Longman, *The empty cradle: how falling birthrates threaten world prosperity and what to do about it* (New York: Basic, 2004), 15–28.

20 Bogenschneider, "Family policy: why we need it and how to communicate its value."

21 See Karen Bogenschneider and Thomas J. Corbett, "Family policy: becoming a field of inquiry and subfield of social policy," *Journal of Marriage and Family* 72 (2010), 783–803.

22 Ibid., 785.

23 Phil A. Cowan and Carolyn Pape Cowan, "Diverging family policies to promote children's well-being in the United Kingdom and United States: some relevant data from family research and intervention studies," *Journal of Children's Services* 3 (2008), 4–16.

This approach has been adopted through the Family Impact Seminars as an alternative to the United States' lack of explicit family policy.[24] In the early years, the focus was on promoting government involvement in families' lives. It has been interpreted over the years as systematically monitoring family trends and their implications on public policy, assessing the impact of a proposed or actual policy on the family and the development of family-centered policies. However, the Family Impact idea has been criticized by American scholars such as Gilbert Steiner who maintain that the concept is broad, elastic and lacking in boundaries.

Family policy is also viewed as an *instrument* to achieve other objectives in other social policy domains. The most popular are income transfers, including child and family allowances, social insurance, social assistance and tax policies. Additional tools are paid and job-protected leaves of absence from employment following childbirth or in the case of a child's illness. Common instruments are cash and tax subsidies to extend access to childcare and laws that regulate inheritance, adoption, guardianship, child protection, foster care, marriage, separation and divorce, custody and child support. Additional instruments include family planning and personal services, housing allowances and maternal or family health services.

TYPOLOGIES OF FAMILY POLICIES

There are efforts not only to define or to discuss dimensions of family policies but to provide typologies, primarily according to the degree of responsibilities to populations in need such as children and the frail elderly.[25] The traditional classification forms four distinct groups of *defamilialization*: (a) generous to the elderly but not to children, as in

[24] The Policy Institute for Family Impact Seminars provides policymakers and professionals with nonpartisan, solution-oriented research and a family and racial equity lens on many of the complex issues being debated in state legislatures across the country. The institute was founded in 1999 at the University of Wisconsin-Madison/Extension and continues the family impact mission of the federal Family Impact Seminar, which operated from 1976 to 1998 in Washington, DC.

[25] Anneli Anttonen and Jorma Sipilä, "European social care services: is it possible to identify models?" *Journal of European Social Policy* 2 (1996), 87–100.

the Netherlands, Norway and Great Britain; (b) generous to children but not to the frail elderly, as in France, Belgium and Italy; (c) generous to both children and the frail elderly, as in Denmark, Finland and Sweden; and (d) generous to neither children nor the frail elderly, as in Greece, Spain, Ireland and Germany. However, this typology has been criticized as too simplistic and completely unrealistic, as most of the policies in Western countries tend to be mixed, and include provisions with different levels of compensations.[26]

There are other typologies that vary according to aim, such as employment support to mothers of young children[27] or generosity of cash benefits or tax credits and services to children in different family situations.[28] In this regard, Kaufmann distinguishes four family policy profiles within Western Europe on the basis of the level of financial and infrastructural support they offer to families irrespective of the explicit or implicit goals.[29] These profiles range from the most generous in terms of both benefits and services (the Nordic countries and France) to the least generous (Italy and the other Southern European countries).

An interesting typology has been offered by Daly according to motivations and the diversity of national philosophical orientations that shape distinct family-market-state relationships.[30] This creates four types of policies: pro-natalist and pro-family orientation countries, such as France and Belgium, linking together fertility, family and national interest; countries with minor intervention in families, mainly through income transfers, such as West Germany; countries in favor of redistribution and social justice, particularly the Nordic states; and

[26] John C. Baldock, Anneli Anttonen and Jorma Sipilä, "Patterns of social care in five industrial societies: explaining diversity," Anneli Anttonen, John C. Baldock and Jorma Sipilä (eds.), *The young, the old and the state: social care systems in five industrial nations* (Cheltenham, UK: Edward Elgar, 2003), 167–97.

[27] Janet C. Gornick and Marcia K. Meyers, *Families that work: policies for reconciling parenthood and employment* (New York: Russell Sage Foundation, 2004).

[28] John Bradshaw, "Child benefit packages in fifteen countries in 2004" Jane Lewis (ed.), *Children, changing families and welfare states* (Cheltenham, UK: Edward Elgar, 2006), 26–50.

[29] Franz X. Kaufmann, "Politics and policies towards the family in Europe: a framework and an inquiry into their differences and convergences," Franz X. Kaufmann (ed.), *Family life and family policies in Europe: volume 2: problems and issues in comparative perspective.* (Oxford: Clarendon, 2002), 419–77.

[30] Mary Daly, "What adult worker model? A critical look at recent social policy reform in Europe from a gender and family perspective," *Social Politics* 18 (2011), 1–3.

those that intend to support low-income families in order to reduce poverty rates, such as the United Kingdom and the United States.

FAMILY POLICIES IN EUROPE AND THE UNITED STATES

European family policies were initiated in the nineteenth century in Germany and Sweden, followed by other European countries that enacted social protection policies just after World War II.[31] The interest in family policy in the United States emerged only in the 1970s and 1980s, but since then has been a divisive issue between liberal and conservative groups.

Neil Gilbert and Rebecca A. Voorhis raised an interesting paradox in family policies between the United States and the EU.[32] In their opinion, although most of the industrial European countries have lower annual rates of marriage and childbearing than the United States, they offer broader and more favorable family policies. If family policies are rational, the expectation is that demographic and social economic changes will be associated with expansion of family-centered policies in the United States as well as in European countries. The following section introduces family policies in the United States and selected industrial European countries.

FAMILY POLICIES IN THE UNITED STATES

Daniel Yankelovich, best known for his seminal work on American social values and public opinion, believes that individualism is as old as the nation state itself. Prior to the 1960s, American individualism focused mainly on the political domain, and only in the 1960s did it

[31] Legislated maternity leave in Germany was adopted in 1883, followed by Sweden in 1891 and France in 1928. For further information about the history of family policy in central Europe, see Tara Zahra, *The lost children: reconstructing Europe's families after World War II* (Cambridge, MA: Harvard University Press, 2011).

[32] Neil Gilbert and Rebecca A. Van Voorhis, "The paradox of family policy," *Social Science and Public Policy* (Sept.–Oct. 2003), 51–6.

broaden from the political domain to personal lifestyles.[33] In his opinion, the majority of Americans believe that family values are the most important values in their lives, and that they are satisfied with their own family life. On the other hand, they express pessimism about the future of the family.[34] In this regard, Bogenschneider believes that Americans' individualism philosophy is responsible for the lack of explicit social policy and a holistic view on families of children.[35] An additional barrier is the idea of family values, as family policy interferes in personal issues and experiences that are highly controversial. Polarized family policy issues such as abortion and same-sex marriage are disputed between liberals and conservatives, and are far from being agreed upon.

The conflicting views of family policy can be interpreted through three worldviews.[36] The "concerned camp" contends that families are in decline and have lost their capacity to carry out socialization of children. Families have become smaller, less stable and more separated from their extended families. The solution, however, is not to return back to the traditional family model, but to promote policies that strengthen families without creating dependence on government institutions.[37] The "impatient camp" argues that the tumultuous changes in family life in the past half century have been insufficient. Public institutions lag behind the changes in family structure, tending to be intolerant to family diversity. The solution is in pluralism, relativism and departure from a one-solution-fits-all-families approach. The "satisfied camp" views demographic changes in families not as a symptom of decline but rather as signs of strength and their capacity to adapt to economic and social conditions. Families today are more egalitarian and

[33] Daniel Yankelovich, "How American individualism is evolving," *The Public Perspective* (Feb.–Mar. 1998). Accessed 2/1/2014 at http://www.ropercenter.uconn.edu/public-perspective/ppscan/92/92003.pdf.

[34] Daniel Yankelovich, "How changes in the economy are reshaping American values," Henry J. Aaron, Thomas E. Mann and Timothy Taylor (eds.), *Values and public policy* (Washington, DC: The Brookings Institution, 1994), 16–53.

[35] See Bogenschneider, *Family policy matters*, 2nd ed.

[36] Bogenschneider, *Family policy matters*, 3rd ed., 91–222.

[37] David Popenoe, "Family decline in America." David Blankenhorn, Steven Bayme and Jean Bethke Elshtain (eds.), *Rebuilding the nest: a new commitment to American family* (Milwaukee, WI: Family Service of America, 1990), 39–51.

have achieved more social rights than in the past. Therefore, the next step is not turning the clock back, but establishing institutional supports for families to enable them to cope with rapid social and economic changes.[38]

The Clearinghouse on International Developments in Child, Youth, and Family Policies at Columbia University summarized 2001 family policy as follows[39]: "The United States has no explicit national, comprehensive family or child policy, nor has there been any such policy or cluster of policies in the past." However, a historical review of enactments related to families reveals that there have been periods of reform such as the Progressive Era (approximately 1895–1920), the New Deal and its aftermaths (1932–1954), and the War on Poverty and the Great Society (1960–1974). A more recent development took place at the beginning of the Clinton administration when there were new child and family initiatives, but the strength of these initiatives decreased during the second half of his presidency and during the Bush administration over concerns about budget constraints. President Barack Obama's first term was characterized by a spelled-out platform of family-friendly policies, but the state of the economy made it difficult to implement them. In a recent review of the past decade in US family policy, Karen Bogenschneider and Thomas S. Corbett concluded that family policy remains undeveloped as a focus of intellectual inquiry despite the growing reach of public policy on families.[40]

Columbia University's Clearinghouse summarized the central themes of US policy toward the family as follows: there is protection of the family as a private unit, discouraging government interference; the puritanical nature of American society encourages voluntarism as opposed to statutory enactment; there is a strict work ethic and a

[38] Janet Z. Giele, "Decline of the family: Conservative, liberal, and feminist views," David Popenoe, Jean Bethke Elshtain and David Blankenhorn (eds.), *Marriage in America* (Totowa, NJ: Rowman and Littlefield, 1996), 89–115.

[39] The Clearinghouse on International Developments in Child, Youth and Family Policies at Columbia University. Accessed 1/12/2013 at http://www.childpolicyintl.org/countries/us01.htm.

[40] Karen Bogenschneider and Thomas S. Corbett, "Family policy becoming a field of inquiry and subfield of social policy," *Journal of Marriage and Family* 72 (2010), 783–803.

relatively open immigration policy, which created population growth while reducing, perhaps eliminating, any case for pro-natalist policies; the late development of a civil service and government bureaucracy limited the national government's capacity for social policy; and, finally, there is ambivalence regarding women's roles, in particular whether public policy should take a position of encouraging women with young children to remain at home and provide care for their children or encourage women to enter the workforce, thus helping to sustain family income.

Social policies affecting children and their families focus primarily on the needy and unfortunate, and the most severely disabled or deprived. Except for free and compulsory public education, the United States has lagged behind in its family policies. Overall, it has placed a heavy emphasis on services and other in-kind benefits for the vulnerable and the neediest families. A brief review of core implicit family policies reveals the following:

FAMILY LEAVE

The United States is one of the few industrialized nations that does not provide paid family leave for new parents. Some parents can take time off under the Family and Medical Leave Act of 1993, which guarantees eligible employees at companies with more than fifty employees twelve weeks of unpaid, job-guaranteed leave for the birth of a child or care of a newborn, adoption of a child, to care for an immediate family member with a serious health condition, or medical leave for a serious health condition. Similar statutes exist in Washington, DC, and some states: California, Connecticut, Hawaii, Maine, Minnesota, New Jersey, Oregon, Rhode Island, Vermont, Washington and Wisconsin. California became the first state to enact a paid family leave act in 2002, allowing employees to take six weeks leave at up to 55 percent of their weekly wages (with a benefit cap) to care for a newborn, newly adopted child or sick family member. Every employee who contributes to the State Disability Insurance is covered, not just those in companies with fifty employees or more. Although some individual companies offer a paid maternity leave benefit, many parents end up using a combination of short-term disability, sick leave, vacation, personal days and unpaid family leave.

EARLY CHILDHOOD EDUCATION AND CARE (ECEC)

The United States has no national system of early childhood education and care (ECEC) nor does any state have a coherent statewide policy or program. ECEC in the United States includes a wide range of part-day, full-school-day and full-workday programs under educational, social welfare and commercial auspices, funded and delivered in a variety of ways in both the public and the private sectors. The result is a fragmented ECEC system of wide-ranging quality and with skewed access, but with some movement in recent years toward the integration of early childhood education and care.[41]

FAMILY ALLOWANCES AND CHILD TAX BENEFITS

The United States stands apart as one of the few industrialized nations that does not provide child or family allowances – cash benefits given to families with children depending on the presence, number, age, and sometimes the ordinal position of children. However, the United States does provide several tax benefits to families with children. Low-income working families can apply for the refundable Earned Income Tax Credit (EITC). There is also the Child Tax Credit (CTC). The credit is per child and is now refundable for low-income families. The government also helps offset childcare (and dependent care) costs by offering a tax credit for up to 30 percent of some of these expenses for working families. For the family living on average earnings, the value of these tax credits is likely to equal about 6 percent of their income. There are also tax credits for families adopting a child, paying for a child's education and for the cost of a child in eligible childcare.

[41] Sheila B. Kamerman and Shirley Gatenio-Gabel, "Early childhood education and care in the United States: an overview of the current policy picture," *Journal of Child Care and Education Policy* 1 (2007), 23–34.

OTHER CHILD-CONDITIONED INCOME TRANSFERS

The most important income transfers for families with children are the tax benefits described in the previous section, means-tested cash and in-kind benefits, and survivor's benefits under social security. Temporary Assistance to Needy Families (TANF) is a means-tested cash benefit funded by the federal government, with contributions by the states as well through federal grants to the states. The grants provide the states with great flexibility in providing cash assistance to poor families with children (or pregnant mothers). TANF has a five-year lifetime limit on receipt, requires poor women with children aged three months and older to participate in work after a maximum of two years, stresses marriage and the reduction of out-of-wedlock pregnancy and childbearing, and has a series of other requirements, some of which vary across the states.

A second important income transfer program of significance to poor children is Food Stamps, the in-kind benefit (a voucher) designed to increase the food purchasing power of eligible low-income families. Families are eligible if at least one member is seeking work or is unemployed, and if the family has a gross monthly income less than 130 percent of the poverty threshold.

A third important benefit is Supplemental Security Income (SSI), a means-tested cash benefit provided by the federal government to poor and disabled children as well as other poor, blind or disabled adults and the aged. As in other countries, children in the United States are also entitled to survivor's benefits under social security.

EXPLICIT AND IMPLICIT FAMILY POLICIES IN SELECTED EUROPEAN COUNTRIES

The overall belief is that European countries are more committed to explicit family policies in responding to changing family needs, whereas the United States, in parallel, represents implicit policies.[42] However, a

[42] Karen Bogenschneider, "Has family policy come of age? A decade review of the state of US family policy in the 1990s," *Journal of Marriage and Family* 62 (2004), 62, 1136–56.

closer look at Western European countries reveals a mixed picture and variation with respect to commitment, scope and provisions. For example, French family policy was institutionalized before World War II and tends toward explicit policies, whereas the United Kingdom has never had explicit family policies.[43] Family policies have been changed over the years, as in Italy and Spain after the end of their fascist regimes. Similarly, Germany had to dramatically change its family policy after the collapse of the Third Reich. Family policies in Nordic countries have been focused primarily on women's and children's issues.[44]

In order to present the range and diversity of concurrent family policies, this section presents typologies of three distinct countries: the United Kingdom, France and Sweden. The United Kingdom is characterized by regulated, means-tested and implicit family policies; France offers the most progressive explicit family policy; and Sweden demonstrates a generous implicit family policy.

UNITED KINGDOM

The United Kingdom does not have constitutional sanctification, thus policies that affect the family reflect a piecemeal approach and segmentation.[45] The dominant culture and ideology is that the state interferes primarily in cases of poverty, distress or inability of the family to take care of itself. The family policy model is classified as a male-breadwinner model with a focus on cash benefits and tax credits for families rather than a system that advocates family growth through the public service system.[46] According to Land and Lewis, women have

[43] There is an international project on Family Change and Family Policy, codirected by Prof. Peter Flora (University of Mannheim, Mannheim Centre for European Social Research) and Profs. Sheila B. Kamerman and Alfred J. Kahn (Columbia University School of Social Work, New York). The project analyzes changes in family structures and family policies from a long-term and comparative perspective in twenty countries in Europe and overseas. This publication was written by Thomas Bahle and Mathias Maucher with contributions by Katherina Fuduli and Beatrix Holzer; *Developing a family policy database for Europe* (Mannheim: Mannheim Centre for European Social Research, 1998).

[44] Ibid., 6. [45] Ibid.

[46] For further reading, see Naomi Finch, "Family policies in the UK," Ilona Ostner and Christoph Schmitt (eds.), *Family policies in the context of family change* (Wiesbaden: VS Verlag, 2008), 129–54. Finch claims that the UK welfare state is moving toward a more

traditionally been treated as dependent wives or mothers looking after their children in their home, while male employment has been assumed to be the main source of family income.[47] Another characteristic of the British policy is the reliance on means-tested benefits and working tax credits.[48] By placing the emphasis on modest cash supports and tax credits, the British system has maintained traditional work divisions between genders.

PARENTAL LEAVE

Maternity leave in the United Kingdom is twenty-six weeks of Ordinary Maternity Leave and twenty-six weeks of Additional Maternity Leave, making one year in total. The combined fifty-two weeks is known as Statutory Maternity Leave. A recent amendment makes it mandatory for women to take a minimum of two weeks' maternity leave immediately after childbirth (four weeks' minimum for factory workers).[49] Pregnant employees may also be eligible for a Sure Start Maternity Grant, a one-time, tax-free payment offered to low-income mothers to buy supplies for the baby that does not have to be repaid.[50]

If employees meet the qualifications, fathers are eligible for Ordinary Paternity Leave (paid) for two consecutive weeks. In addition, twenty-six weeks of Additional Paternity Leave are available on top of the 2 weeks' ordinary leave.[51]

individualistic state but this shift has been hindered because social policies are still based on earlier principles.

47 Hilary Land and Jane Lewis, "Gender, care and the changing role of the state in the UK." Jane Lewis (ed.), *Gender, social care and welfare state restructuring in Europe* (Aldershot, Hants, England: Ashgate, 1998), 51–84.

48 Finch, "Family policies in the UK," 142.

49 See overview of "Statutory Maternity Leave." Accessed 10/10/2013 at https://www.gov.uk/maternity-pay-leave/overview.

50 See overview of "Sure Start Maternity Grant." Accessed 10/10/2013 at https://www.gov.uk/sure-start-maternity-grant/overview.

51 See overview of "Ordinary Paternity Leave." Accessed 10/10/2013 at https://www.gov.uk/paternity-pay-leave/overview.

CHILD BENEFIT/GUARDIAN'S ALLOWANCE[52]

Child Benefit is a tax-free, non-means-tested benefit administered by Her Majesty's Revenue and Customs (HMRC) and paid to people who are responsible for, or treated as responsible for, children or qualifying young persons. There are two rates of payment: (a) higher rate payable for the eldest or only child or qualifying young person in the family unit; (b) basic rate payable for all other children or qualifying young persons in the family unit. If the eldest children or qualifying young persons are twins, the higher rate is payable only for the elder twin. If two children or qualifying young persons in the same family unit qualify, the higher rate is payable only for the eldest child or qualifying young person.

Child Benefit is payable to only one person for a particular child or qualifying young person in any one week. Where two people satisfy the entitlement conditions, only one of them can be entitled and receive payment. The law provides rules to decide which one of them it will be. The child or qualifying young person must be present, or treated as being present, in Great Britain or Northern Ireland as the case may be in that week, and the claimant must be both present and ordinarily resident in Great Britain or Northern Ireland. From January 7, 2013, the High Income Child Benefit charge was introduced. This means that if a person or their partner, if they have one, has an individual adjusted net income of more than £50,000, the person with the higher income will be liable to a tax charge on some or all of the Child Benefit they are entitled to receive.

Where a person or their partner is liable for the High Income Child Benefit charge from January 7, 2013, the person who is the Child Benefit claimant can decide to stop their Child Benefit payments. This means a person remains entitled to Child Benefit but does not receive payment and so they, or their partner, do not have to declare the Child Benefit they are entitled to receive as a tax charge or continue to receive their Child Benefit payments. This means the person or their partner will have to declare some or all of the Child Benefit they are

[52] See overview and purpose of "Child Benefit and Guardian's Allowance." Accessed 10/10/2013 at http://www.hmrc.gov.uk/manuals/cbtmanual/cbtm01020.htm.

entitled to receive as a tax charge through the Self-Assessment process. Where more than one child is included in a Child Benefit award, the Child Benefit claimant's decision to stop or start their Child Benefit payments applies to every child in their award. The tax charge will be 1 percent of the Child Benefit paid for every £100 of income received over £50,000 and up to £60,000 or a charge equal to the full amount of Child Benefit paid for income over £60,000. *Guardian's Allowance* is a tax-free allowance, administered by HMRC. It is paid in addition to the Child Benefit to people bringing up a child or qualifying young person whose parents have died, but can sometimes be paid when only one parent has died. It is paid at one rate for all children or qualifying young persons.

CHILDCARE[53]

Childcare is inspected and regulated by the Office for Standards in Education, Children's Services and Skills (OFSTED). The British preschool options for parents consist of day nurseries, toddler groups and preschools. In addition, there are *crèches* (for children up to 8 years old), or child minders and nannies (for children up to twelve years old). Parents also have the option of sending their child to playgroups or out-of-school clubs after they have started school. All childcare has to be registered and inspected by OFSTED. The UK government offers three- and four-year-olds 12.5 hours of free early learning a week; this should apply to all forms of childcare for at least 38 weeks of the year, but there is no guarantee of getting a place with a particular provider.

The government provides means-tested funding to help families. Claims of up to 80 percent of childcare costs can be made through the United Kingdom's Working Tax Credit (WTC). There are also job

[53] For further information about the early years and childcare, see the OFSTED site. OFSTED is the United Kingdom's independent and impartial Office for Standards in Education, Children's Services and Skills. It reports to Parliament about inspections and regulated services which care for children and young people, and those providing education and skills for learners of all ages. Accessed 11/10/2013 at http://www.ofsted.gov.uk/early-years-and-childcare.

grants for those who have been unemployed and are returning to work, or a child maintenance premium for those receiving income support or jobseekers' allowance. In addition, there is a tax-efficient employer-supported childcare system.

A recent study by the Daycare Trust released in 2012 revealed that working parents were spending up to £15,000 a year on childcare and fewer families were receiving help with the financial burden.[54] According to this report, the cost of a nursery place for a two-year-old had increased more than twice the rate of inflation.

FRANCE

According to Rachel Henneck's review, French family policy is probably the most progressive and comprehensive in Europe in its commitment and scope.[55] France was the first country to offer paid maternity, prior to World War I, and has the most affordable and widely available childcare system.[56] In addition, the country offers generous family allowances and parental leave, benefits that have been conceived as replacement for forgone wages.[57] Regardless of the generous parental leave benefits and universal family allowances, French women have an impressive employment rate (46%).[58]

In recent years, the government has had to change its policy and now offers means-tested benefits. This departure from horizontal redistribution has increased the tendency of lower income women to stay at

[54] The report appears on the Daycare Trust site. The Family and Childcare Trust is a research-led charity with more than forty years' experience of campaigning and research into family life. The organization supports the well-being of families in the United Kingdom by identifying and alleviating the pressures on family life and childcare and campaigning for a more family-friendly United Kingdom. Accessed 12/1/2012 at http://www.daycaretrust.org.uk/.

[55] Rachel Henneck, "Family policy in the US, Japan, Germany, Italy and France: parental leave, child benefits/family allowances, child care, marriage/cohabitation, and divorce" (briefing paper, the Council on Contemporary Families, 2003). Founded in 1996 and based at the University of Miami, the council's mission is to enhance the national understanding of how and why contemporary families are changing, what needs and challenges they face and how these needs can best be met.

[56] See Jane Lewis, "Gender and the development of welfare regimes," *Journal of European Social Policy* 2 (1995), 165.

[57] Ibid., 166. [58] Ibid., 164, 170.

home, especially when these women also receive pro-natalist benefits that pay more and give longer leave for third births. Means-tested allowances have benefited single wage earners more than working wives because single mothers' income is likely to be lower, so they are more likely to qualify for additional benefits.[59] However, despite the reduction in economic growth, France still offers significantly high rates of social expenditures and increased basic universal family benefits, and constrains spending on pensions and health care instead.

PARENTAL LEAVE

Parental leave policy in France is probably the most advanced in Europe. The government offers all women workers paid, job-protected maternity leave six weeks before and ten weeks after the births of the first two children, eight weeks before and eighteen weeks after the birth of the third child, thirty-four weeks (twelve prenatally) for twins and forty-two weeks (twenty-four prenatally) for multiple births. Maternity leave, pre- and after birth, is mandatory.[60] The benefit paid over maternity leave is equal to the woman's net salary, within certain limits. The government offers paid parental leave for either parent at the end of the maternity leave until the child turns three or if at least two children at home need care.

CHILD BENEFITS/FAMILY ALLOWANCES

The family allowance policy in France is the most generous in the world. Child benefit is paid to families with two or more dependent children living in France. It is neither means tested nor related to previous employment periods. Child benefit rates since April 1, 2012, are 32 percent of the monthly benefit base (€127.68) for two children and

[59] Ibid., 167.

[60] Christopher J. Ruhm and Jackqueline L. Teague, "Parental leave policies in Europe and North America," Francine Blau and Ronald G. Erhenberg (eds.), *Gender and family issues in the workplace* (New York: Russell Sage Foundation, 1997), 135.

41 percent (€163.59) for each additional child.[61] The rates increase for each child except the eldest in families with fewer than three children. The increase depends on the age and dates of birth of the children: for children born before or on April 30, 1997, the increase is 9 percent of the calculation base (€35.91) for children aged between eleven and sixteen, and the increase is 16 percent for children aged sixteen or older (€63.84). For children born on or after May 1, 1997, the increase is 16 percent of the calculation base (€63.84) for children aged fourteen or older. In addition, there are several means-tested benefits for income supplementation, single parents, adoption, parents who reduce their professional activity to stay home with children, special education, schooling of children and housing.

CHILDCARE

The French model is based on the idea that childcare responsibility is shared between the state and the family.[62] The basic assumption is that parents are pivotal to government family policy and it must provide them with optimal preferences for working or caring. No wonder that the childcare system is available from birth to the age of two and a half to three years. A child can be placed in either a *crèche* (communal nursery) or in the home of an *assistante maternelle* (nanny). Once a child reaches the age of between two and a half and three he or she can be enrolled in an *école maternelle* (preschool). None of these options is compulsory, as schooling in France is not obligatory until a child reaches the age of five. Families pay on a sliding scale; however, lower income families usually pay nothing, and better-off families pay no more than 10 to 15 percent of their income for this service.[63] The underlying rationale for this comprehensive policy is that early childhood education is an

[61] For information about the French Social Security System and particular Family Benefits, see its site. Accessed 5/3/2013 at http://www.cleiss.fr/docs/regimes/regime_france/an_4.html.

[62] Marie Therese Letablier and Jeanne Fagnani, "Caring rights and responsibilities of families in the French welfare state." Birgit Pfau-Effinger and Birgit Geissler (eds.), *Care arrangements and social integration in European Societies* (Berlin: Policy, 2005), 153–72.

[63] Janet C. Gornick and Marcia K. Meyers, "Welfare regimes in relation to paid work and care." Janet Zollinger Giele and Elke Holst (eds.), *Changing life patterns in western industrial societies* (Amsterdam: Elsevier Science, 2004), 45–67.

effective mode of socialization, education and cultural reproduction. France also offers allowances to defray the costs of childcare, at home or in registered facilities, for children younger than three. In one of the most progressive provisions, known as *nourrices*, child minders look after between one and three children aged between two and a half months and three years in their own homes. They can be independent or attached to a *crèche.*

SWEDEN

Sweden is a welfare state and as such offers policies supporting women and children. The country is a front-runner in and a model of progressive social policy, encouraging parents' employment and the sharing of unpaid childcare work. The country's welfare policy is based on the dual-earner family and asserts the same rights and obligations regarding family and labor market work for both women and men.[64] Interestingly, since the 2006 election and the rise of the center-right coalition, Sweden has been in the process of reassessing its social welfare policies and adjusting it to changes in demography and the economic system.[65] The current governing center-right coalition came to power in 2006 after twelve years of uninterrupted Social Democratic governments. During the election campaign of 2006, the coalition advocated a number of reforms to family policy, including a gender equality bonus in the earnings-related part of parental insurance; a flat-rate home care allowance; a voucher system for day care; boosted pedagogical curriculum standards in public day-care centers; and tax deductions for household services. Some of these reforms can be expected to strengthen the earner-carer orientation of policy, while others leave greater room for market solutions, as well as more pronouncedly traditional family orientations.

Nevertheless, Sweden is marked by a dual-earner family policy model with strong support for dual earners and low general family

[64] Ann-Zofie Duvander, "Family policy in Sweden 2008," *Social Insurance Report* 15 (2008), Stockholm: Swedish Social Insurance Agency.

[65] Tommy Ferrarini and Ann-Zofie Duvander, "Earner-carer model at the crossroads: reforms and outcomes of Sweden's family policy in comparative perspective," *International Journal of Health Services* 40 (2010), 373–98.

support. Most social policies in Sweden are based on residential rather than citizenship rights. Therefore, policies toward family members apply to all individuals permanently residing in Sweden.

PARENTAL LEAVE BENEFIT

Enacted in 1974, paternity benefits were initially part of the country's proactive approach to encouraging women to join the workforce, but have since come to reflect Sweden's philosophical emphasis on gender equality. Fathers aren't leaving work simply to relieve mothers' burdens, but rather to bond with their children and experience parenting. Essentially, this means that fathers should take a greater share of child-care responsibility by using more parental leave. This is related not only to children's rights to access to both parents, but also to gender equality in that fathers' leave facilitates women's return to and involvement in labor market work. The parental leave policy is thus related to the goals of increasing employment levels, gender equality and children's rights. Paid parental leave is 480 days (16 months). For 390 days the allowance is equivalent to the parent's qualifying income (80 percent of income up to a certain ceiling). A parent can stay at home for a further ninety days on the minimum benefit level.[66]

CHILD ALLOWANCE AND OTHER BENEFITS

Swedish social insurance also includes child allowance, a flat-rate benefit to which all children residing in Sweden are entitled. Parents receive approximately 1,000 SEK per child per month, with a supplement for families having two or more children. The supplement increases with the number of children. This benefit was introduced in 1948 as a result of a concern over declining birth rates in the 1930s.

[66] A brief review, "Social insurance in Sweden," was published by the Ministry of Health and Social Affairs, No 20, 2005. Accessed 1/8/2013 at http://faculty.law.ubc.ca/myoung/poverty/Social%20Insurance%20in%20Sweden.pdf. Information about Sweden's social insurance is available on the government site. Accessed 2/7/2013 at http://www.government.se/sb/d/15473/a/183495.

Families may receive a care allowance for sick and disabled children and maintenance support in the case of parents separating. Finally, Sweden provides a housing allowance to single parents, mostly women. It is a means-tested benefit based on household income, the number of individuals in the household and the cost and size of housing. The housing allowance is of major importance in increasing the income level of many one-parent households.

CHILDCARE

Childcare in Sweden includes preschools (day nurseries), family day-care homes and open preschools and leisure time centers. All preschool programs have to be assessed by the government and meet certain standards. Swedish nurseries are financed partly by central government grants, partly by tax revenue and partly by parental fees. In 2002, the government reformed the childcare market by establishing maximum fees. This regulation is intended to increase both the labor supply among parents and their economic well-being. Research that examined the possible effect of the reform found positive but small effects on the labor supply.[67]

RECENT REFORMS

As mentioned earlier, in 2007 Sweden initiated a tax deduction for household services, providing a tax deduction of 50 percent of the cost of such services up to a fairly high ceiling.[68] This reform is intended to assist families where both parents are career-oriented and work full-time, as well as to create a formal market for care services. The reform is a departure from Sweden's traditional universal family policy

[67] For additional information about the study, see Anna Brink, Katarina Nordblom and Roger Wahlberg, "Maximum fee vs. child benefit: a welfare analysis of Swedish childcare fee reform," *International Tax Public Forum* 14 (2007), 457–80.

[68] For further reading of the tax deduction for household services of 2007, see *Tax deductions for domestic service work*, Sweden. Accessed 7/9/2013 at https://eurofound.europa.eu/areas/labourmarket/tackling/cases/se015.htm.

because it allowed higher income families to have greater tax deductions than lower income families.

Two new additional reforms released in 2008 were the gender equality bonus and the home care allowance,[69] the result of a political compromise emanating from conflicting interests within the center-right government, in particular between the Christian Democratic Party and the Liberal Party. For decades the Christian Democrats encouraged the home care allowance that allows parents (primarily mothers) to stay at home instead of working and utilizing public day care, while the Liberal Party favored greater gender equality of earner-carer policies.

The home care allowance is an untaxed benefit of 3,000 SEK per month, designed to be used after the earnings-related parental leave period. It is paid to parents who want to extend their time at home and delay the start of day care.

CONCLUSION

The chapter introduces the paradox of family policy; in spite of the growing recognition of family policy by politicians and policymakers, it is narrowly used primarily by academics and policy specialists. The family is at the center of controversies regarding values and whether to adopt the structural or functional definition approach. The chapter introduces the difficulties in defining family policy in Western societies, which are torn between individualism and communitarianism (familism) approaches. There is an extensive review and demonstration of US and selected European core family policies that vary in their approaches to families. The chapter reveals that there is lack of consensus as to whether family policy is a solid concept with clear boundaries or a loose one, used primarily in practice to characterize policies that touch on family matters. There is basic agreement among researchers that family policy can be differentiated between explicit and implicit; the

[69] For additional reading about the gender equality bonus and the home care allowance 2008, see Kimberly Earles, "Aims and outcomes of recent changes to Swedish family policy: contradictions within a social democratic welfare model" (paper presented at the Canadian Political Science Association Annual Conference, 2010).

first is aimed at family concerns while the second (implicit) is any public policy that has relevance or implications for the family.[70]

The chapter's second challenge is to introduce three common conceptual interpretations of family policy as a domain, a perspective or an instrument. Domain covers the family's function, creation, provision of basic economic support, supporting cohesion and relationships and promoting child development. The use of perspective is more common in capitalist or neoconservative countries, which lack explicit and regulated family policies. It is often used as a recommendation or a call to consider family matters in the formulation of any public policy. Family policy is also viewed as an instrument to promote family policies such as child or family allowance, tax subsidies and services and programs.

If the first part of the chapter intends to provide a conceptual base, the second introduces US and selected European family policies and discusses major differences between the two. Overall, European policies reflect greater commitment to families than those of the United States. The latter perceives the family as a private institution that deserves intervention only in exceptional circumstances. The chapter also presents the diversity of family policies within Europe, such as in France, which has probably the most progressive explicit family policy; Sweden, which has adopted generous implicit policies; and the United Kingdom, with a more conservative and regulated implicit policy, offering a mixed approach.

The chapter ends with reference to family disability policy and raises two core questions: does family policy cover all families, including those with children with disability, and is there a need for specific family disability policies or can they be added as supplements? These questions will be responded to in the next chapters in discussing US and European family policies toward families of children with disability.

[70] See Kamerman, "Families and family policies," 115–21.

3 FAMILIES OF CHILDREN WITH DISABILITY: CORE NEEDS

FAMILIES OF CHILDREN WITH DISABILITY: STATISTICAL OVERVIEW

Perceptions of childhood disability have changed dramatically over the past century, as have conceptualizations of health and illness, medical developments, threats to children's health and development, and expectations for child functioning. Neal Halfon and others have examined how these changes have influenced the risk of poor health and disability and how recent policies to address the needs of children with disability have evolved.[1] They found that childhood disability is increasing and that emotional, behavioral and neurological disabilities are now more prevalent than physical impairments. This progressive shift also involves changes in the image of children with disability.

Until the 1960s, the iconic image of a child with disability was the Easter Seals Poster Child with Polio, projecting an image of innocence, dependency and neediness.[2] This has changed, and the perceived image is of a range of ubiquitous and not as easily recognizable mental health and neurodevelopmental disabilities.

It is difficult to provide an acceptable definition and estimate of the prevalence of childhood disability. Various national surveys have been carried out in the United States and the United Kingdom to determine

[1] See Neal Halfon et al., "The changing landscape of disability in childhood," *Future of Children* 21 (2012), 13–42.

[2] See comprehensive review of media images of disability in the author's recent book, Rimmerman, *Social inclusion of people with disabilities*, 61–3.

TABLE 3.1 *Disability prevalence estimates in childhood*[3]

Survey	Year	Measure of disability or related concept	Prevalence estimate (and age group)
National Health Interview Survey[(a)]	1992–1994	Disability: a long-term reduction in ability to conduct social role activities such as school or play because of a chronic physical or mental condition	6.5% (under 18)
Family Resources Survey (United Kingdom)[(b)]	2004–2005	Disability: the presence of a physical or mental illness or disability that limits the child and creates significant difficulties within defined areas of life	7.3% (under 18)
National Health Interview Survey[(c)]	2009	Disability: a defined activity limitation	8.0% (under 18)

the prevalence of chronic conditions, impairments and disabilities among children. We introduce here (Table 3.1) three different national surveys that incorporate medical and functional or activity limitation. Interestingly, the prevalence of disability among children and youth (up to eighteen years) ranges between 6.5 percent and 8.0 percent.

Detailed statistics on children with developmental disabilities in the United States have shown that from 2006 to 2008 one out of six children in the United States had a developmental disability, and the prevalence of this population increased 17.1 percent from 1997 to 2008.[4] The most significant change between 1997 to 1999 and 2006

[3] (a) Paul W. Newacheck and Neal Halfon, "Prevalence and impact of disabling chronic conditions in childhood," *American Journal of Public Health* 88 (1998), 610–7.
(b) Clare M. Blackburn, Nick J. Spencer and Janet M. Read, "Prevalence of childhood disability and the characteristics and circumstances of disabled children in the U.K.: secondary analysis of the Family Resources Survey," *BMC Pediatrics* 10 (2010), 1471–2431.
(c) Child Trends Data Bank, "Children with limitations." The Child Trends Data Bank examines and monitors more than 100 indicators that focus on risks and positive developments for children. Accessed 3/8/2013 at www.childtrendsdatabank.org/?q=node/73.

[4] For additional information, see *America's Children in Brief: Key National Indicators of Well Being 2012*, Forum on Child and Family Statistics. Since 1997, the Federal Interagency

to 2008 has been in autism and attention deficit hyperactivity disorder (ADHD). Table 3.2 presents the prevalence of specific developmental disabilities in US children aged three to seventeen years between 1997 and 2008.

One out of nine children under the age of eighteen receives special education services. There are about 2.8 million families that live with two or more children receiving special education services. Unfortunately, 28 percent of US children with disability live below the federal poverty threshold, as contrasted with 16 percent of children without disability.[5]

Almost the same figures are reported in the United Kingdom.[6] In 2011, there were 770,000 children with disability under the age of sixteen, equating to one in twenty children. It is estimated that around 748,000 children and young people aged five to sixteen in the United Kingdom have mental health conditions; around 78,000 of these have autistic spectrum disorders; around 132,000 have a learning disability, and 51,000 of those with a learning disability also have mental health conditions. Similar to the United States, more children with disability (29%) live in poverty than households with no disabled children (21%).[7]

Forum on Child and Family Statistics has published a report on the well-being of children and families. Accessed 5/8/2013 at http://childstats.gov/pdf/ac2012/ac_12.pdf.

[5] Glenn T. Fujiura and Kiyoshi Yamaki, "Trends in demography of childhood poverty and disability," *Exceptional Children* 66 (2000), 187–99.

[6] Disability in the United Kingdom 2011: Facts and figures. This statistical summary gives an overview of the current key facts and figures surrounding disability in the United Kingdom today. It covers important areas such as employment, housing, transportation and education. Published by the Papworth Trust, Cambridge, July 2011. Accessed 11/10/2013 at http://www.papworth.org.uk/downloads/factsandfigures_disabilityintheuk_july2011_110721132605.pdf.

[7] The Institute for Public Policy Research (IPPR) 2007: Disability 2020. The aim of this project was to make an assessment of a possible "state of affairs" concerning disabled people in the year 2020. The research was undertaken in partnership with the Personal Social Services Research Unit at the London School of Economics and Faculty of Actuarial Science and Statistics at City University. The final report, *Disability 2020: Opportunities for the full and equal citizenship of disabled people in Britain in 2020*, brings together demographic projections on the size and composition of the disabled population by 2020 and evidence on health trends, with an assessment of the key trends in the policy environment influencing the dynamics of disabled people's citizenship. Accessed 6/2/2013 at http://www.efds.co.uk/assets/0000/3420/OOO54.pdf.

TABLE 3.2 *Trends in the prevalence of specific developmental disabilities in US children aged three to seventeen years, 1997–2008*

Disability	*n* (unweighted)	All years,%	1997–1999,%	2000–2002,%	2003–2005,%	2006–2008,%	Percentage change 1997–1999 versus 2006–2008[c]
Any developmental disability	15,956	13.87	12.84	13.70	13.88	15.04	17.1[c]
ADHD	7,652	6.69	5.69	6.71	6.77	7.57	33.0[c]
Autism	537	0.47	0.19	0.35	0.59	0.74	289.5[c]
Blind/unable to see at all	160	0.13	0.11	0.15	0.12	0.13	18.2
Cerebral palsy	305	0.39	0.39	0.43	[b]	[b]	[b]
Moderate to profound hearing loss	533	0.45	0.55	0.44	0.42	0.38	30.9
Learning disability	8,154	7.04	6.86	7.24	6.82	7.24	5.5
Intellectual disability[a]	868	0.71	0.68	0.73	0.75	0.67	−1.5
Seizures, past twelve months	792	0.67	0.66	0.65	0.66	0.72	9.1
Stutter or stammer, past twelve months	1,924	1.60	1.63	1.40	1.69	1.68	3.1
Other developmental delay	3,978	3.65	3.40	3.28	3.67	4.24	24.7[c]

Source: Centers for Disease Control and Prevention, National Center for Health Statistics, NHIS.
[a] Survey question asked about mental retardation, but we refer to the condition as intellectual disability.
[b] We excluded cerebral palsy from the analysis for 2004–2007.
[c] Because of the high likelihood of interviewer error arising from a questionnaire change in 2004.

CHALLENGES EXPERIENCED BY FAMILIES OF CHILDREN WITH DISABILITY

Families caring for children with disability experience significant personal and marital challenges, financial burdens and curtailed employment opportunities. In addition, they are required to cope with special concerns related to their children's type of disability. This chapter discusses these important challenges and also examines service provisions and their importance for family preservation. The conclusion summarizes core concerns raised by caregiving families and conceptualizes their priorities for family policy.

FAMILIES' PERSONAL AND MARITAL CHALLENGES

Families are considered the primary caregivers and critical source of support for their children with disability. Most of the studies on caregivers of children with disability relate to mothers, while only portions of them relate to fathers, siblings or the family as a whole.

PERSONAL IMPACT ON PARENTS

Research carried out in the past three decades reveals that raising a child with disability drains a family's emotional resources and increases stress and depression among parents.[8,9] These studies compare mothers of children with intellectual disability with those without disability, showing that they experience more caregiving demands, emotional distress, and physical health and mental health problems.[10] Although families of children with disability share common concerns, there are unique

[8] See Christine Baxter, Robert A. Cummins and Lewi Yiolitis, "Parental stress attributed to disabled family members: a longitudinal study," *Journal of Intellectual and Developmental Disability* 25 (2000), 105–18.

[9] See, for example, Malin B. Olsson and Philip C. Hwang, "Depression in mothers and fathers of children with intellectual disability," *Journal of Intellectual Disability Research* 45 (2001), 535–43.

[10] See, for example, Robert M. Hodapp et al., "Health outcomes of infants and toddlers with Down syndrome," *International Review of Research in Mental Retardation* 39 (2010), 37–66.

responses associated with a child's type of disability. For example, parents of children with Down syndrome appear to be less depressed than parents of children with other types of developmental disabilities, in particular autism.[11,12] Similarly, a comparative study of families of children with physical disability versus families of children with cancer showed that the latter experience greater emotional stress.[13] Parents of children with behavioral disorders or complicated health problems experience the most unresolved challenges at home.[14]

THE IMPACT ON MARITAL RELATIONS

In addition to personal concerns, caring for children with disability has a significant impact on their parents' marital relations. Parents often complain that children's maladjustment, particularly behavior and conduct disorders, interfere in their intimacy and create problems in their marriage.[15] However, findings are inconclusive, probably because there are other issues that may exist in their lives. For example, in the early 1980s, Friedrich and Friedrich found that mothers of children with developmental disability reported less satisfaction with their marital relationship than a matched sample of mothers of typically developing children.[16] However, recent studies have demonstrated

[11] See, for example, a study by Leonard Abbeduto et al., "Psychological well-being and coping in mothers of youths with autism, Down syndrome, or fragile X syndrome," *American Journal of Mental Retardation* 109 (2004), 237–54.

[12] See Leila A. Ricci and Robert M. Hodapp, "Fathers' perceptions, stress, and involvement with children with Down syndrome versus with other types of mental retardation," *Journal of Intellectual Disability Research* 47 (2003), 273–84.

[13] See Jen Wen Hung, Yee-Hwa Wu and Chao-Hsing Yeh, "Comparing stress levels of parents of children with cancer and parents of children with physical disabilities," *Psycho-Oncology* 13 (2004), 898–903.

[14] See, for example, S. Herring et al., "Behaviour and emotional problems in toddlers with pervasive developmental disorders and developmental delay: association with parental mental health and family functioning," *Journal of Intellectual Disability Research* 50 (2006), 874–82.

[15] See Donna Ruane Morrison and Mary J. Coiro, "Parental conflict and marital disruption: do children benefit when high-conflict marriages are dissolved?" *Journal of Marriage and the Family* 61 (1999), 626–37.

[16] William N. Friedrich and Wanda L. Friedrich, "Psychosocial assets of parents of handicapped and non-handicapped children," *American Journal of Mental Deficiency* 85 (1981), 551–53.

that the difference in separation and divorce rates is marginal.[17] A meta-analysis confirmed that children's intellectual disability had a much smaller effect on parents' marital relationships than would be expected under older assumptions about disability and family.[18]

GENDER DIFFERENCES BETWEEN MOTHERS AND FATHERS

Mothers and fathers have different roles and experiences with their children's disability. In an interesting review of the literature, Susan L. Neely-Barnes and David A. Dia of the University of Tennessee found that mothers of children with disability reported greater rates of burden of care and depression than did their spouses.[19] However, a UK study on fathers of children with disability found that they were more emotionally reactive to the diagnosis of disability in the newly born child than their wives.[20] In addition, their adjustment process to their child's disability could be more turbulent and long-lasting.[21] Fathers' sense of "inferiority" seems to be related, in part, to their gender stereotypes and breadwinning role. They often work overtime in order to

[17] Chris Hatton et al., "Changes in family composition and marital status in families with a young child with cognitive delay," *Journal of Applied Research in Intellectual Disabilities* 23 (2010), 14–26.

[18] Don Risdal and George H. S. Singer, "Marital adjustment in parents of children with disabilities: a historical review and meta-analysis," 2004. Accessed 4/6/2012 at http://www.atyponlink.com/TASH/doi/abs/10.2511/rpsd.29.2.95. See, also, Don Risdal and George H. S. Singer, "Marital adjustment in parents of children with disabilities: a historical review and meta-analysis," *Research & Practice for Persons with Severe Disabilities* 29 (2004), 95–103.

[19] Susan Neely-Barmes and David L. Dia, "Families of children with disability: a review of research and recommendations for intervention," *Journal of Early and Intensive Behavior Intervention* 5 (2008), 93–107.

[20] See research summary on fathers of disabled children published September 21, 2007, by the Fatherhood Institute located at Warren Courtyard, Savernake, Marlborough, Wiltshire, SN8 3UU, UK. The Fatherhood Institute is a UK charity and think-and-do-tank considered to be the most respected fatherhood organization in the world. Accessed 5/7/2013 at http://www.fatherhoodinstitute.org/2007/fatherhood-institute-research-summary-fathers-and-disabled-children/.

[21] See, for extensive reading, Jill Harrison, Matthew Henderson and Rob Leonard, *Different dads: fathers' stories of parenting disabled children* (London: Jessica Kingsley, 2007).

avoid being involved with their children.[22] Mothers, on the other hand, feel that their spouses are incapable of openly discussing their own child's problems.

THE IMPACT ON OTHER FAMILY MEMBERS

The birth of a child with a disability or chronic illness has a critical effect on other family members, particularly siblings. They have to adjust to a brother or sister who, because of their condition, may require a large portion of family time, attention, money and psychological support. Their reactions to a sibling with a disability can affect the overall adjustment and development of self-esteem in both children.[23] According to National Dissemination Center for Children with Disability (NICHCY), the positive or negative nature of the relationships between siblings and among family members may be influenced by factors such as family resources, lifestyle, child-rearing practices, type and severity of the disability, number of children in the family and age differences, as well as the coping mechanism and family support.

However, findings regarding the impact of the sibling with disability on other siblings vary. There is a consensus among scholars that there are some concerns, such as feelings of guilt, shame, stigma, and that they have to bear extra responsibilities.[24] In general, though, most of the nondisabled siblings do not pay an emotional price, and can even gain from their unique experience. However, siblings may need support to understand their feelings about their experiences with their disabled brother or sister and to differentiate their experiences from their own parents.

Grandparents are also being asked to serve as caregivers for their disabled grandchildren. The new grandparents, often called the

[22] See the classical study by Thomas T. Cummings, "The impact of the child's deficiency on the father: a study of fathers of mentally retarded and chronically ill children," *American Journal of Orthopsychiatry* 46 (1976), 246–55.

[23] Thomas H. Powell and Peggy Ahrenhold-Ogle, *Brothers and sisters: a special part of an exceptional family* (Baltimore, MD: Paul Brookes, 1985).

[24] Debra J. Lobato, *Brothers, sisters, and special needs: information and activities for helping young siblings of children with chronic illnesses and developmental disabilities* (Baltimore, MD: Paul Brookes, 1990).

skip-generation, are grandmothers in their late 50s and 60s who provide daily care for their grandchildren with developmental delays, learning and intellectual disabilities, and chronic illnesses.[25]

ECONOMIC CHALLENGES

Childhood disabilities have direct and indirect immediate and long-term economic costs to the family and society but are difficult to measure. Mark Stabile and Sara Allin provide the most updated review on the cost of children with disability to their families.[26] The two professors from the University of Toronto examined three kinds of costs – direct, out-of-pocket costs incurred as a result of the child's disability; indirect costs incurred by the family as it decides how best to cope with the disability; and long-term costs associated with the child's future economic performance.

DIRECT COSTS

Direct monetary costs include expenditures on health care, clinical, behavioral or educational services; transportation; caregivers; and other special needs services. Estimated costs for families are associated with type (physical, cognitive, sensory and mental) and severity of disability. The availability of benefits and services varies from one country to another and may decrease or increase direct cost. Stabile and Allin provide an updated and comprehensive review of seventeen studies from 1989 to 2005 that estimated the annual direct (consumption) costs associated with severe physical childhood disabilities (such as cerebral palsy and spina bifida). They have demonstrated that the range is extremely wide (from $108 to $8,742), and they reflect the

[25] See, for example, a study by Matthew P. Janicki et al., "Grandparent caregivers I: characteristics of the grandparents and the children with disability for whom they care," *Journal of Gerontological Social Work* 33 (2000), 33, 35–55.

[26] Mark Stabile and Sara Allin, "The economic costs of childhood disability," *Future of Children* 22 (2012), 65–96. Accessed 1/3/2014 at http://futureofchildren.org/futureofchildren/publications/journals/journal_details/index.xml?journalid=77.

complexity of the matter.[27] Similarly, an earlier review reported average annual expenditures in the 1980s ranging from $334 for families of children with cystic fibrosis to $4,012 for families of children with cancer.[28]

There is no doubt that calculating estimated direct costs of caring for children with different types of disabilities is a difficult task. Using the 2001 National Survey of Children with Special Health Care Needs (NS-CSHCN), one study reported an average annual cost of medical care (excluding insurance premiums and reimbursable costs) of $752 (or $620 if the 17.5 percent of families with no expenditures are factored into the estimate).[29] More recent estimates from the 2005–2006 wave of this survey were similar at approximately $832.[30]

Aside from including type or severity of disability in the estimated calculation, it is important to understand the context and background of the family. A good example is a study carried out by Susan Parish and her colleagues on a sample of low-income families. Using the 1999 National Survey of America's Families, they found that children with disability living with single parents spent significantly more hours in childcare than did children with disability living with two parents and children without disability in single- and two-parent households.[31] Interestingly, children with disability in single-parent households

27 Donna Anderson et al., "The personal costs of caring for a child with a disability: a review of the literature," *Public Health Reports* 122 (2007), 3–16; Stabile and Allin, "The economic costs of childhood disability," updated in 2012. The literature search using the same search terms yielded fifty-two new studies of the cost of child disabilities to families from 2000 to 2010, only seventeen of which estimated the direct or indirect costs associated with children with disability. Of these, nine were focused on a specific disability. Therefore, we include the results of eight of these studies in our review.

28 Philip Jacobs and Suzanne McDermott, "Family caregiver costs of chronically ill and handicapped children: method and literature review," *Public Health Reports* 104 (1989), 158–63.

29 Paul T. Shattuck and Susan L. Parish, "Financial burden in families of children with special health care needs: variability among states," *Pediatrics* 122 (2008), 13–18.

30 Lisa C. Lindley and Barbara A. Mark, "Children with special health care needs: impact of health care expenditures on family financial burden," *Journal of Child and Family Studies* 19 (2010), 79–89. The authors report health expenditures in six categories, so this estimate is calculated by combining the midpoint of each range with the proportion reporting an amount in that range.

31 Susan L. Parish et al., "Child care, disability, and family structure: use and quality in a population-based sample of low-income preschool children," *Children and Youth Services Review* 27 (2005), 905–19.

had the lowest monthly childcare costs, suggesting that single parents were compelled to use cheaper (and perhaps lower quality) childcare. Estimated monthly childcare costs averaged $179 for single-parent families of children with disability, $250 for single-parent families of children without disability and $271 for two-parent families with a child with disability (compare this with $225 for two-parent families with healthy children). Using the 2002 wave of this survey, Parish and her associates examined indicators of material hardship and found that having a child with a disability was associated with twice the odds of experiencing hardship after controlling for family income, maternal education, family structure and race.[32]

Overall, estimates of the direct costs to families associated with childhood disability present a very wide range. These estimates depend on definition of disability and kind of measurement used, the types of costs that are included in the estimate and the population that is sampled. The direct monetary costs may be the smallest component of costs to families given a range of indirect costs that are associated with children with disability.

INDIRECT COSTS

Indirect costs consist primarily of reductions in parents' ability to sustain paid employment. This loss of productivity could relate to the additional time that is required to care for a child with a disability combined with high costs or unavailability of adequate childcare. Stabile and Allin reviewed studies that tried to estimate the indirect cost of child disability. The majority of these studies focus on the probability that a mother is employed as a function of predicted wages, regional economic measures, availability of other sources of income (such as husband's income), receipt of benefits (such as social assistance or benefits for the disabled child), mother's health, child's health and age, and other socioeconomic factors such as maternal education. Some studies also look at hours of

[32] Susan L. Parish et al., "Material hardship in U.S. families raising children with disabilities," *Exceptional Children* 75 (2008), 71–92.

work, and others control for whether and how much the mother worked before the birth of her child.

Several studies find that having a child with disability restricts a mother's work activity.[33] Fewer mothers of young children with disability work (3 to 11 percent), and the effect is even larger (13 to 15 percentage points) when the child has severe disability.

However, indirect costs are difficult to measure basically because they are linked to children's type and severity of disability and family background and context. For example, it is almost impossible to distinguish between the effect of having a child with a disability and the effects of other correlated measures of socioeconomic status, including education and family income on maternal employment.[34] In addition, indirect costs have to take into consideration the association between child-rearing and employment by time. As children age, the caregiving burden falls for parents of healthy children relative to parents of disabled children.[35]

Researchers try to overcome these difficulties by using panel data and direct questioning of parents. Panel data measured over time is used in order to disentangle the effect of having a child with disability from the effects of other correlated factors related to the family. For example,

[33] See, for example, the following studies: Katherine E. Heck and Diane M. Makuc, "Parental employment and health insurance coverage among school-aged children with special health care needs," *American Journal of Public Health* 90 (2000), 1856–60; Elizabeth T. Powers, "New estimates of the impact of child disability on maternal employment," *American Economic Review* 91 (2001), 135–9; Marji E. Warfield, "Employment, parenting, and well-being among mothers of children with disabilities," *Mental Retardation* 39 (2001), 297–309; Jean Kimmel, "Child care costs as barrier to employment for single and married mothers," *Review of Economics and Statistics* 80 (1998), 287–99; Barbara L. Wolfe and Steven C. Hill, "The effect of health on the work effort of single mothers," *Journal of Human Resources* 30 (1995), 42–62; Pamela Loprest and Amy Davidoff, "How children with special health care needs affect the employment decisions of low-income parents," *Maternal and Child Health Journal* 8 (2004), 171–82; Karen A. Kuhlthau and James M. Perrin, "Child health status and parental employment," *Archives of Pediatrics & Adolescent Medicine* 155 (2001), 346–50.

[34] See Janet Currie and Mark Stabile, "Mental health in childhood and human capital," Jonathan Gruber (ed.), *An economic perspective on the problems of disadvantaged youth* (University of Chicago Press for National Bureau of Economic Research, 2009); Greg J. Duncan and Jeanne Brooks-Gunn, *Consequences of growing up poor* (New York: Russell Sage Foundation, 1997); Paul W. Newacheck and Margaret A. McManus, "Financing health care for disabled children," *Pediatrics* 81 (1988), 385–94.

[35] Kelly Noonan, Nancy E. Reichman and Hope Corman, "New fathers' labor supply: does child health matter?" *Social Science Quarterly* 86 (2005), 1399–417.

Nazli Baydar and others used the Medical Expenditure Panel Survey to assess the indirect costs of a child with asthma on the mothers' employment status.[36] The findings revealed that mothers who had a child with asthma were less likely to be employed full-time or part-time, and if single, they were less likely to retain their full-time jobs than other mothers. The effects of having a child with asthma depended on the marital status of the mother and the well-being of the child. Employment behaviors of single mothers were affected more than those of married mothers. Furthermore, children with unexpected asthma attacks or difficulties in breathing reduced the prevalence and continuation of full-time employment for single and married mothers.

Several studies used direct questioning to assess indirect costs such as the causal pathway and mechanisms underlying the relationship between childhood disability and maternal employment.[37] Interestingly, this method offers a validity check on panel data studies. Stabile and Allin, who have reviewed these economic studies, concluded that between 10 to 30 percent of mothers reported across studies that they had to stop working entirely, and the range of those that claim that they had to reduce work hours was between 15 and 68 percent.[38] It is evident that the wide range of findings reflects the common problems in estimating the indirect costs paid by mothers, as discussed earlier.

OUT-OF-POCKET EXPENDITURES

Naturally, out-of-pocket expenditures are higher among families of children with a disability and special health-care needs. This is probably related to the inability to cover all needs or due to restrictions associated

[36] Nazli Baydar et al., "Employment behaviors of mothers who have a child with asthma," *Journal of Family and Economic Issues* 28 (2007), 337–55

[37] Naomi Breslau, David Salkever and Kathleen S. Staruch, "Women's labor force activity and responsibilities for disabled dependents: a study of families with disabled children," *Journal of Health and Social Behavior* 23 (1982), 169–83; David S. Salkever, "Parental opportunity costs and other economic costs of children's disabling conditions," Nicholas Hobbs and James Perrin, *Issues in the care of children with chronic illness* (San Francisco: Jossey-Bass, 1985), 864; Shirley L. Porterfield, "Work choice of mothers in families with children with disabilities," *Journal of Marriage and Family* 64 (2002), 972–81.

[38] Stabile and Allin, "The economic costs of childhood disability," 77.

with medical regulations. Newachek and McManus[39] estimated that the expenses of parents of children with disability were two to three times higher than those of children without disability. In a newer study, Newacheck, Inkelas and Kim established an out-of-pocket costs threshold of 5 percent exceeding family income as an indication of unfair burden.[40] They found that the financial burden carried by low-income families exceeded that of the higher income families. Specifically, low-income families with a child with disability are approximately nineteen times more likely to incur expenses exceeding 5 percent of their family income than their higher income counterparts.

In an interesting article, Lukemeyer, Meyers and Smeeding estimated the out-of-pocket expenditures of parents caring for children with disability and chronic illness in welfare families.[41] They concluded that most of these expenditures are related to unreimbursed medical expenses and childcare.

However, the out-of-pocket cost to families of children with disability is also related to the type and severity of the disability or illness. Tsimicalis and associates claimed in a recent review that the quality of appraisal indicated that the derived cost estimates failed to reflect the magnitude of families' true costs.[42] Being specialists in caring for children with cancer they indicated that out-of-pocket expenses have to also include nonmedical costs such as continual travel to the hospital, purchasing supplies or hiring help. In a new study, they calculated that nearly three quarters of the total costs of parents are attributed to travel and food, followed by domestic labor, supplies and equipment.[43] Another new study carried out in Israel showed that out-of-pocket expenditures for children with autism spectrum disorder (ASD) are

[39] Newachek and McManus, "Financing health care for disabled children," 385–94.

[40] Paul W. Newacheck, Moira Inkelas and Sue E. Kim, "Health services use and health care expenditures for children with disability," *Pediatrics* 114 (2004), 79–85.

[41] Anna Lukemeyer, Marcia K. Meyers and Timothy M. Smeeding, "Expensive children in poor families: out-of-pocket expenditures for the care of disabled and chronically ill children in welfare families," *Journal of Marriage and the Family* 62 (2000), 399–415.

[42] Argerie Tsimicalis et al., "The cost of childhood cancer from the family's perspective: a critical review," *Pediatric Blood & Cancer* 56 (2011), 707–17.

[43] Argerie Tsimicalis et al., "A mixed method approach to describe the out-of-pocket expenses incurred by families of children with cancer," *Pediatric Blood & Cancer* 60 (2013), 438–45.

high regardless of the existing National Health Insurance system.[44] The average annual out-of-pocket expenditure per child was $8,289, with a median of $4,473 and a range of $0–89,754. Interestingly, allied medical treatments such as hydrotherapy, hippotherapy and art therapy totaled up to 41 percent of the total out-of-pocket expenditure, followed by alternative educational interventions and employing personal aides.

AVAILABLE AND ACCESSIBLE RESOURCES TO FAMILIES

A recent national survey on family and individual needs for disability supports prepared for the ARC by University of Minnesota provides an overall view of the unmet support needs of family caregivers of children with intellectual disability and developmental disability (ID/DD).[45] It seems that more than 40 percent of all family caregivers of children, adolescents and young adults with ID/DD have had unmet support needs for assistance in getting outside of the home to run errands or to see a doctor (48%), managing finances (46%), transportation (45%) and household management (41%). Interestingly, family caregivers of those with ASD were less likely to have unmet support needs than people with ID/DDs. Severity of disability was associated with more likelihood to have unmet needs for support in managing finances and transportation (57% vs. 42% for those with ID/DDs).

The same survey reported that family caregivers have been less satisfied with government-funded services. The dissatisfaction rate from therapy services was 49 percent.[46] Similar findings have been found with respect to family caregivers of ASD children and young adults. The core complaint is that government-funded services received by a person with ID/DD were lower than expected, in particular those

[44] Raanan Raz et al., "A survey of out-of-pocket expenditures for children with autism spectrum disorder in Israel," *Journal of Autism and Developmental Disorders* 43 (2013), 295–302.

[45] See Lynda Anderson, Sheryl A. Larson and Allise Wuorio, with Peter Berns, Ann Cameron Caldwell and K. Charlie Lakin, *2010 FINDS National survey family and individual needs for disability supports*, Technical Report Part 1, prepared for the Arc of the United States by the Research and Training Center on Community Living, University of Minnesota, May 2011, 9–10.

[46] Ibid., 12–13.

related to the number of therapy services (79% were dissatisfied), respite care (78%) and housing supports (77%). Interestingly, family caregivers reported greater satisfaction with the quality of private-pay services. Overall, 70 percent were satisfied with the quality of personal support services paid for with private funds, 66 percent were satisfied with the quality of therapy services, 64 percent were satisfied with the quality of transportation services, 61 percent were satisfied with the quality of private-pay respite care and 60 percent were satisfied with the quality of privately paid housing supports.

EDUCATION

The University of Minnesota report finds that family caregivers of children with ID/DD tend to be satisfied with their quality of education.[47] Eighty percent of family caregivers reported being satisfied or very satisfied with the quality of education the person with ID/DD received in preschool, but only 60 percent to 67 percent of family caregivers reported being satisfied or very satisfied with the quality of kindergarten through high school. However, the picture is less satisfactory in the ASD group, particularly with respect to the quality of kindergartens. Overall, family caregivers of people with ASD or ID were satisfied with the quality of the high school education. Finally, there were significant differences in caregiver satisfaction with the quality of education across all grade levels when considering the severity level of the person with ID/DD. Family caregivers of children and adolescents with severe ID/DD were less satisfied with school experiences than those with moderate ID/DD.

CHILDCARE AND RESPITE CARE

Childcare is important for children with disability and provides a stable and healthy environment in which they can learn, grow and develop

[47] Cathryn Booth-LaForce and Jean F. Kelly, "Childcare patterns and issues for families of preschool children with disabilities," *Infants and Young Children* 17 (2004), 6.

relationships with other children. It is a central provision that enables parents to work, rest, study or attend to their other responsibilities. However, families of children with disability experience a variety of childcare issues such as finding good-quality, affordable care that is within a reasonable distance from home or work.[48] Additionally, they are faced with logistical problems such as transportation to childcare programs and limited availability of childcare options because of their children's special care needs. Many programs do not provide professional care and are not geared to meeting the needs of these children.[49]

Another helpful service needed by families of children with disability is respite care, which is defined as "the shared care of a person with an illness or disability, either at home, in the community, or in a short-term residential setting, in order to give the family a break from the routine of caregiving."[50] Respite care is not familiar to all parents of children with disability and special needs. A comprehensive study carried out in South London found that 38 percent of parents were not familiar with the availability of this service. Most of the studies that examine parental needs indicate that parents wish to have access to a wide variety of respite care options.[51] The preferences vary between families and within families across time as circumstances change. Families place a child's need for respite as the primary reason for using it and not necessarily their own preference. They look for trustworthy and quality service carried out by professional and dedicated staff.

Parents prefer in-home services as they prefer that their child remains in his or her natural environment. In addition, in-home respite facilitates monitoring of the quality of care provided. However, in case of emergency or need for long-term support, parents prefer respite outside the home. In cases where the children are seriously ill or medically fragile, parents prefer skilled and trained caregivers who can

[48] Ibid.

[49] Marji Erickson-Warfield and Penny Hauser-Cram, "Childcare needs, arrangements, and satisfaction of mothers of children with developmental disabilities," *Mental Retardation* 34 (1996), 294–302.

[50] Medelon Treneman et al., "Respite care needs met and unmet: assessment of needs of children with disability," *Developmental Medicine and Child Neurology* 39 (1997), 548.

[51] See, for example, Barbara J. Leonard, Ann Louise Johnson and Janny Dwyer Brust, "Caregivers of children with disability: a comparison of those managing 'OK' and those needing more help," *Children's Health Care* 22 (1993), 93–105.

provide more intensive services. However, the most frequent use of respite care is for shorter duration services, for example, care provided for a few hours to free the caregiver for running errands, attending to other children's needs or taking a night off. However, the impact of short break provisions on children with disability and their parents is fairly limited. A recent review of fifty-six studies found that although short breaks enable parents to carry out what are relatively mundane activities, such as sleeping and social contact, short breaks in isolation are unlikely to impact on many other areas of their well-being.[52] It appears that respite care has a limited but consistent merit for siblings who report being able to spend time with their peers. There is evidence that short breaks enable them to take part in activities that may otherwise be impossible.[53]

HOUSING AND TRANSPORTATION NEEDS

One of the neglected areas is the availability of decent and appropriate housing for families of children with disability. There is no doubt that poor housing conditions, lack of access to and in the house, and lack of space to use equipment or carry out therapies dramatically reduce the well-being of the child with disability and the family. A recent campaign, Every Disabled Child Matters (EDCM) and the Joseph Rowntree Foundation (JRF), which have come together to highlight the housing needs of families with disabled children, touches upon the housing problem for families of children with disability in the United Kingdom.[54] Their comprehensive report sheds light on the housing needs of families of children with disability.[55] The report indicates that families of children with disability are more likely to be renting

[52] Janet Robertson et al., *The impacts of short breaks provision on disabled children and families: an international literature review* (London: Department for Education, 2010), 29. Accessed 3/11/2012 at https://www.gov.uk/government/uploads/system/uploads/attachment_data/file/221938/DCSF-RR222.pdf.

[53] Ibid., 30.

[54] See JRF 2008 report titled *Disabled children housing*. Accessed 4/6/2013 at http://www.edcm.org.uk/media/8104/disabled_children_and_housing.pdf.

[55] Department for Communities and Local Government (DCLG) (2007), *Housing in England 2005/6.*

their homes than families with nondisabled children, and they are more likely to live in overcrowded accommodation and to rate their home as being in a poor state of repair. The great majority of families of children with disability report that their homes are unsuitable for their child's needs and the associated needs of other family members. The sorts of problems with housing most frequently reported by families include lack of family space and lack of space for storing and using therapeutic equipment. Other common problems are difficulties with location and unsuitable or inaccessible kitchens, toilets and bathrooms. Living in unsuitable housing has been found to be associated with increased levels of parental stress. Parents describe the negative impact that living in unsuitable housing has on their child's well-being and development as well as on their own well-being and that of their other children.

The housing needs of US families of children with disability cannot be separated from other material hardships.[56] Examination of material hardship in US families raising children with disability found that families that had food insecurity and lack of access to care also had poor housing conditions. As family income rose above the federal poverty level, hardship declined sharply for families of children without disability but not for families raising children with disability. Thus, the US federal poverty level was found to be a particularly poor predictor of hardship for families. An additional report released by the Department of Housing and Urban Development (HUD) reveals that households of people with disability face serious difficulties finding safe and affordable housing for several reasons, such as being subjected to housing discrimination and encountering limited availability of accessible housing units.[57] Ambulatory, cognitive and independent living limitations were the most prevalent restrictions among households with the most severe case needs and with people with disability. Visual, hearing and self-care limitations were found in a smaller share of those same households.

[56] Parish et al., "Material hardship in U.S. families raising a child with disability."

[57] US Department of Housing and Urban Development, Office of Policy Development and Research, *Report to Congress of 2009 worst case housing needs of people with disabilities: supplemental findings*. Accessed 4/10/2013 at http://www.huduser.org/portal/publications/WorstCaseDisabilities03_2011.pdf.

Transportation is another important need of people with disability, and in particular families of children with special needs.[58] The greatest need is that of children with physical disability and complicated health problems. They often lack an appropriate vehicle, the equipment needed for transportation or guidance regarding safe seating in vehicles. Unfortunately, poor families often cannot access services because of lack of resources, including transportation.[59]

NEEDS OF FAMILIES WITH DIFFERENT TYPES OF DISABILITY

Families of children with disability have common personal and economic concerns, including difficulties in obtaining and accessing services. There are specific and unique needs related to the type of disability or illness. The following section summarizes the service needs of families of children with physical, ASD, intellectual and learning disabilities and medical complexities.

SERVICE NEEDS OF FAMILIES OF CHILDREN WITH PHYSICAL DISABILITIES

Families of children with a physical disability experience a large variety of needs over and above those of families with typically developing children. A recent review of the literature on families of children with physical disability through December 2011 revealed that the top need was information about available services and benefits and professional help.[60] Most of the studies have been focused on cerebral palsy (CP),

58 Torbjörn Falkmer, J. Fulland and Nils Petter Gregersen, "A literature review of road vehicle transportation of children with disability," *Journal of Traffic Medicine* 29 (2001), 54–62.

59 Beth M. McManus et al., "Modeling the social determinants of caregiver burden among families of children with developmental disabilities," *American Journal on Intellectual and Developmental Disabilities* 116 (2011), 246–60.

60 Renate C. Siebes et al., "Needs of families with children who have a physical disability: a literature review," *Critical Reviews™, Physical and Rehabilitation Medicine* 24 (2012), 85–108.

the most prevalent childhood physical disability with a rate of 3.6 per 1000, which accounts for approximately 2 percent of children with special health-care needs (CSHCN) in the United States.[61] CP is defined as a nonprogressive disturbance of the developing fetal or infant brain that results in movement and posture disorders that cause activity limitations.[62]

Parents of children and youth who use wheeled mobility expressed the highest number of family needs, while parents of children/youth who walk without restrictions expressed the fewest needs.[63] Families reporting need for information, support, community services and finances differed based on children's gross motor function level. More than half of the parents studied looked for information on current and future services, planning for the future, and how they could locate community activities and gain more personal time. Parents of children and youth who use wheeled mobility were more likely to ask for financial assistance for home modifications, equipment and respite care services. Similarly, a recent study has shown that mothers of high social economic status with children with CP who are able to walk reported strong family relationships and less need for community, financial and family support and services.[64]

SERVICE NEEDS OF FAMILIES OF AUTISM SPECTRUM DISORDERS (ASD) CHILDREN

Autism spectrum disorders are a group of developmental disabilities that can cause significant social, communication and behavioral challenges. Parents of ASD children feel that they have to cope with unique challenges and unmet needs. Their most reported need is for

[61] Jessica Sun et al., "Prevalence of cerebral palsy in 8-year-old children in three areas of the US in 2002: a multisite collaboration," *Pediatrics* 121 (2008), 547–54; Sarah Winter et al., "Trends in the prevalence of cerebral palsy in a population-based study," *Pediatrics* 110 (2002), 1220–25.

[62] Peter Rosenbaum et al., "A report: The definition and classification of cerebral palsy," *Developmental Medicine & Child Neurology* 109 (2007), 8–14.

[63] Robert J. Palisano, "Physical activity of children with cerebral palsy: what are the considerations?" *Developmental Medicine & Child Neurology* 54 (2012), 390–91.

[64] Nihad Almasri et al., "Profiles of family needs of children and youth with cerebral palsy," *Child Care, Health & Development* 40 (2011), 130–54.

information about available services and how to handle their children's difficult behaviors or teach them skills.[65] Parents are often required to serve as case managers for their children and struggle for access and better coordination of services. They often complain about difficulties in obtaining adequate services. In one of the American studies, 60 percent of parents of three- to nine-year-old children with ASD reported that the agencies that provided services to them failed to communicate adequately with them, respond to family functioning problems or provide for home-based respite care.[66] In a Canadian study, Hilary K. Brown and her colleagues found that family needs were far from being met in three major areas: social activities for the child, information about services and continuous service provision.[67] Finally, a study that examined Northern Ireland's demonstrated needs for services[68] revealed that families lacked information and statutory service provisions, there were prolonged waiting times for diagnosis and there was an absence of a coherent view on science-based policy and practice. The research uncovered that the considerable lack of knowledge and application of the science of behavior analysis amongst professionals can be directly linked to the noninclusion of suitably qualified behavior analysts in local governmental reviews and reports.

SERVICE NEEDS OF FAMILIES OF CHILDREN WITH INTELLECTUAL OR DEVELOPMENTAL DISABILITIES (ID/DD)

Research that compares families of children with ID/DD with those without recognized disability finds greater stress in parents of children

[65] Warren Mansell and Kathleen Morris, "A survey of parents' reactions to the diagnosis of an autistic spectrum disorder by a local service: access to information and use of services," *Autism* 8 (2004), 387–407.

[66] James T. Ellis et al., "Families of children with developmental disabilities: assessment and comparison of self-reported needs in relation to situational variables," *Journal of Developmental and Physical Disabilities* 14 (2002), 191–202.

[67] Hilary K. Brown et al., "Unmet needs of families of school-aged children with an autism spectrum disorder," *Journal of Applied Research in Intellectual Disabilities* 25 (2012), 497–508.

[68] Mickey Keenan et al., *Meeting the needs of families living with children diagnosed with autism spectrum disorder: final report* (Coleraine: University of Ulster, 2007).

with ID/DD than in parents of children without disability.[69] It appears that parents of children with Down syndrome express less stress and depression than parents of children with other diagnoses, particularly autism.[70] Families of children and youth with intellectual disability have ongoing service needs. In probably the largest survey carried out in the United States by the University of Minnesota for the ARC, the researchers studied ongoing challenges of 5,287 family members regarding their met and unmet needs.[71] The Family and Individual Needs for Disability Supports (FINDS) survey reported that most family caregivers (58%) provided more than forty hours of care per week. This interfered with their work (71%) and caused tremendous financial strain (81%). Family caregivers reported on unmet services in getting help outside of the home for errands or to see a doctor (48%), managing finances (46%), transportation (45%) and household management (41%). Whether private-pay or government-funded, family caregivers were not satisfied with the amount of assistance they received. They reported paying for more services out of pocket (47%) and were providing more support than they used to (41%). Finally, they were more satisfied with the quality of private-pay services than with government-funded services. Families of children with intellectual disability and challenging behavior demonstrated the greatest need for support.[72] They thought that disability services should respond better to their concerns in obtaining relevant professional information and adjusted respite care provision. Specifically, parents looked for effective strategies to handle challenging behavior.

[69] See Douglas Barnett et al., "Building new dreams: supporting parents' adaptation to their child with special needs," *Infants and Young Children* 16 (2003), 184–200.

[70] See, for example, Pamela Lewis et al., "Cognitive, language and social-cognitive skills of individuals with Fragile X Syndrome with and without autism," *Journal of Intellectual Disability Research* 50 (2006), 532–45.

[71] See Executive Summary of FIND's survey *Still in the shadows with their future uncertain on family and individual needs for disability support*, ARC 2011. Accessed 7/8/2013 at http://www.thearc.org/document.doc?id=3672

[72] G. Wodehouse and Peter McGill, "Support for family carers of children and young people with developmental disabilities and challenging behaviour: what stops it being helpful?" *Journal of Intellectual Disabilities Research* 53 (2009), 644–53.

SERVICE NEEDS OF FAMILIES OF CHILDREN WITH CHRONIC ILLNESS AND MEDICAL COMPLEXITIES (CMC)

A chronic health condition is a health problem that lasts more than three months; affects children's normal activities; and requires a lot of hospitalizations, home health care, and in some cases extensive medical care. Chronic condition is an "umbrella" term; children with chronic illnesses may be ill or well at any given time, but they are always living with their condition. Some examples of chronic conditions include (but are not limited to) asthma (the most common), diabetes, sickle cell anaemia, cystic fibrosis, cancer, epilepsy and congenital heart problems. Families of children with chronic illness face challenges that are related to the type and severity of the illness. In one of the early studies on service needs of families of young children with chronic illness, Axtell and her colleagues assessed parents' satisfaction with services their families received and identified families' unmet service needs as well as the reasons for these unmet needs.[73] Although families' ratings of the adequacy of services were relatively high, 28 percent of the families reported unmet service needs, which included occupational, physical or speech therapy and respite care/childcare. Lack of funding was the most commonly given reason for unmet needs, while children with multiple impairments were at highest risk for unmet needs.

The most significant challenges are experienced by families of children with CMC, which refers to congenital or acquired multisystem disease, a severe neurologic condition with marked functional impairment and/or technology dependence for activities of daily living. Regardless of their underlying diagnoses, they share similar functional and resource-use consequences, including intensive hospital or community-based service needs, reliance on technology and home care, risk of frequent and prolonged hospitalizations and ongoing need for care coordination.[74] In a recent article, Eyal Cohen and his colleagues addressed parental areas of concern, among them elevated stress, marital difficulties, employment challenges and financial

[73] Sara A. M. Axtell et al., "Unmet service needs of families of young children with chronic illnesses and disabilities," *Journal of Family and Economic Issues* 16 (1995), 395–411.

[74] Rajendu Srivastava, Bryan L. Stone and Nancy A. Murphy, "Hospitalist care of the medically complex child," *Pediatric Clinics of North America* 52 (2005), 1165–87.

consequences. In addition, parents have to be familiar with a child's condition and utilize community medical care services.[75]

FAMILIES OF CHILDREN WITH MENTAL ILLNESS

Families of children with mental health disorders experience greater economic burden of care than those with other special health-care needs.[76] Mental disorders tend to be less predictable than other child health disorders, and they potentially lead to greater parental labor-market disruption. According to Gould, parents, particularly mothers, cannot plan for associated medical expenses or taking time away from work. Gould found that only 17 percent of married mothers can work if their child has an illness with an unpredictable time component.[77] A child's mental illness tends to stigmatize the family as a whole and reduces the social acceptability of parents taking time off to care for the child or to obtain appropriate services from family members and friends. In addition, parents have to cope with the fact that private health insurance companies provide less generous services for mental health care than for general health care. Therefore, parental expectation is for equalizing private insurance coverage and the provision of cash support to ease the economic toll of care for their children with mental health disorders.[78]

FAMILIES THAT TURN TO OUT-OF-HOME PLACEMENT

An interesting way to understand needs of families of children with disability is to examine extreme cases such as parents who have difficulties keeping their child at home. Families that opt to seek out-of-home

[75] Eyal Cohen et al., "Children with medical complexity: an emerging population for clinical and research initiatives," *Pediatrics* 127 (2011), 529–38.
[76] Susan H. Busch and Colleen L. Barry, "Mental health disorders in childhood: assessing the burden on families," *Health Affairs* 26 (2007), 1088–95.
[77] Elise Gould, "Decomposing the effects of children's health on mother's labour supply: is it time or money?" *Health Economics* 13 (2004), 525–41.
[78] Busch and Barry, "Mental health disorders in childhood," 1094.

placement reported fewer family resources and more stress.[79] Critical resources include financial and professional assistance for associated medical problems and family social support. There is a consensus among current researchers that the decision to seek out-of-home placement is related to three multidimensional variables associated with the characteristics of the child and family and available services.[80]

The most significant characteristics associated with parental inability to keep a child at home are severity of a child's disability, a child's challenging behavior and caring for an adolescent with serious physical disability.[81] Family characteristics associated with out-of-home placement include caregiver's increased stress and parental concern about the impact on siblings.

A leading clinical assumption is that the provision of appropriate educational programs and sufficient respite care services may prevent families of young children with disability from seeking out-of-home placement.[82] An interesting study carried out in-depth interviews with parents of young children with medical complexities in order to understand the dynamics of placement decisions.[83] Results indicate that

[79] Arie Rimmerman, "Alternatives to institutions and family support," Stanley S. Herr, Lawrence O. Gostin and Harold Hongju Koh (eds.), *The human rights of persons with intellectual disabilities: different but equal* (Oxford: Oxford University Press, 2003), 415–28.

[80] Gwynnyth Llewellyn et al., "Out-of-home placement of school-age children with disabilities and high support needs," *Journal of Applied Research in Intellectual Disabilities* 18 (2005), 1–6.

[81] See, for example, Arie Rimmerman and Ilana Duvdevany, "Parents of children and adolescents with severe mental retardation: stress, family resources, normalization and their application for out-of-home placement," *Research in Developmental Disabilities* 17 (1996), 487–94. In this particular study the researchers examined out-of-home applications of eighty-eight Israeli parents who had younger children and adolescents with severe mental retardation and, in particular, the question of whether parental application for placement is a function of their marital status, level of education, children's age, parental stress, family environment (climate), social support, or attitudes toward normalization. Multiple regression analysis showed that five predictors had significant correlations with parental application: parental stress (high), social support (less), attitudes toward normalization (favorable), family environment or climate (low) and children's age (adolescents). However, only the first three predictors (stress, social support and attitudes toward normalization) contributed to the model of prediction of placement.

[82] Jan Blacher and P. Prado, "The school as respite for parents of children with severe handicaps," Christine L. Salisbury and James Intagliata (eds.), *Respite care: support for persons with developmental disabilities and their families* (Baltimore, MD: Paul Brookes, 1986), 217–34.

[83] Deborah A. Bruns, "Leaving home at an early age: parents' decisions about out-of-home placement for young children with complex medical needs," *Mental Retardation* 38 (2000), 50–60.

parents experience a common process: recognition that they cannot cope with their children's medical problems without additional support, realization that these provisions are inappropriate or unsatisfactory in solving their immediate needs and mounting financial concerns. The decision to turn to out-of-home placement is triggered by a sense that they have no choice but to give up.

A retrospective study that explores families' thoughts prior to placement reveals that there is a typical explanation shared by most parents, for example, "We did realize that sooner or later he would have to go, though we put it off as long as possible because, you know, he's part of the family."[84] Similarly, a study of out-of-home placement of school-age children with high support needs indicated that parental placement tendency was associated with difficulty balancing the demands of caring and the needs of other family members, sharing workload and responsibility and integrating the child into the everyday world. The conclusion was that available resources were not enough and the most important issue was their capacity to continue balancing the demands of caring and responding to the needs of other family members.[85]

CONCLUSION: FAMILY NEEDS AND PRIORITIES FOR FAMILY POLICY

The chapter sheds light on the needs of families of children with disability and their personal, marital and financial challenges. Overall, one out of six children in the United States had a developmental disability in 2006–2008, and the prevalence of this population increased 17.1 percent from 1997 to 2008. Parents of children with disability carry a significant emotional burden, and their needs are associated with the type and severity of the disability and the context and policies existing in each country. The research review shows inconclusive findings regarding the impact on marital relations and siblings, with most of the reports showing that the negative effect, if it exists, is marginal.

[84] Brigit Mirfin-Veitch, Ann Bray and Nicola Ross, "It was the hardest and most painful decision of my life!: Seeking permanent out-of-home placement for sons and daughters with intellectual disabilities," *Journal of Intellectual & Developmental Disability* 28 (2003), 103.

[85] Llewellyn et al., "Out-of-home placement of school-age children with disability," 6.

The more evident burden is financial; childhood disabilities have direct and indirect economic costs to the family and society that are strongly linked to the type and severity of disability. It is easier to measure the direct monetary costs, including expenditures on health care, clinical, behavioral or educational services and transportation, than indirect or out-of-pocket costs. It is more complicated to estimate reductions in parents' ability to sustain paid employment or the cost of unavailability of adequate childcare. These estimates vary from one country to another and are greatly dependent on explicit and implicit policies.

Aside from the financial burden on families, surveys of families' needs demonstrate that parents mostly complain about inadequate and inaccessible services.[86] Relatively, the most met needs are education, and to some degree childcare and respite. The unmet needs are medical, financial, housing and transportation. There is no doubt that poor and inadequate housing dramatically reduces the well-being of the child with disability. An examination of material hardship in US families raising children with disability shows that those with poor housing conditions also reported food insecurity and lack of access to care and transportation.

There is no doubt that there is great variability among disabilities; parents of children with ASD, CMC and mental illness require information, special guidance and additional care as compared with those of children with physical or intellectual disability. They face more financial demands and experience greater labor market disruption. In addition, these families, in particular parents of children with behavioral challenges, are more vulnerable to considering out-of-home placement.

[86] 2010 FINDS National Survey *Family and Individual Needs for Disability*, which was earlier cited in the chapter, found that about 20 percent of families had no source of income. Overall, 62 percent reported experiencing decreases in services and nearly a third were waiting for government-funded services (32%), most for more than five years. They reported paying for more services out of pocket (47%) and were providing more support than they used to (41%). Most family caregivers (58%) provided more than forty hours of care per week (including 40% who provided more than eighty hours of care per week). This interfered with their work (71%) and caused physical (88%) and financial strain (81%). One-fifth of family caregivers reported that someone in their family had to quit work to provide care. Nearly two-thirds of family caregivers (62%) were paying for some care out of pocket. Family caregivers also struggled to find afterschool care (80%), reliable home-care providers (84%) and community-based care (82%).

4 FAMILY POLICIES RELATED TO CHILDREN AND YOUTH WITH DISABILITY IN THE UNITED STATES

The United States has no explicit family policy, nor has there been any such policy or cluster of policies in the past.[1] Nonetheless, over the years, the federal government has developed provisions and regulations for family conservation and support. Overall, US federal policy leans toward individualism, strict work ethics and protection of the family as a private entity. Within this context, social policies affecting children and their families focus primarily on the children with disability, particularly those with severe conditions living in poor families. The impression is that legislation and regulations lean toward services and in-kind benefits with modest and inconsistent cash benefits to some low-income families and tax benefits to the middle and upper classes.[2]

The chapter consists of two parts; the first provides a review of core provisions (policies, legislations and regulations) covering generic and explicit policies and legislations relating to families of children and youth with disability. The second assesses and discusses three themes reflected in these legislations and policies: means testing and taxation, public accommodations and recognized rights of working parents, and parents' rights to participate in educational decision making.

[1] See extensive review of US family policy in Karen Bogenschneider, *Family policy matters: how policymaking affects families and what professionals can do*, 3rd ed. (New York: Routledge, 2014).

[2] Neil Gilbert and Rebecca Van Voorhis, "The paradox of family policy," *Social Science and Public Policy* (September/October 2003), 51–6.

GENERIC POLICIES AND LAWS

Tax law

The core generic provision for families of young children and youth with disability is through the tax system. Following is a discussion of the common deductions and credits that are permitted in tax law.

The dependency exemption

The US tax system allows taxpayers to claim a dependency exemption ($3,900 for 2013) for a "qualifying child." With the passage of the Working Families Tax Relief Act of 2004, P.L. 108–311 (effective 2005)[3] the definition of a qualifying child in Sec. 152(a) was amended to provide a uniform definition for purposes of the dependency exemption and for the child tax, dependent care and EITCs.

Under the definition, to be a qualifying child, in addition to meeting the relationship test (taxpayer's child; stepchild; eligible foster child; adopted child or descendant, for example, grandchild), an individual (Sec. 152(c)) must meet any one of the following three requirements: the child must be under the age of nineteen at the end of the year, permanently and totally disabled, or unable to engage in any substantial gainful activity by reason of any medically determinable physical or mental impairment that can be expected to result in death or that has lasted or can be expected to last for a continuous period of not less than twelve months (Sec. 22(e)(3)). A physician must certify in writing that the individual is permanently and totally disabled.

Attending special schools as qualified medical expenses

In general, taxpayers who exceed the 10%-of-adjusted-gross-income (AGI) floor in 2013 (7.5% of AGI for 2012) can deduct qualifying

[3] Working Families Tax Relief Act of 2004, P.L. 108-311, was signed by President George W. Bush on October 4, 2004, extending various personal income tax reductions for middle-class taxpayers that had been scheduled to expire. The act also extends several business-related provisions that had been scheduled to expire at the end of 2004 and 2005. Accessed 11/11/2013 at http://www.gpo.gov/fdsys/pkg/PLAW-108publ311/pdf/PLAW-108publ311.pdf.

medical expenses including those of dependent children. The expenses of a special school that are deductible as medical expenses include amounts paid for lodging, meals, transportation and the cost of ordinary education that is incidental to the special services the school provides. Also, any costs incurred for the supervision, care, treatment and training of a physically and/or neurologically handicapped individual are deductible if the institution provides the services.

Taxpayers participating in tax-advantaged plans through work for funding medical expenses (for example, flexible spending accounts or health savings accounts) can set aside limited amounts of money to finance medical care expenses on a pretax basis, thereby avoiding the 10%-of-AGI limitation. The amounts that can be set aside pretax are under $3,250 for employees with single coverage and $6,450 for those with family coverage. It is important to note that the IRS considers the medical facilities and therapeutic orientation of a school as critical factors in determining whether a school qualifies for a medical care deduction. A regular school with special curricula can also be considered as a special school for those individuals benefiting from a special curriculum.

Capital expenditures

In general, US tax law does not permit the use of capital expenditure as a medical expense deduction. However, a medical expense deduction is available when the capital expenditure is made primarily for the medical care of the taxpayer, the taxpayer's spouse and/or the taxpayer's dependents. To secure a current medical expense deduction for a capital expenditure, the cost must be reasonable in amount and incurred out of medical necessity for primary use by the individual requiring medical care. These capital expenditures for medical expense deductions fall into two categories: (1) expenditures improving the taxpayer's residence while also providing medical care (for example, a central air conditioning system for an individual suffering from a chronic respiratory illness) and (2) expenditures removing structural barriers in the home of an individual with physical limitations (for example, construction costs incurred for an entrance ramp, widening doorways and halls, customizing bathing facilities, lowering kitchen cabinets and adding railings).

Earned income tax credit (EITC)

Sec. 32 of the EITC[4] has been offered to encourage disadvantaged populations to work by partially offsetting the social security taxes on wages. Appropriately, it is not available to taxpayers who have unearned income (that is, dividends, interest, gains on sales of securities) above a specified threshold ($3,300 for 2013). For EITC purposes, a qualifying child has the same definition as for the dependency exemption – an individual who has the requisite relationship with the taxpayer, who resided with the taxpayer for more than six months during the calendar year and who is under the age of nineteen at the end of the year, under the age of twenty-four and a full-time student, or is permanently and totally disabled (Sec. 32(c)(3)). A child with severe disability is considered a qualifying child regardless of age, even into adulthood, as long as the child continues to live at home with a parent or another person who meets the relationship test with respect to the child. The maximum EITC for 2013 is $6,044 for families with three or more qualifying children, $5,372 for families with two qualifying children and $3,250 for families with one qualifying child.

HEALTH

Children's Health Insurance Program (CHIP)

The Children's Health Insurance Program (CHIP), formerly the State Children's Health Insurance Program (SCHIP), was created by the Balanced Budget Act of 1997, enacted Title XXI of the Social Security Act, and has allocated about $20 billion over ten years to help states insure low-income children who are ineligible for Medicaid but cannot afford private insurance. States receive an enhanced federal match (greater than the state's Medicaid match) to provide for this coverage. In 2007, after President Bush and Congress could not agree on CHIP reauthorization details, the program was extended through March 2009. In February

[4] The United States federal earned income tax credit (EITC) is a refundable tax credit for low- and medium-income individuals and couples, primarily for those who have qualifying children.

2009, the Children's Health Insurance Program Reauthorization Act of 2009 was approved by Congress and signed by President Obama. President Obama signed the Patient Protection and Affordable Care Act, H.R. 3590, on March 23, 2010, and the Reconciliation Act of 2010, H.R. 4872, on March 30, 2010.[5] Among many provisions, the laws extend the authorization of the federal CHIP program for an additional two years, through September 30, 2015. The laws require states, upon enactment, to maintain current income eligibility levels for CHIP through September 30, 2019. States are prohibited from implementing eligibility standards, methodologies or procedures that are more restrictive than those in place as of March 23, 2010, with the exception of waiting lists for enrolling children in CHIP.

Family and Medical Leave Act

The Family and Medical Leave Act of 1993 (FMLA) is a federal law that enables employers to provide employees job-protected and unpaid leave for qualified medical and family reasons, among which are personal or family illness (including a child with disability).[6] President Bill Clinton signed the bill into law on February 5, 1993, (P. L. 103–3; 29 U.S.C. sec. 2601; 29 CFR 825) and it took effect on August 5, 1993, six months later. The act allows eligible employees to take up to twelve work weeks of unpaid leave during any twelve-month period to attend

[5] See the combined full text of Public Law 111-148. Accessed 4/2/2014 at http://www.gpo.gov/fdsys/pkg/PLAW-111publ148/pdf/PLAW-111publ148.pdf and PL 111–152 at http://www.gpo.gov/fdsys/pkg/PLAW-111publ152/pdf/PLAW-111publ152.pdf.

[6] See Purposes of 29 U.S.C. §2601. The purposes are as follows: (1) to balance the demands of the workplace with the needs of families, to promote the stability and economic security of families, and to promote national interests in preserving family integrity; (2) to entitle employees to take reasonable leave for medical reasons, for the birth or adoption of a child, and for the care of a child, spouse, or parent who has a serious health condition; (3) to accomplish the purposes described in paragraphs (1) and (2) in a manner that accommodates the legitimate interests of employers; (4) to accomplish the purposes described in paragraphs (1) and (2) in a manner that, consistent with the Equal Protection Clause of the Fourteenth Amendment, minimizes the potential for employment discrimination on the basis of sex by ensuring generally that leave is available for eligible medical reasons (including maternity-related disability) and for compelling family reasons, on a gender-neutral basis; and (5) to promote the goal of equal employment opportunity for women and men, pursuant to such clause. Accessed 2/3/2014 at http://www.dol.gov/whd/regs/statutes/fmla.htm.

to the serious health condition of the employee, parent, spouse or child; for pregnancy or care of a newborn child; or for adoption or foster care of a child. On February 6, 2013, the act was signed into law – the Wage and Hour Division, the arm of the US Department of Labor that enforces the FMLA, published new regulations updating its rules.

EDUCATION

Elementary and Secondary Education Act (ESEA)

The Elementary and Secondary Education Act (ESEA) emphasizes equal access to education, establishes high standards and accountability, and requires the inclusion of all students with disability in the student achievement system. The law authorizes federally funded education programs that are administered by the states. In 2002, Congress amended ESEA and reauthorized it as the No Child Left Behind Act (NCLB), which authorizes several federal education programs that are administered by the states. Under the 2002 law, states are required to test students in reading and math in grades 3–8 and once in high school. All students are expected to meet or exceed state standards in reading and math by 2014. The major focus of No Child Left Behind is to close student achievement gaps by providing all children with a fair, equal and significant opportunity to obtain a high-quality education. The US Department of Education emphasizes four pillars within the bill: accountability, ensuring that those students who are disadvantaged achieve academic proficiency; flexibility, allowing school districts flexibility in how they use federal education funds to improve student achievement; evidence-based education, emphasizing educational programs and practices that have been proven effective through scientific research; and parent options, increasing the choices available to the parents of students attending Title I schools.

The legislation provides the following provisions for students with disability. The No Child Left Behind Act provides unprecedented new flexibility for all fifty states and every local school district in America in the use of federal education funds. States will receive the freedom to target up to 50 percent of federal non-Title I dollars under the act to programs that will have the most positive impact on the students they serve, including students with disability; assessments have to include adaptations and accommodations for students with disability as defined in the Individuals with Disabilities Education Act (IDEA); and assessment results and state progress objectives must be broken out by student groups, including those with disability, to ensure that no group is left behind.

Head Start

Head Start is a federally funded preschool program that provides comprehensive services to children and poor families. Children from birth to five and pregnant women are eligible for Head Start (3–5) or Early Head Start (0–3 and pregnant women) if they are homeless, receiving Temporary Assistance for Needy Families (TANF) benefits or Supplemental Security Income (SSI), or if they are in foster care. Another way they are considered eligible is if the family's income is determined to be at or below the federal poverty level. Some grantees enroll a percentage of children from families with incomes above the Poverty Guidelines as well. Its aim is to prepare children for success in school through an early learning program. The Office of Head Start (OHS), within the Administration of Children and Families of the Department of Health and Human Services, awards grants to public and private agencies on a competitive basis to provide these comprehensive services to specific communities. The Head Start program is managed by local nonprofit organizations in almost every county in the country. Children who attend Head Start engage in various educational activities, receive free medical and dental care, have healthy meals and snacks, and enjoy playing indoors and outdoors in a safe setting. Head Start–funded enrollment is more than 820,000 children since 2003. Figures from 2010 indicate that 128,157 of children determined to have a disability comprise about 12 percent of all Head Start children.[7]

[7] Based on Stephanie Schmit and Danielle Ewen, CLASP (Center for Law and Social Policy) Report No. 10, 2012, *Putting children and families first: Head Start Programs 2010*. The nonpartisan and nonprofit organization advocates for public policies that will improve the lives of low-income people. The organization focuses on policy solutions in the areas of

The Federal Education Rights and Privacy Act (FERPA)

The Family Educational Rights and Privacy Act (FERPA) (20 U.S.C. §1232g; 34 CFR Part 99) is a federal law that protects the privacy of student education records. The law applies to all schools that receive funds under an applicable program of the US Department of Education. FERPA gives parents certain rights with respect to their children's education records. These rights transfer to the student when he or she reaches the age of eighteen or attends a school beyond high school level. Students to whom the rights have transferred are "eligible students." Parents or eligible students have the right to inspect and review the student's education records maintained by the school. It should be noted that Section 504 of the Rehabilitation Act[8] protects the civil rights of persons with disability, prohibiting discrimination against a person with a disability by an agency receiving federal funds. Students who are defined as "handicapped" but do not require special education services can be provided with a 504 plan.

HOUSING

The Fair Housing Act of 1968 (FHA) prohibits discrimination in the sale or rental of private housing on the basis of race, religion, color or sex.[9] The main thrust of the 1988 amendments to the FHA was to strengthen

childcare and early education, child welfare, postsecondary education, workforce development, income and work supports, employment strategies and disadvantaged youth. Accessed 2/4/2014 at http://www.clasp.org/admin/site/publications/files/Head-Start-Trend-Analysis-Final2.pdf.

8 Section 504 of the Rehabilitation Act is a civil rights law which prohibits discrimination against individuals with disabilities. It ensures that the child with a disability has equal access to an education. The child may receive accommodations and modifications. Unlike the IDEA, Section 504 does not require the school to provide an individualized educational program (IEP) designed to meet the child's unique needs and provide the child with educational benefit. Under Section 504, fewer procedural safeguards are available to children with disability and their parents than under IDEA. On September 25, 2008, the president signed the Americans with Disabilities Act Amendments Act of 2008 (ADAAA). The act, effective January 1, 2009, emphasizes that the definition of disability should be construed in favor of broad coverage of individuals to the maximum extent permitted by the terms of the ADA. Section 504 accessed 12/2/2012 at http://www.dol.gov/oasam/regs/statutes/sec504.htm.

9 Federal Fair Housing Act, P. L. No. 90–284, 82 Stat. 73, 81 (1968) (codified as amended at 42 U.S.C. §3601–3631 (1994)). The Fair Housing Act (FHA) was enacted "to provide, within constitutional limitations, for fair housing throughout the United States." The original 1968 act prohibited discrimination on the basis of "race, color, religion, or national origin" in the sale or rental of housing, the financing of housing or the provision of brokerage services. In 1974, the act was amended to add sex discrimination to the list of prohibited

the enforcement mechanisms of the law for these protected classes. In 1994, the Fair Housing Amendments Act (FHAA) included, for the first time, prohibitions on discrimination against persons based on disability. Much of the language of the FHAA was taken directly from Section 504 of the Rehabilitation Act. The passage of the FHAA, combined with Section 504, meant that individuals with disability (including families of children with developmental or other disability) were covered in the public sector context as well as private housing.

NUTRITION

The Supplemental Nutrition Assistance Program (SNAP)

Formerly known as the Food Stamp Program, SNAP is the most important antihunger program. The majority of SNAP households include low-wage working families, low-income seniors and people with disability with fixed incomes (76%).[10] The federal government pays the full cost of SNAP benefits and splits the cost of administering the program with the states, which operate the program. The average monthly SNAP benefit per person in 2011 is $133.85, or less than $1.50 per person per meal.[11]

WELFARE REFORM

Personal Responsibility and Work Opportunity Reconciliation Act of 1996

The enactment of the Personal Responsibility and Work Opportunity Reconciliation Act in 1996 replaced Aid for Families with Dependent Children with Temporary Assistance for Needy Families (TANF). The act is known as The Welfare Reform Act and represents the federal

activities. Likewise, in 1988 the act was amended to prohibit discrimination on the additional grounds of physical and mental handicap, as well as familial status.

[10] US Department of Agriculture, Food and Nutrition Service, *Characteristics of Supplemental Nutrition Assistance Program Households: Fiscal Year 2011*. Table A.14. November 2012. Accessed 2/2/2014 at http://www.fns.usda.gov/ora/menu/Published/snap/SNAPPartHH.htm.

[11] US Department of Agriculture, Food and Nutrition Service, *Characteristics of Supplemental Nutrition Assistance Program Households: Fiscal Year 2011*. Table D.3. November 2012. Accessed 3/1/2014 at http://www.fns.usda.gov/ora/menu/Published/snap/SNAPPartHH.htm.

government's attempt to reform the welfare system by "encouraging" recipients to leave welfare and go to work and by turning over primary responsibility for administering the welfare system to the states. Under the Welfare Reform Act, the following rules apply: most recipients are required to find jobs within two years of first receiving welfare payments, and they are allowed to receive welfare payments for a total of no more than five years.

DISABILITY POLICIES AND LAWS

The Rehabilitation Act of 1973 – Section 504

Section 504 is a part of the Rehabilitation Act of 1973 that prohibits discrimination based on disability. Section 504 is an antidiscrimination, civil rights statute that requires the needs of students with disability to be met as adequately as the needs of the nondisabled. It states that "No otherwise qualified individual with a disability in the United States, as defined in section 706(8) of this title, shall, solely by reason of her or his disability, be excluded from the participation in, be denied the benefits of, or be subjected to discrimination under any program or activity receiving Federal financial assistance" [29 U.S.C. §794(a), 34 C.F.R. §104.4(a)].

The act is divided into seven subparts. Subpart D applies to K–12 schools and Subpart E applies to postsecondary institutions. A 504 plan is developed when a K–12 student needs certain accommodations and modifications to either the physical space in the school or the learning environment. However, a 504 plan indicates that there is no need for special education (if there was a need for special education, the student would have been given an Individualized Education Program (IEP) as discussed later in this chapter). Subpart E states that postsecondary students must be granted the opportunity to compete with their non-disabled peers.

The Developmental Disabilities Assistance and Bill of Rights Act

Also known as the DD Act, this act ensures that individuals with developmental disability and their families have access to community-based services and supports to promote opportunities for independence, productivity and inclusion. Title I of the act established four components, including the State Councils on Developmental Disabilities to represent and advocate for people with developmental disability; Protection and Advocacy (P&A) Systems to protect the legal and human rights of individuals with developmental disability within each state and US territory; University Centers for Excellence in Developmental Disabilities to provide training, technical assistance, service, research and information sharing, with a focus on sustainable living for people with disability; and Projects of National Significance to support the development of national and state policy that enhances the independence, productivity, inclusion and integration of individuals with developmental disability in the community.

Individuals with Disabilities Education Act (IDEA) (Public Law 101–119), Part B and Part C

IDEA is a main federal law passed by Congress in 1986; it provides children with disability or delays in development the right to appropriate and needed developmental and educational services from birth to the age of twenty-one. The law has four different parts, but parts B and C most directly affect families.

Part B of IDEA, known as Assistance for Education of All Children with Disability, is set up to help states, territories and the District of Columbia with providing special education and related services to children ages three to twenty-one. Children who are entitled to services must have one of the thirteen following disabilities: autism, deafness, deaf-blindness, emotional disturbance, hearing impairment, mental retardation, multiple disabilities, orthopedic impairment, other health impairment, specific learning disability, speech or language impairment, traumatic brain injury, or visual impairment. The services require collaboration between family and a school team, with both agreeing on a written plan, known as the Individualized Education Program (IEP).

Part C of IDEA, also called Infants and Toddlers with Disabilities, is set up to assist states, territories and the District of Columbia with developing a comprehensive and coordinated system of early intervention services that are provided to infants and toddlers with disability or developmental delay from birth to twenty-four months and their families. Early intervention services and supports include an evaluation of the child's development and, if the child's development is delayed, the creation of a plan with the family to help the child overcome those delays. This plan is called the Individualized Family Service Plan (IFSP), which determines the type of services the infant or toddler may need. The services are given in the child's natural environment or place that the child spends the majority of his or her time.

National statistics of children and youth underserved by IDEA show that the number of children and youth served under IDEA increased to 6.7 million in 2004–2005, or about 14 percent of total public school enrollment, but by 2009–2010[12] this number declined to 6.5 million, corresponding to about 13 percent of total public school enrollment. Interestingly, in 2009–2010, some 38 percent of all children and youth receiving special education services had specific learning disabilities, 22 percent had speech or language impairments and 11 percent had other health impairments.

THE AMERICANS WITH DISABILITIES ACT (ADA) OF 1990 AND AMERICANS WITH DISABILITIES ACT AMENDMENTS ACT (ADAAA) OF 2008

The Americans with Disabilities Act signed by President George H. W. Bush in 1990 is the most comprehensive disability rights legislation in the United States. President Bush described it as a "historic new civil rights act . . . the world's first comprehensive declaration of equality for people with disabilities."[13] The ADA prohibits discrimination on the basis of disability in employment, in state and local government activities and in public accommodations and services, including

[12] *The Condition of Education* reports trends in enrollments across all levels of education. Enrollment is a key indicator of the scope of and access to educational opportunities and functions as a basic descriptor of American education. Changes in enrollment have implications for the demand for educational resources such as qualified teachers, physical facilities, and funding levels, all of which are required to provide high-quality education for our nation's students. Accessed 1/7/2014 at http://nces.ed.gov/pubs2012/2012045_2.pdf.

[13] Remarks of President George H. W. Bush at the signing of the Americans with Disabilities Act. Accessed 1/10/2011 at http://www.eeoc.gov/eeoc/history/35th/videos/ada_signing_text.html.

transportation. The 1990 legislation includes five titles, which are discussed in the following sections.

Employment (Title I)

> Title I requires covered employers to provide reasonable accommodations for applicants and employees with disability and prohibits discrimination on the basis of disability in all aspects of employment.

Public Services (Title II)

> Under Title II, public services (which include state and local government agencies, the National Railroad Passenger Corporation and other commuter authorities) cannot deny services to people with disability or deny participation in programs or activities that are available to people without disability. In addition, public transportation systems, such as public transit buses, must be accessible to individuals with disability.

Public Accommodations (Title III)

> Public accommodations include facilities such as restaurants, hotels, grocery stores, retail stores, and others, as well as privately owned transportation systems. Title III requires that all new construction and modifications must be accessible to individuals with disability. For existing facilities, barriers to services must be removed if readily achievable.

Telecommunications (Title IV)

> Telecommunications companies offering telephone service to the general public must offer telephone relay service to individuals who use telecommunication devices for the deaf (TTYs) or similar devices.

Miscellaneous (Title V)

> This title includes a provision prohibiting either (a) coercing or threatening or (b) retaliating against individuals with disability or those attempting to aid people with disability in asserting their rights under the ADA.

The ADA has two core implications for children with disability and their parents. First, it provides the right of children with disability to have access to public settings and to participate alongside their peers in all aspects of community life, including childcare settings. Secondly, it prohibits most employers from firing a parent or excluding a parent from a job opportunity or benefit because the parent has a child with a disability. In a little-used aspect of the ADA, the law prohibits employers from discrimination against employees who have an "association" with someone with a disability. The law, 42 U.S.C. Sec. 12112(b)(4), would prohibit discrimination against "a qualified individual because of the known disability of an individual with whom the qualified individual is known to have a relationship or association." Thus, a parent is protected under this act since he or she has a relationship with a child with a disability.[14]

The Americans with Disabilities Act Amendments Act of 2008 (ADAAA) was passed by Congress in December 2008 and became effective January 1, 2009. This significant piece of legislation corrected what Congress considered to be a departure from the intent of the original ADA (passed in 1990) brought about by several narrow interpretations of the law through Supreme Court rulings.[15] These rulings weakened the law and made it difficult for people with disability to receive the protection the law intended. The ADAAA also has a direct and substantial impact on Section 504 of the Rehabilitation Act of 1973. However, the ADAAA did not change the basic definition of disability but rather the manner in which the definition is to be interpreted.

[14] There are two cases from the Seventh Circuit Court of Appeals in Chicago; the court noted that an employer cannot fire, demote or harass a parent because the employer thinks that parent *may* be "somewhat inattentive" during work hours. Employees who are distracted by family needs, but still manage to get the job done without accommodations, are protected. *Larimer v. IBM*, 370 F.3d 698 (7th Cir. 2004). In *Washington v. Illinois Department of Revenue*, 420 F. 3d 658, 662 (7th Cir. 2005), the Seventh Circuit ruled that an employer cannot make a work change that exploits a worker's special vulnerability. In Washington's case, she needed to get home early to care for her child with disability. The employer could not spitefully change her work schedule when it knew she had to leave early. The court even cited the evil human resources character Catbert from the cartoon strip *Dilbert*, who delights in pouncing on the workers' vulnerabilities! On June 22, 2006, the United States endorsed the approach of the Seventh Circuit when it held the scope of the anti-retaliation provision extends beyond workplace-related or employment-related retaliatory acts and harm. *Burlington Northern Santa Fe Railway Co. v. White*, 548 U.S. 53 (2006).

[15] In particular, most notably *Sutton v. United Airlines, Inc.* (1999) and *Toyota Motor Manufacturing v. Williams* (2002).

The ADAAA continues to define a disabled person as an individual with a physical or mental impairment that substantially limits one or more major life activities and who has a record of such an impairment or is regarded as having such an impairment. With respect to the definition of major life activities, the ADAAA added eating, sleeping, walking, standing, lifting, bending, reading, concentrating, thinking and communicating. While the list of major life activities has been expanded, it remains "illustrative," and an activity not listed may be covered.

The legislation clarified that an impairment substantially limiting one major life activity does not need to limit others to be considered a disability. For example, students with learning disability and their parents who may receive informal or undocumented accommodations should not be denied coverage by the law.[16] The Supreme Court rulings had resulted in a narrow interpretation of "substantially limits," both in scope and conditions on which the determination was made. While the ADAAA did not change the term "substantially limits," the new law clearly establishes that the term is to be interpreted broadly and inclusively. The law clarifies that the measurement for impairments that are episodic or in remission must be considered at the time they are active. For example, a student with depression, diabetes, asthma or anxiety that is in remission is "substantially limited" and this would need to be determined when the student's condition is active. Other Supreme Court decisions in 1999 indicated that the ADA must take into account the effects, both positive and negative, of any "mitigating measures" used by that individual.[17] The ADAAA requires the "substantially

[16] Representative George Miller raised the matter in Congress on the floor of the House (see Congressional Record 9/17/2008, Page: H8294). Accessed 3/10/2013 at http://www.govtrack.us/congress/record.xpd?id=110-h20080917-24.

[17] The Supreme Court's rulings were in *Sutton v. United Airlines, Inc.* (97-1943) 527 U.S. 471 (1999) and *Murphy v. United Parcel Service, Inc.* (97-1992). In *Sutton v. United Airlines, Inc.*, the Supreme Court had to rule whether nearsightedness that can be corrected with glasses or contact lenses was a "disability" under the Americans with Disabilities Act. The court ruled that the Americans with Disabilities Act does not cover people whose disabilities can be sufficiently corrected with medicine, eyeglasses or other measures. In the *Murphy v. United Parcel Service* case, the Supreme Court had to rule whether medication or other mitigating measures should be considered in assessing if an individual is disabled under the terms of the Americans with Disabilities Act. The justices ruled that the condition the petitioner suffers and controls with medication is not considered disabling under the ADA. The condition and medication preclude him from performing only a particular job and do not substantially limit him in employment.

limits" decision to be made without regard to any impact or ameliorative effects of mitigating measures. For example, schools can no longer consider the effect of medication on a student with ADHD, asthma or diabetes, among others. Finally, it provides an expansive list of mitigating measures. Such measures include but are not limited to medication, medical supplies, equipment or appliances, low-vision devices (except eyeglasses or contact lenses), hearing aids, cochlear implants, assistive technology, and reasonable accommodations. This fairly new legislation has relevance to Section 504. There is no doubt that the expanded list of major life activities – now including reading, concentrating and thinking, in addition to learning – provides a basis for more students to be considered for eligibility under Section 504. Additionally, the clear and concise language regarding mitigating measures and the expansive list of measures included in the ADAAA provides a different framework for eligibility decisions. Since most Section 504 plans are currently being provided for students with ADHD, many more students may be eligible when the effects of medication are not part of the consideration of "substantially limits." The same is true for the change clarifying that the impact of an impairment is to be measured at the time the impairment is active.

SOCIAL SECURITY AVAILABLE FOR CHILDREN WITH DISABILITY

Supplemental Security Income (SSI)

Social security provides three optional disability benefits for children. All benefits are cash benefits paid to disabled children or to the children of disabled or retired workers. SSI benefits are authorized under Title XVI of the Social Security Act. SSI benefits are available for certain children with disability under the age of eighteen if their families have low incomes and minimal assets. SSI benefits are paid out of general revenues providing cash to meet basic needs for food, clothing and shelter. Children who are younger than eighteen (or nineteen if a full-time student) and have a parent who is currently receiving Social Security Disability Income (SSDI) or social security retirement benefits (or who had earned enough social security credits to earn one of these benefits before dying) may be able to collect dependents' benefits on the basis of their parents' records, whether they have a disability or not. Finally, children with a disability who are older than eighteen but who became disabled before they turned twenty-two can collect disability benefits if they have a parent collecting SSDI or social security retirement income (or a deceased parent who was entitled to one of these benefits before his or her death).

In October 2012, the SSI provided monthly cash benefits to 1.3 million disabled children under the age of eighteen whose families had low incomes and few assets (these are basic eligibility criteria) – or about 1.7 percent of all children in the United States.[18] The number of children on SSI represents about one-fifth of the 8 to 9 percent of US children who are estimated to have serious disability.[19] SSI benefits, which average $615 a month for a disabled child (the federal maximum is $698)[20] lift more than 300,000 children with disability from below 50 percent of the poverty line to above that threshold.[21]

The SSI is linked to income, and a child's benefits are terminated once a parent's earnings pass the threshold or a dollar in benefits is deducted for each added dollar that a parent earns. It counts half, rather than all, of a parent's earnings when gauging a child's eligibility and benefit level. In addition, SSI rules assume that some portion of a parent's earnings may be needed to support other family members, not just the child with disability. Therefore, if a parent goes to work or

[18] Social Security Administration, "SSI Monthly Statistics, October 2012," accessed 6/1/2014 at http://www.ssa.gov/policy/docs/statcomps/ssi_monthly/2012-10/index.html; Office of the Chief Actuary, *Annual Report of the Supplemental Security Income Program*, May 2012, Table IV.B7, accessed 7/22/2014 at http://www.ssa.gov/OACT/ssir/SSI12/ssi2012.pdf.

[19] Shawn Fremstad and Rebecca Vallas, *Supplemental security income for children with disabilities* (National Academy of Social Insurance, November 2012). Accessed 1/8/2013 at http://www.nasi.org/sites/default/files/research/SSI_For_Children_Disabilities.pdf.

[20] Average amount from SSI Monthly Statistics, October 2012; maximum amount from SSI Federal Payment Amounts, 1975–2013. Accessed 1/2/2014 at http://www.ssa.gov/OACT/COLA/SSIamts.html.

[21] CBPP analysis of the March 2010 Current Population Survey and SSI income data from the Urban Institute/HHS Transfer Income Model Version 3. Accessed 12/10/2012 from trim3.urban.org. This result is consistent with earlier statistics presented in Anne DeCesaro and Jeffrey Hemmeter, "Characteristics of non-institutionalized DI and SSI program participants," Social Security Administration Research and Statistics Note No. 2008-02, Table 11. Accessed 2/3/2013 at http://www.socialsecurity.gov/policy/docs/rsnotes/rsn2008-02.html.

increases the number of hours worked, it will have a smaller effect on the SSI benefits, and hence the added work will yield a substantial net increase in the family's income.

Medicaid and the Home and Community-Based Services Waiver (HCBS)

Medicaid is a health-care program for people with low incomes and limited resources implemented under Title XIX of the Social Security Act.[22] It is a public insurance program that provides mandatory services for patients such as inpatient/outpatient hospital resources; transportation for nonemergency medical care; home health services; laboratory procedures; physician services; family planning; nursing facilities; Early Periodic Screening, Diagnosis, and Treatment (EPSDT) programs; and tobacco cessation programs for pregnant women. Medicaid requires no co-payment or deductibles. To be eligible for the program one must be in one of four categories: income level, disability criteria, eligibility for institutional level of care or out-of-home placement. Many Children with Special Health Care Needs (CSHCN) qualify for Medicaid on the basis of low-income level, but some children qualify independently of income level because of their disability. Medicaid has a more restrictive definition of disabilities and special health-care needs than the Maternal and Child Health Bureau (MCHB), which defines special needs as needs that must impede daily functioning. Medicaid accepts children who need to receive SSI program money and children who are defined as medically needy,[23] that is, children whose families have above the maximum income to receive Medicaid but because of health expenditures their income is lowered to the level required. Forty states currently offer this program.[24] Medicaid programs in each state

[22] United States. TITLE XIX—Grants to States for Medical Assistance Programs. Social Security Act §1900. Web. 29 Nov. 2012. Accessed 3/6/2013 at http://www.ssa.gov/OP_Home/ssact/title19/1900.htm.

[23] For additional information, see Jill Rosenthal et al., "Public insurance programs and children with special health care needs: a tutorial on the basics of Medicaid and the Children's Health Insurance Program," 2011. Accessed 1/2/2014 at http://www.nashp.org/sites/default/files/Medicaid_101_tutorial.pdf.

[24] Jeff Crowley, *Medicaid medically needy programs: an important source of Medicaid coverage* (Washington, DC: Henry J. Kaiser Family Foundation, 2003). Accessed 1/3/2014 at http://www.kff.org/medicaid/loader.cfm?url=/commonspot/security/getfile.cfm.

are administered differently, and federal dollars go to each state on the basis of per capita income levels.

The 1915(c) waivers are one of many options available to states to allow the provision of long-term care services in home and community-based settings under the Medicaid program. States can offer a variety of services under an HCBS Waiver program. Programs can provide a combination of standard medical services and nonmedical services. Standard services include but are not limited to case management (that is, supports and service coordination), homemaker, home health aide, personal care, adult day health services, habitation (both day and residential) and respite care. States can also propose other types of services that may assist in diverting and/or transitioning individuals from institutional settings into their homes and community.

The Tax Equity and Fiscal Responsibility Act (TEFRA) of 1982

TEFRA allows states to cover home care services under Medicaid for children with disability, even when family income and resources exceed that of the state's financial eligibility standards.

The Family Opportunity Act of 2006 (FOA) (contained in P.L. 109–171, the Deficit Reduction Act)

The FOA gives states the option of allowing families with annual incomes between approximately $17,050 and $60,000 for a family of four who have children with significant disability (those who meet the Social Security definition of disability or have the potential to meet it) to buy into Medicaid. The FOA also includes authorization and funding for Family to Family Health Information Centers (F2F HICs), which are nonprofit, family-staffed organizations that help families of children and youth with special health-care needs navigate the health-care system to get appropriate services. The MCHB provides the primary funding support for the centers in all states and the District of Columbia.

Title V Maternal and Child Health Services Block Grant

This program, authorized under Title V of the Social Security Act, improves the health of all mothers, children and their families. These legislated responsibilities reduce health disparities, improve access to health care and improve the quality of health care. Specifically, the program assures access to quality care, especially for those with low incomes or limited availability of care; reduces infant mortality; provides and ensures access to comprehensive prenatal and postnatal care for women (especially low-income and at-risk pregnant women); increases the number of children receiving health assessments and follow-up diagnostic and treatment services; provides and ensures access to preventive and childcare services as well as rehabilitative services for certain children; implements family-centered, community-based systems of coordinated care for children with special health-care needs; and provides toll-free hotlines and assistance in applying for services to pregnant women with infants and children who are eligible for Medicaid. The program also administers discretionary grant programs that focus on key issues in maternal and child health, support research and train maternal and child health professionals.

The Children's Health Act of 2000 (P.L 106–310)

The act amends and reauthorizes the Traumatic Brain Injury Act of 1996 and establishes the National Center on Birth Defects and Developmental Disabilities. It authorizes funding to the Centers for Disease Control and Prevention (CDC) to expand state surveillance, national education and prevention; to the National Institutes of Health to carry out applied research related to cognitive disorders and neurobehavioral consequences; and to the Health Resources and Services Administration for state capacity building grants. The law also authorizes funding for state protection and advocacy services to provide legal advocacy for people with traumatic brain injuries (PATBI).

Improving long-term care under Medicaid of 2006 (contained in P.L. 109–171, the Deficit Reduction Act)

This provision gives states the option of creating home and community-based services, and it supports the Medicaid plan within the state without obtaining a waiver. States are permitted to allow individuals to choose self-directed services. States must establish a more stringent eligibility standard for placement of individuals in institutions than for services in a home and community-based setting. Unfortunately, provisions added to the act before passage allows states to impose caps on services and to establish waiting lists for the new home- and community-based optional services.

The Affordable Care Act (ACA) of 2010, known as the Health Care Reform Law (P.L. 111–148, as amended by P.L. 111–152)

The ACA actually refers to two separate pieces of legislation – the Patient Protection and Affordable Care Act (P.L. 111–148) and the Health Care and Education Reconciliation Act of 2010 (P.L. 111–152) – which together expand Medicaid coverage to millions of low-income Americans and make numerous improvements to both Medicaid and CHIP.

The Lifespan Respite Care Act of 2006 (P.L. 109–442, 42 U.S.C. 201)

The legislation, which was passed under Title XXIX of the Public Health Service Act, expands and enhances respite care services to family caregivers. It improves the statewide dissemination and coordination of respite care to provide, supplement or improve access and quality of respite care services to family caregivers, thereby reducing family caregiver strain. The act also created the National Lifespan Respite Resource Center designed to maintain a national database on lifespan respite care; provide training and technical assistance to state, community and nonprofit respite care programs; and provide information, referral and educational programs on lifespan respite care to the public.

In terms of use, funding is allocated to state and local governments in order to provide services at the state and local levels for family caregivers caring for children or adults with special needs. The budget also covers training and recruitment of respite care workers and volunteers. Funds may also be used for training programs for family caregivers to assist them in making informed decisions about respite care services.

The Assistive Technology Act of 2004 (P.L. 108–364)

This legislation reauthorized the Assistive Technology Act of 1998. Aimed at "getting more assistive technology into the hands of more consumers," the legislation mandates state Tech Act programs to provide, with at least 60 percent of their federal dollars, Alternative Financing and Device Loan programs, and it makes Demonstration Centers and Device Recycling programs discretionary. The act authorizes a minimum level of funding to all state assistive technology programs and also authorizes resources to fund national technical assistance activities.

Combating Autism Reauthorization Act of 2011 (P.L. 112–32)

The act will continue to support the programs established by the Combating Autism Act of 2006, which include screening and surveillance of ASD and educating professionals about proper screening, diagnosis and intervention for children with ASD, as well as many other developmental disabilities. The act authorizes $231 million a year from fiscal year (FY) 2012 through 2014 for these efforts.

US POLICIES TOWARD FAMILIES OF CHILDREN WITH DISABILITY: CHARACTERIZATION AND DISCUSSION

Tax versus means-tested entitlements

Federal budget and census data for 2010 shows that 91 percent of the benefit dollars from entitlement and other mandatory programs went to the elderly (people sixty-five and older), the disabled (including families of children with disability) and members of working households.[25] Only 9 percent of the people who were neither elderly nor disabled and did not live in a working household received benefits. Interestingly, the distribution of entitlement benefits stands in contrast to the distribution of benefits for tax expenditures, also known as "tax entitlements." The

[25] Arloc Sherman, Robert Greenstein and Kathy Ruffing, "Contrary to entitlement society rhetoric over nine-tenth of entitlement benefits go to elderly, disabled, or working households" (Washington, DC: Center on Budget and Policy Priorities, February 10, 2012). Accessed 3/4/2014 at http://www.cbpp.org/cms/?fa=view&id=3677.

Tax Policy Center finds that in the tax year of 2011, the top fifth of the population received 66 percent of the tax-expenditure benefits as compared to 10 percent of the entitlement benefits[26]; the middle 60 percent of the population received about 31 percent of tax expenditure benefits compared to 58 percent of entitlement benefits, while the bottom fifth received just 2.8 percent of the tax-expenditure benefits as compared to 32 percent of entitlement benefits. Interestingly, the top 1 percent of the population received 23.9 percent of the tax-expenditures benefits – more than eight times as much as the bottom fifth of the population, and nearly as much as the middle 60 percent of the population.

If we look only at entitlement programs that are targeted to people with low incomes, the percentage of benefit dollars going to people who are elderly, disabled (including families of children with disability) or members of working households remains high. However, if we examine "tax entitlements," it is clear that the above figures contrast sharply with the distribution of the extensive deductions, credits and other write-offs in the federal tax code, known as tax expenditures (or tax entitlements). The Urban Institute-Brookings Institution Tax Policy Center estimates that for tax year 2011 the top fifth of the population received 66 percent of the $1.1 trillion in individual tax-expenditure benefits (the top 1% alone received 23.9% of the benefits), the middle 60 percent of the population received a little more than 31 percent of the benefits and the bottom 20 percent of the population received only 2.8 percent of the benefits.

There is a clear division between families with middle-high to high income regarding provisions for their children with disability. Families of children with disability with high income get credits and extensive deductions from their reported income whereas those with low income don't have enough reported income to claim deductions. They eventually need to apply for means-tested social programs in order to obtain benefits and services for their children. The exceptions are educational provisions (such as IDEA), which are provided regardless of income, and universal legislation such as the ADA and ADAAA. In fact,

[26] The figures are for individual tax expenditures and do not include corporate tax expenditures. If corporate tax expenditures were included, the results would be skewed even more heavily to the top of the income spectrum.

these legislations offer new conceptualizations of family policy with respect to disability rights and inclusion and parental involvement and empowerment.

The SSI reflects the debate between conservatives and liberals regarding the desired policy related to children with disability and their families.[27] Conservatives believe that the SSI requires budget restraint, arguing that the program has to be restricted to disability services for children rather than providing families with cash. They believe that parents and states are highly motivated to enroll even mildly impaired children in SSI. Liberals complain that the program is limited to children with severe disability and that more children with disability and their families need to be included. They argue that about 6.6 million school-age children have activity limitations that result from one or more chronic health conditions, but only about 1.3 million US children receive SSI benefits.[28] Most children with disability do not qualify for Supplemental Security either because their disabilities are not severe enough to meet the Social Security Administration's strict standards or their families do not meet the program's financial eligibility criteria. Under the Social Security Administration's definition of childhood disability, a child may qualify for Supplemental Security if he or she has a medically determinable physical or mental impairment that results in marked and severe functional limitations and if he or she lives in a household with very low income and less than $3,000 in assets. According to a 2012 Government Accountability Office report, the Social Security Administration has consistently denied a majority of children's applications for Supplemental Security over the past decade using this stringent definition of disability.[29] In addition, the income

[27] Ron Haskins is a senior editor of the *Future of Children*, a senior fellow in economic studies, codirector of the Center on Children and Families at the Brookings Institution and a senior consultant at the Annie E. Casey Foundation. See his policy brief for Spring 2012. Accessed 1/2/2014 at http://futureofchildren.org/futureofchildren/publications/docs/22_01_PolicyBrief.pdf.

[28] For further reading, see online article by Rebecca Vallas and Shawn Fremstad of the Center of American Progress, September 10, 2012, "Maintaining and strengthening supplemental security income for children with disabilities." Accessed 4/2/2014 at http://www.americanprogress.org/issues/poverty/report/2012/09/10/37115/maintaining-and-strengthening-supplemental-security-income-for-children-with-disabilities.

[29] 2012 Government Accountability Office report accessed 1/3/2014 at http://www.gao.gov/assets/660/650902.pdf.

supplement for eligible recipients is modest. The maximum monthly supplement in 2012 was $698, about three-quarters of the monthly poverty threshold for an individual. Between one-third and one-half of children with severe disability receiving Supplemental Security have family incomes below the federal poverty line. Income is a significant criterion for obtaining Medicaid services for children with disability. In fact, children with disability who also qualify for Medicaid because of their medical circumstances are being justified by using financial augmentation. Their families are recognized for having excessive medical expenditures that actually lower the household's income.

Means testing is central to the provision of services to children with disability and their families. Although the Family Opportunity Act of 2006 has expanded the number of families of children with disability able to buy into Medicaid, it allows it only in families with annual incomes between approximately $17,050 and $60,000 for a family of four with children with significant disability.

Similarly, means testing is central to families applying for CHIP. The family's gross income must be below 200 percent of the federal poverty level (FPL) for the children to get CHIP coverage. Generally, a family's gross income must be below 133 percent FPL for children age one to five years to get Medicaid. The family's gross income must be below 100 percent FPL for children age six to eighteen to receive Medicaid. Family income includes the income of all children aged eighteen or younger, with all parents and all stepparents living in the home. Finally, eligibility for the Head Start program serving children from birth to age five or a pregnant woman is determined by income. Family income is determined to be below the income figures published annually by the federal government as the Poverty Guidelines.

Public accommodations and recognized rights of working parents

Aside from the means-testing restriction, US legislation since the ADA has recognized the civic rights of children with disability and their parents' to accessibility and inclusion in society. The ADA was the first comprehensive law prohibiting disability discrimination by privately owned *public accommodations* nationwide.[30] Public accommodations, a term that includes private childcare facilities, are subject to the requirements of Title III of the ADA, regardless of funding source.[31] This law clearly defines reasonable accommodation for children with disability and encourages providers to offer adjustments in order to integrate them.

In addition, the ADA protects the right of working parents of children with disability, as seen in two cases from the Seventh Circuit Court of Appeals in Chicago.[32] In *Larimer v. IBM*, 370 F.3d 698 (7th Cir. 2004), the court noted that an employer cannot fire, demote or harass a parent because the employer thinks that parent *may* be "somewhat inattentive" during work hours. Employees who are distracted by family needs but still manage to get the job done without accommodations are protected. In *Washington v. Illinois Department of Revenue*, 420 F. 3d 658, 662 (7th Cir. 2005), the Seventh Circuit ruled that an employer cannot make a work change that exploits a worker's special vulnerability. Chrissie Washington worked from 7 a.m. until 3 p.m. instead of the standard 9 to 5 schedule at the Illinois Department of Revenue. The earlier hours allowed her to care for her son, who has Down syndrome, when he arrived home.

Parents' rights to participate in educational decision making

One of the most progressive legislations related to families of children with special needs and disability is the right of parents to be informed and participate in the educational decision-making process. For example, in No Child Left Behind, parent involvement means the

[30] See Marilyn Golden, Linda D. Kilb and Arlene B. Mayerson, "Americans with Disabilities act: An Implementation Guide," The Disability Rights and Education and Defense Fund, 1993.

[31] Public accommodations under the ADA cover a wide variety of private businesses that are open to the public, including (but not limited to) hotels, restaurants, retail stores, amusement parks, recreational programs and childcare programs.

[32] See *Larimer v. IBM*, 370 F.3d 698 (7th Cir. 2004) and *Washington v. Illinois Department of Revenue*, 420 F. 3d 658, 662 (7th Cir. 2005). Accessed 3/5/2012 for *Larimer v. IBM* at http://law.justia.com/cases/federal/appellate-courts/F3/370/698/522116/; for *Washington v. Illinois Department of Revenue* at http://caselaw.findlaw.com/us-7th-circuit/1034067.html.

participation of parents in regular, two-way and meaningful communication involving the student's academic learning and other school activities including ensuring that (a) parents play an integral role in assisting their child's learning; (b) parents are encouraged to be actively involved in their child's education at school; and (c) parents are full partners in their child's education and are included, as appropriate, in decision making and on advisory committees to assist in the education of their child.[33]

IDEA gives families of special education children the right to have their child assessed or tested to determine special education eligibility and needs, inspect and review school records relating to their child, attend an annual individualized education program (IEP) meeting to develop a written IEP plan with representatives of the local school district, and resolve disputes with the school district through an impartial administrative and legal process. Parent participation has been a core concept since the inception of IDEA in 1997.[34]

Two Supreme Court rulings can demonstrate parental rights when challenging school districts in a due process hearing. In *Schaffer v. Weast* (2004),[35] Brian's parents contacted the Montgomery County Public School System regarding their son's diagnosed disability. An IEP was developed for implementation in that public school system. Even though Brian's parents were involved in the development of his IEP they rejected it. Initially, Brian's parents unsuccessfully took their IEP

[33] See Title IX Section 9101(32). The text is as follows: "(32) PARENTAL INVOLVEMENT – The term 'parental involvement' means the participation of parents in regular, two-way, and meaningful communication involving student academic learning and other school activities ensuring

(A) that parents play an integral role in assisting their child's learning;
(B) that parents are encouraged to be actively involved in their child's education at school;
(C) that parents are full partners in their child's education and are included, as appropriate, in decision making and on advisory committees to assist in the education of their child;
(D) the carrying out of other activities, such as those described in section 1118."

Accessed 4/1/2013 at http://www2.ed.gov/policy/elsec/leg/esea02/pg107.html.

[34] Audrey Trainor, "Reexamining the promise of parent participation in special education: an analysis of cultural and social capital," *Anthropology and Education Quarterly* 42 (2010), 245–63.

[35] Weast v. Schaffer, 377 F.3d 449 (4th Cir. 2004). Accessed 3/1/2012 at http://www.wrightslaw.com/law/caselaw/04/4th.schaffer.weast.md.htm.

issue and a request for tuition reimbursement to a due process hearing where an administrative judge ruled in favor of the school system. They next went to the federal district court where, convinced that the burden of proof should have been placed on the school officials, the judge remanded the case back to the administrative judge. On remand, the administrative judge held for the parents and ordered that Brian's parents be reimbursed for the private school tuition. On appeal to the Fourth Circuit the ruling was reversed.[36]

In *Arlington Central School District v. Murphy* (2006), the plaintiff parents sought reimbursement for tuition paid for their child's education at a private school from a federal district court.[37] The parents prevailed at trial and requested that the fees for their consultant be paid by the school system. Subsequently, the district court's decision was appealed to the Second Circuit where the following narrow question was before the court: may a prevailing plaintiff recover consultant/expert fees under the IDEA's fee shifting provision, 20 U.S.C. 1415 (i)(3)(B), which authorizes a court to award "costs"? The Second Circuit held that "expert fees are compensable as costs under IDEA." The lower court decision was affirmed.[38]

CONCLUSION

U. S. family policy leans toward individualism, strict work ethics, protection of the family as a private entity and the limited role of federal government. Within this context, social policies affecting children with disability and their families focus primarily on in-kind benefits with modest and inconsistent cash benefits to some low-income families and tax benefits to the middle and upper classes. Overall, families of children with disability with adequate income can benefit from tax

[36] See Joint Appendix Filed in the US Court of Appeals for the Fourth Circuit in *Weast v. Schaffer*. Accessed 3/1/2012 at http://www.wrightslaw.com/law/caselaw/04/4th.schaffer.weast.md.pdfURL: http://www.harborhouselaw.com/law/plead/schaffer.4th.jtappendix.pdf.

[37] *Arlington Central School District Board of Education v. Murphy*, 548 U.S. 291 (2006). Accessed 3/1/2012 at http://www.law.cornell.edu/supct/html/05-18.ZO.html.

[38] *Arlington Central School District v. Murphy* (2nd Cir. 2005). Accessed 7/2/2013 at http://www.wrightslaw.com/law/caselaw/05/2nd.arlington.murphy.htm.

entitlements including dependency exemptions, capital expenditures (primarily excessive medical bills) and EITCs. Families whose income is low need to apply for means-tested cash benefit and service provisions. The extensive review of these services reveals that the most used are SSI, Medicaid and IDEA. In 2012, the SSI provided monthly cash benefits to 1.3 million children with disability under the age of eighteen whose families had low incomes and few assets. A significantly larger proportion of SSI-eligible children qualified on the basis of a mental or intellectual disability. Two-thirds (67%) qualified on the basis of a mental or intellectual disability. Twenty percent of the qualifying children had developmental disorders and 8 percent had autistic disorders. Another 19 percent qualified on the basis of a childhood or adolescent disorder, including attention deficit hyperactivity disorder.[39] In fiscal year 2013, which covers the school year 2012–2013, total IDEA funding was $11.98 billion, of which $10.97 billion was dedicated to IDEA Part B Section 611 state grants.

The chapter discusses three themes that reflect family policies in this area. The first introduces the division between families with middle-high to high income regarding provisions for their children with disability. Families of children with disability with high income get credits and extensive deductions from their reported income whereas those with low income don't have enough reported income to claim deductions. They eventually need to apply for means-tested social programs in order to obtain benefits and services for their children. The second theme addresses the ADA and children with disability and their parents' right for accessibility and inclusion in society. An additional contribution is the protection of the rights of working parents of children with disability, demonstrated by two court decisions.[40] Finally, the chapter discusses the progressive legislation of IDEA and the right of parents to be informed and participate in the educational decision-making process.

[39] See Chapter 2 "Medicaid, managed care, and people with disabilities," in *Medicaid managed care for people with disabilities*, National Council on Disability. Accessed 6/3/2013 at http://www.ncd.gov/publications/2013/20130315/20130315_Ch2.

[40] See *Larimer v. IBM*, 370 F.3d 698 (7th Cir. 2004), accessed 6/3/2013 at http://law.justia.com/cases/federal/appellate-courts/F3/370/698/522116/, and *Washington v. Illinois Department of Revenue*, 420 F. 3d 658, 662 (7th Cir. 2005).

US policies aimed toward families of children with disability express limited support to families on means testing, sending a message to working families that they can receive credits only through annual tax returns. On the other hand, policies and legislation recognize society's responsibility to provide accessible accommodation and protect the rights of parents in employment and the educational system.

5 FAMILY POLICIES AND DISABILITY IN SELECTED EUROPEAN COUNTRIES

European family policies vary with respect to the way they are organized and the way they have developed. The prevailing policy in continental Europe ties benefits to the breadwinner's income, traditionally fathers. The chapter will focus on family policies of three different countries in Europe (see Table 5.1). According to "The comparative macro-sociology of welfare states" by Esping Andersen, the United Kingdom represents the liberal and social democratic approaches of the welfare state, French policy is a mixture of liberal and conservative corporatist principles, and Sweden is a typical social democratic welfare state.[1]

In terms of childcare policies, France is known as providing the most generous provisions, and the United Kingdom and Sweden are known as being moderate.[2] Finally, these three countries differ also in their disability policies; Sweden, like other Nordic countries, is known for its commitment to human rights and equality of opportunity for all citizens. This results in provision of benefits and inclusive services by the government. The United Kingdom and France vary in their commitment to human rights and equality of opportunity and in their provisions and benefits.[3]

[1] See Gøsta Esping-Andersen, *The three worlds of welfare capitalism* (Princeton, NJ: Princeton University Press, 1990). The book led to a plethora of research on the merits of fitting real welfare states across Europe and beyond into his three ideal-type categories. The direction of Esping-Andersen's analysis becomes clearer in his book, *Social foundations of postindustrial economies* (Oxford: Oxford University Press, 1990).

[2] John Ditch et al., *A synthesis of national family policies* (Brussels: DGV, 1998).

[3] For extensive review and analysis, see Franz-Xaver Kaufmann, *Variations of the welfare state: Great Britain, Sweden, France and Germany between capitalism and socialism* (New

TABLE 5.1 *Esping-Andersen comparative macro-sociology of welfare states*[4]

Country typology	UK	France	Sweden
Liberal welfare state: Means testing, modest universal transfers or social insurance, strict entitlement rules, focus on market economy	Medium	Medium	Low
Conservative corporatist state: Strong state welfare orientation, minimal private insurance, family is central	Low	High	Low
Social democratic welfare state: State is committed to social rights universal insurance system, committed to full employment policy	Medium	Low	High

UK POLICY AND LEGISLATION TOWARD FAMILIES OF CHILDREN WITH DISABILITY

In general, the United Kingdom has a mixed social policy of liberalism and welfare state, with means-tested programs and modest universal transfer. For example, its social security system provides a means-tested and highly regulated assessment for people with low income and disability. The National Health Service (NHS) and the compulsory education system are universal.

UK policy and legislation aimed toward children with disability and their families is highly regulated by the government in terms of determining eligibility and provisions. The first section of the chapter provides a comprehensive review of general and specific legislations that are relevant to children with disability and their families. In addition, the review presents tax credit and housing entitlements relevant to families of children with disability. The second section discusses core issues related to UK policies toward families of children with disability.

York-Heidelberg: Springer, 2013). Translated from the German. Originally published as *Geschichte der Sozialpolitik in Deutschland seit 1945* (Baden-Baden: Nomos, 2001).

4 Gøsta Esping-Andersen, "The comparative macro-sociology of welfare states," in Luis Moreno (ed.), *Social exchange and welfare development* (Madrid: Csic, 1993), 123–36.

GENERAL LEGISLATION

The Children Act 1989 reinforces the autonomy of families through its definition of parental responsibility.[5] One of the central changes introduced by the Children Act 1989 was the substitution of the concept of parental responsibility for that of parental rights. The act defines parental responsibility as "all the rights, duties, powers, responsibilities and authority which by law a parent of a child has in relation to the child and his property" [Children Act 1989, s3(1)]. Parental responsibility is given to both the child's father and mother in the case where they are married to each other at, or after, the child's conception. In the case of unmarried parents, the mother has parental responsibility; the father does not have parental responsibility for his child unless he acquires it. This is achieved by the father's successful application to a court, a parental responsibility agreement negotiated between the mother and father, or (when the relevant provisions of the Adoption and Children Act 2002 are implemented) if the father's name is on the child's birth certificate. A guardian who is appointed by the court or by a parent also acquires parental responsibility on taking up appointment (Children Act 1989, s5). More than one person may have parental responsibility for the same child at the same time. Any person who has parental responsibility does not cease to have that duty solely because some other person subsequently acquires parental responsibility. In brief, parental responsibility is something that parents have and, short of adoption (or freeing for adoption), do not lose. Two additional principles that are emphasized are the welfare of the child and the encouragement of greater cooperation between those responsible for children and statutory or voluntary agencies.

Part III of the Children Act gives powers and duties to local authorities to provide services for children and their families. Services for children in need and disabled children are brought under one statute. Under Part III, local authorities are required to produce plans setting out their provision of children's services. Strategic health authorities,

[5] The Children Act 1989 was implemented for the most part on October 14, 1991. See details in government site. Accessed 1/2/2013 at http://www.legislation.gov.uk/ukpga/1989/41/contents.

local health boards, primary care trusts and NHS trusts should be consulted in this process.

The NHS and Community Care Act 1990[6] provides a statutory framework for community care that forms the cornerstone of community care law. It places a duty on local authorities to assess an individual's need for "community care services." If the need is urgent, the services can be provided without prior assessment of need, although an assessment should be done as soon as possible. The legislation splits the role of health authorities and local authorities by changing their internal structure so that local authority departments assess the needs of the local population and then purchase the necessary services from "providers." To become "providers" in the internal market, health organizations became NHS trusts, competing with each other. Community care ensures people in need of long-term care are now able to live either in their own home, with adequate support, or in a residential home setting.

The Children Act 2004, presented earlier, provides the legislative foundation for whole-system reform to support this long-term and ambitious program. It outlines new statutory duties and clarifies accountabilities for children's services. But legislation by itself is not enough: it needs to be part of a wider process of change. Every Child Matters[7] is a government policy published as a result of concerns raised by Lord Laming in his inquiry into the death of Victoria Climbié.[8] The report sets out a framework to improve outcomes for all children and their families, to protect them, to promote their well-being and to support all children to develop their full potential. It focuses on four main areas: early intervention and effective protection, supporting parents and carers, accountability and integration (locally, regionally and nationally),

[6] See content of the NHS and Community Care Act 1990. Accessed 3/9/2013 at http://www.legislation.gov.uk/ukpga/1990/19/contents.

[7] HM Treasury, *Every child matters* (London, The Stationery Office, 2003). Accessed 7/9/2013 at http://www.everychildmatters.gov.uk/key-documents/.

[8] Victoria Climbié died in February 2000 with 128 separate injuries on her body after months of abuse at the hands of her great aunt Marie Therese Kouao and her aunt's boyfriend Carl Manning. Despite coming into contact with health, police and social services on several occasions and twice being taken to the hospital, the abuse was not discovered until her death. In the aftermath of her death and the court case convicting Kouao and Manning of murder, Lord Laming was instructed to undertake an inquiry into the circumstances leading up to Climbié's death and make recommendations on how the system should change.

and workforce reform. It also introduces the five outcome aims for children and young people, identified through previous consultation with children and young people and their families: being healthy, staying safe, enjoying and achieving, making a positive contribution and achieving economic well-being. This policy is significant for the government's statement of its intention to focus on parents and carers with the goal of improving children's lives. However, the policy focuses on the support needed from parents to achieve the desired outcomes for children, rather than the support needed for parents in carrying out their roles as parents.

The Childcare Act 2006 is a pioneering legislation, implementing the aims set out in *Choice for parents, the best start for children: a ten-year strategy for childcare.*[9] The act imposes a range of general obligations on local authorities in relation to childcare for younger children in particular. The obligations are designed to ensure that local authorities take an active strategic role in managing the provision of childcare within their areas with a view to ensuring that local childcare provisions support the Every Child Matters agenda. There are three new local authority duties of particular importance: improving five Every Child Matters outcomes for all preschool children and reducing inequalities in these outcomes; securing sufficient childcare for working parents; and providing a better parental information service.

The children's plan: building brighter futures,[10] released in 2007, is the government's grand plan to underpin and inform all future policy relating to children, their families and schools. The central goal is to eradicate child poverty and reduce illiteracy and antisocial behavior by 2020. It has five principles: (a) government does not bring up children – parents do – so government needs to do more to support parents and families; (b) all children have the potential to succeed and should go as far as their talents can take them; (c) children and young people need to enjoy their childhood as well as grow up prepared for adult life; (d) services need to be shaped by and responsive to children, young people

[9] The strategy published in 2004 by HM Treasury sets out the government's long-term vision to ensure that every child gets the best start in life, and to give parents more choice about how to balance work and family life.

[10] Department of Children, Schools and Families, *The children's plan: building brighter futures* (presented to Parliament by the Secretary of State for Children, Schools and Families by Command of Her Majesty, December 2007). Accessed 5/10/2012 at http://www.educationengland.org.uk/documents/pdfs/2007-childrens-plan.pdf.

and families, not designed around professional boundaries; and (e) it is always better to prevent failure than tackle a crisis later.[11] The plan introduced ten goals to be achieved by 2020:

- Enhance children and young people's well-being, particularly at key transition points in their lives.
- Every child ready for success at school, with at least 90 percent developing well across all areas of the Early Years Foundation Stage Profile by age five.
- Every child ready for secondary school, with at least 90 percent achieving at or above the expected level in both English and mathematics by age eleven.
- Every young person with the skills for adult life and further study, with at least 90 percent achieving the equivalent of five higher level GCSEs by age nineteen and at least 70 percent achieving the equivalent of two A levels by age nineteen.
- Parents satisfied with the information and support they receive.
- All young people participating in positive activities to develop personal and social skills, promote well-being and reduce behavior that puts them at risk.
- Employers satisfied with young people's readiness for work.
- Child health improved, with the proportion of obese and overweight children reduced to 2000 levels.
- Child poverty halved by 2010 and eradicated by 2020.
- Significantly reduce by 2020 the number of young offenders receiving a conviction, reprimand or final warning for a recordable offense for the first time, with a goal to be set in the Youth Crime Action Plan.[12]

The Children and Families Bill 2013[13] is the recent government legislation that underpins wider reforms to ensure that all children and young people can succeed regardless of their background. The bill

[11] See The Department for Children, Schools and Families (DCSF), *Schools and pupils in England: January 2007 (Final)*, 5–6. The final report accessed 7/8/2013 at http://webarchive.nationalarchives.gov.uk/20130401151655/http://media.education.gov.uk/assets/files/pdf/sfr302007v2pdf.pdf.

[12] DCSF 2007, 14.

[13] Children and Families Bill 2013. Content of the bill accessed 8/9/2013 at http://www.education.gov.uk/a00221161/children-families-bill.

intends to reform the systems for adoption, looked-after children, family justice and special educational needs. It encourages growth in the childcare sector, introduces a new system of shared parental leave and ensures children in England have a strong advocate for their rights. The section that is relevant to children with disability is the effort to transform the special education system. Specifically, the bill will extend the Special Educational Needs (SEN) system from birth to twenty-five, giving children, young people and their parents greater control and choice in decisions and ensuring needs are properly met. Shared parental leave and flexible working is an additional general component of the bill that applies to families of children with disability and special needs.[14] The government is committed to encouraging the full involvement of both parents from the earliest stages of pregnancy, including promoting a system of shared parental leave and extending the right to request a flexible work schedule.

SPECIFIC LEGISLATION

The Chronically Sick and Disabled Persons Act 1970[15] was a groundbreaking step on the road to equality, and it forms a basis for much of the subsequent UK legislation. It was revolutionary in transforming official policy, setting down specific provisions to improve access and support for people with disability. Briefly, the act placed responsibilities on local authorities for the provision of welfare services and housing, extending to the provision of practical assistance for people in their own homes, meals at home or community centers, and the adaptation of houses to meet their needs. The act gave people with disability the right to equal access to recreational and educational facilities, including providing assistance with transportation, which would be provided by local authorities. The law transferred to local authorities the duty to set

[14] The Employment Act 2002 included flexible working hours for family members of children with disability. The person being cared for must be a relative or live at the same address as the carers. Carers also have the right to take (unpaid) time off work for dependents in cases of emergency.

[15] See content of The Chronically Sick and Disabled Persons Act 1970. Accessed 5/9/2013 at http://www.legislation.gov.uk/ukpga/1970/44/pdfs/ukpga_19700044_en.pdf.

up special educational facilities for children who are both blind and deaf. This provision was extended to include children with learning disability, with the expectation that the level of education provided was the same as that available in other local authority schools. Local authorities were also required to provide disabled accessibility in all public facilities such as universities, railway stations, shops and offices. Disabled badges for cars were introduced with exemptions for parking and other access.

The Disabled Persons (Services, Consultation and Representation) Act 1986[16] strengthened the legislation laid down in the Chronically Sick and Disabled Persons Act. The law is important because it contained a requirement to recognize carers' input; under the act, social services had to provide a written assessment and look at the abilities of informal carers when deciding what services to provide to the person with disability.

The Disability Living Allowance (DLA)[17] was introduced in 1992 as the main benefit for disabled children; it helps to cover any extra costs of being disabled. It is not means tested, so an applicant's financial situation will not be taken into account. The DLA is also not taxable or treated as income for other benefits. Instead, the DLA can sometimes lead to an increase in other benefits or help families qualify for benefits they are not yet receiving. In short, the DLA can make a real difference to a family's overall income.

The DLA has two main parts called components. The care component is paid for children who need extra care and attention and can be paid at one of three weekly rates, depending on how much extra help the child needs. The mobility component can be paid for children who either have problems with walking or with getting around in unfamiliar areas. It is paid at one of two weekly rates and a child can get one or both components at the same time. The Welfare Reform Act 2012 introduced the Personal Independence Payment (PIP).[18] PIP replaces the DLA for people aged sixteen to sixty-four but not for children younger

[16] Disabled Persons (Services, Consultation and Representation) Act 1986. Accessed 7/9/2013 at http://www.legislation.gov.uk/ukpga/1986/33/contents.

[17] Disability Living Allowance (DLA) 1992. Accessed 4/8/2013 at https://www.gov.uk/dla-disability-living-allowance-benefit/overview.

[18] Personal Independence Payment (PIP) 2013. Accessed 4/8/2013 at https://www.gov.uk/pip/overview.

than sixteen with disability. Two pieces of legislation – The Carers (Recognition and Services) Act 1995[19] and The Carers and Disabled Children Act 2000[20] – are important in establishing the rights of carers. The first piece of legislation, The Carers Act 1995, was viewed as a major step forward for carers, giving them important new rights and a clear legal status. Under the act, individuals who provide or intend to provide a substantial amount of care on a regular basis are entitled to request (at the time the person they care for is being assessed for community-care services) an assessment of their ability to care and to continue caring. Local authorities are required to take into account the results of that assessment in making decisions about the type and level of community-care services to be provided to the cared-for person. The assessment under the 1995 act is of the carer's ability to provide care and of his or her ability to sustain the care that he or she has been providing. The 1995 act applies to carers of all ages. The 2000 act made four principal changes to the law with the objective of enabling local authorities to offer new support to carers to help them maintain their own health and well-being. The 2000 act applies to carers aged sixteen and older and people with parental responsibility for disabled children. Under the 2000 act, local authorities have the power to supply certain services (those services which help the carer to care) directly to carers following assessment. It gives carers the right to an assessment independent of the community-care assessment for the cared-for person. This enables a local authority to carry out an assessment in circumstances where the cared-for person has refused an assessment for, or the provision of, community-care services.

The 2000 act empowered local authorities to make direct payments to carers (including sixteen- and seventeen-year-old carers) for the services that meet their own assessed needs. The 2000 act, the legislative framework relating to direct payments for carers, was updated through Section 57 of the Health and Social Care Act 2001.[21] In addition, the

[19] The Carers (Recognition and Services) Act 1995. Accessed 4/8/2013 at http://www.legislation.gov.uk/ukpga/1995/12/pdfs/ukpga_19950012_en.pdf.

[20] The Carers and Disabled Children Act 2000. Accessed 4/8/2013 at http://www.legislation.gov.uk/uksi/2001/510/pdfs/uksi_20010510_en.pdf.

[21] Social Security Adjudications Act 1983. Accessed 4/8/2013 at http://www.legislation.gov.uk/ukpga/1983/41/pdfs/ukpga_19830041_en.pdf.

2000 act provides for local authority social services departments to run short-term break voucher schemes, which are designed to offer flexibility in the timing of carers' breaks and choice in the way services are delivered to cared-for people while their usual carer is taking a break. And, finally, the 2000 act amends the Health and Social Services and Social Security Adjudications Act 1983 to give local authorities the power to charge carers for the services they receive. Although the Carers (Equal Opportunities) Act 2004,[22] known as the 2004 act, was enacted after 2000, it is considered as being linked to the previous two pieces of legislation. The legislation has three sections. The first gives carers more choice and better opportunities to lead a more fulfilling life by ensuring that carers receive information about their rights to an assessment under the 2000 act. The second section ensures that those assessments now consider the carer's wishes in relation to leisure, education, training and work activities. The third provides for cooperation between local authorities and other public authorities, including housing, education and health, in relation to the planning and provision of services that may help support the carer in his or her caring role.

The Special Educational Needs (SEN) and Disability Act 2001 was created to help establish legal rights for disabled children and children with special educational needs in compulsory and post-sixteen years of age education, training and other student services. It extended the Disability Discrimination Act 1995[23] and sought to remove unjustified discrimination against children and students with disability, making such cases of discrimination unlawful. The Disability Discrimination Act 2005,[24] which was enacted later, ensured that public authorities were given a duty to promote and reinforce equality for people with disability.

The Disability Discrimination Act (DDA) 1995 legislated that it is against the law for goods, services and facility providers to discriminate against disabled people by treating them less favorably because of their

[22] The Carers (Equal Opportunities) Act 2004. Accessed 4/8/2013 at http://www.legislation.gov.uk/ukpga/2004/15/pdfs/ukpga_20040015_en.pdf.

[23] Disability Discrimination Act 1995. Accessed 4/8/2013 at http://www.legislation.gov.uk/ukpga/1995/50/contents.

[24] The Disability Discrimination Act 2005. Accessed 4/8/2013 at http://www.legislation.gov.uk/ukpga/2005/13/pdfs/ukpga_20050013_en.pdf.

disability. However, the DDA 1995 did not cover education providers. The Special Educational Needs and Disability Act 2001 was created in order to tackle discrimination in this sphere and extend the DDA 1995. Under the 2001 act, all education facilities were required to make the same sort of reasonable adjustments for disabled people as stipulated in the DDA 1995.

Removing Barriers to Achievement outlined the government's new long-term strategy for SEN.[25] This document, published in 2004, presented the government's vision for the education of children with special education needs and disability. It reinforced the commitment made in the green paper entitled *Every Child Matters:* a commitment to early intervention, inclusion, raising expectations and achievement, and developing partnership networks. It identified the weaknesses in the services offered at present, set out objectives for improvement and made specific commitments for future action. The document also included numerous case studies and summarized the findings of other relevant reports.

Aiming high for disabled children: better support for families[26] was published in 2007 by Her Majesty's Treasury and the Department for Education and Skills. The document was intended to improve service provision across the board for children with disability and their families, in addition to enhancing equality and opportunity. There were three priority areas to improve the lives of disabled children and their families: access and empowerment – establishing a clear standard of service provision for children and their families from public services; responsive services and timely support – health, social services and education are required to provide a coordinated, timely, integrated service provision to disabled children and their families; and improving quality and capacity – the government is required to increase the provision and

[25] HM Treasury, Department for Education and Skills, *Removing barriers to achievement: the government's strategy for SEN*, 2004. Accessed 6/8/2013 at http://webarchive.nationalarchives.gov.uk/20130401151715/https://www.education.gov.uk/publications/eOrderingDownload/DfES%200117%20200MIG1994.pdf.

[26] HM Treasury, Department for Education and Skills, *Aiming high for disabled children: better support for families*, 2007. Accessed 4/8/2013 at http://webarchive.nationalarchives.gov.uk/20130401151715/https://www.education.gov.uk/publications/eOrderingDownload/PU213.pdf.

quality of key services for disabled children and their families, including short breaks and childcare provision.

The Equality Act 2010 (EA)[27] aims to streamline and strengthen antidiscrimination legislation and provides the legal framework that protects all people from discrimination. It replaces a range of antidiscrimination legislation, including the DDA 1995, and is intended to be easier to operate and understand than previous equality legislation. The act provides a legal framework of equality law for all people with protected characteristics, including disability, age, race and gender.

Short breaks for disabled children, young people and their families[28] have been offered since April 2011 by local authorities. More than £800 million in non-ring-fenced grants has been provided to local authorities for the provision of short breaks in 2011–2012 and 2014–2015. The regulations require local authorities to offer breaks as a preventive early intervention, offer a range of services for parents and publish a statement of those services to parents.

TAX CREDIT

Tax credits are paid by Her Majesty's Revenue and Customs (HMRC) to lift millions of families out of poverty, but the system is complex and not everyone claims the credits to which they are entitled. There are two types of tax credits: Working Tax Credit (WTC) and Child Tax Credit (CTC). The latter is a means-tested payment for people who have responsibility for children younger than sixteen whether they are working or not. It replaces the previous support in the benefit and tax system for those with childcare responsibilities. Interestingly, parents of children with disability can obtain extra CTC if they receive the DLA or PIP for their children, if their children are registered as blind or if their children came off the blind register in

[27] The Equality Act 2010 (EA). Accessed 4/8/2013 at http://www.legislation.gov.uk/ukpga/2010/15/pdfs/ukpga_20100015_en.pdf.

[28] For additional information see "Short breaks for disabled children and young people and their carers." Accessed 4/8/2013 at http://www.bromley.gov.uk/info/260/disabled_children_and_young_people-short_breaks/168/short_breaks_for_disabled_children_and_young_people_and_their_carers.

the twenty-eight weeks before tax credits were claimed. They may get additional payment for their children's severe disability if one of the following is paid for them: Highest Rate Care Component of Disability Living Allowance and/or Enhanced Daily Living Component of Personal Independence Payment.

HOUSING

Housing Benefit (HB) is provided by the government to persons with low income to help with rent and some other housing costs.[29] Like income support, it is means-tested and provided to those who do not have capital/savings above £16,000. Local housing allowance (LHA) is a set amount of housing benefit paid if the person rents private accommodation. The amount is dependent on the area, number of bedrooms needed, means testing and whether there are nondependents living there. Responsiveness of LHA regulations to families of children with disability has been disputed in court. The case, represented by Child Poverty Action Group, was *Richard Gorry v. (1) Wiltshire Council (2) Secretary of State for Work and Pensions.*[30] The Court of Appeal ruled on May 15, 2012, that the Local Housing Allowance (LHA) size criteria discriminated unlawfully against the children in the Gorry family on the grounds of disability. The Court judged that children with severe disability – in this case a child with spina bifida and another with Down syndrome – could not always be expected to share a bedroom because of additional needs related to their disability. There is no doubt that the Court of Appeal's judgment represents a rare, important and very welcome victory for a discrimination argument in a social security context.

[29] "The Housing Benefit Regulations of 2006," in *Social Security*, 2006, No. 213. Accessed 4/8/2013 at http://www.legislation.gov.uk/uksi/2006/213/pdfs/uksi_20060213_en.pdf.
For those who have reached the qualifying age for Pension Credit (regardless of whether it has been claimed), the credit is governed by the Housing Benefit Regulations of 2006.

[30] *Richard Gorry v. (1) Wiltshire Council (2) Secretary of State for Work and Pensions.* Look at background and overview of the case. Accessed 4/8/2013 at http://www.cpag.org.uk/content/gorry-v-secretary-state-work-and-pensions.

UK POLICIES TOWARD FAMILIES OF CHILDREN WITH DISABILITY: A DISCUSSION

United Kingdom family policy has changed since 1997 under New Labour. According to Mary Daly, there is a range of measures demonstrating focus on children's early education and care, services to stabilize and improve the quality of family relations and greater flexibility in work and family life.[31] However, while the sense is that New Labour has been more receptive to the family, the United Kingdom continues to be a market-oriented family policy model.

UK MIXED FAMILY POLICY

The general impression is that Britain has a mixed family policy. On the one hand, the state declares universalist ambitions, viewing families as an asset for stability and social order. On the other hand, in practice, entitlements and provisions continue to be selective and are still employing needs assessment. A recent households study using 2004/2005 data demonstrated that 7.3 percent of the child population had disability.[32] The majority lived at home with their families of origin, with two-thirds in two-parent households.

The past decade has seen significant changes in legislation in the UK as well as at the global level, in particular the adoption of the UN CRPD.[33] Children with disability and their families are perceived as citizens with legal and human rights rather than being referred to as recipients of social services. This change has been the center of debate

[31] Mary Daly, "Shifts in family policy in the UK under New Labour," *Journal of European Social Policy* 20 (2010), 433–43.

[32] Clare M. Blackburn, Nick J. Spencer and Janet M. Read, "Prevalence of childhood disability and the characteristics and circumstances of disabled children in the UK: Secondary analysis of the Family Resources Survey," *BMC Pediatrics* 10 (2010), 1471–2431.

[33] The CRPD and its Optional Protocol were adopted on December 13, 2006, at the United Nations Headquarters in New York, and they were opened for signature on March 30, 2007. The Convention is intended as a human rights instrument with an explicit, social development dimension. It adopts a broad categorization of persons with disabilities and reaffirms that all persons with all types of disabilities must enjoy all human rights and fundamental freedoms. The CRPD coverage of family disability policy is discussed in Chapter 8.

in the United Kingdom among scholars who believe that the conventional human rights model is more favorable than the social welfare model.[34] Supporters of the conventional human rights model believe that children with disability and their families have to be equal and receive the same recognition as the nondisabled. However, social welfare specialists raise concern that this equal approach may fail to recognize special provisions for children with disability and their families.

Universalists versus specialists

The heart of the debate is between universal and specialist policy. Good examples are the Children Act of 1989 and the Childcare Act 2006. The first is one of the main pieces of legislation governing support services for children with disability. Some have argued that while having a universal legislation that encompasses all children has merit, only Part III of the Children Act can be adapted to children with disability.[35] Similarly, the Childcare Act 2006 imposes a range of general obligations on local authorities in relation to childcare for younger children in particular. The obligations are designed to ensure that local authorities take an active strategic role in managing the provision of childcare within their areas with a view to ensuring that local childcare supports the Every Child Matters: Change for Children agenda.[36] The latter stands for a universal and preventative approach to children and the elimination of child poverty by 2020.[37]

It is evident that the past fifteen years have also changed the legislation and policy relevant to children with disability and their families.

[34] Dan Goodley and Katherine Runswick-Cole, "Problematising policy: conceptions of 'child,' 'disabled' and 'parents' in social policy in England," *International Journal of Inclusive Education* 15 (2011), 71–85.

[35] Luke Clements, "The disability rights convention and the right to independent living," *Legal Action* 2008, 27–9.

[36] Richard Barker, *Making sense of Every Child Matters: multi-professional practice guidance* (University of Bristol, UK: Policy, 2009). Accessed 6/9/2013 at www.everychildmattersbook.co.uk.

[37] Every Child Matters is often compared to the US Department of Education strategy No Child Left Behind 2002. However, the US program is narrowly focused, aimed at educational achievement.

There is no doubt that the two pieces of disability rights legislation –The Disability Discrimination Act 1995 and The Equality Act 2010 – aimed toward people with disability have also recognized the rights of children with disability and their families. If the Disability Discrimination Act 1995 intended to protect them from discrimination, the Equality Act 2010 sought to eliminate their discriminatory treatment in all areas of public life.[38] A reflection of the change is seen in the Aiming High for Disabled Children policy,[39] with government efforts to set new standards on information, transparency, participation, assessment and feedback. The policy tried to communicate to families of children with disability that it has been attentive and responsive to their individualized need for access and support. An additional development associated with Aiming High for Disabled Children is the promotion of personalized social care, offering more choice and control to consumers including personal and individual budgets. However, this endeavor is at an early stage and has to cope with resistance and obstacles from the current service delivery system.

Most of the provisions for children with disability and their families are still based on needs assessment and means-tested policies and legislation. The CTC, for example, is a means-tested credit for parents with a low income, whether working or not; it is paid for each child, with additional amounts for a child who is registered as blind or receiving the DLA. The Housing Benefit and the Council Tax Benefit are also means-tested benefits intended to help with rent or council tax. Both benefits are paid to welfare recipients or based on income. An interesting example is the Carer's Allowance paid to caring parents if their child receives the middle or highest rate DLA care component, if the parent cares for the child for thirty-five hours a week or more, and if the parent earns less than a set amount (currently £100 per week) after deducting tax.

[38] See Janet Read, Claire Blackburn and Nick Spencer, "Disabled children and their families: a decade of policy change," *Children & Society* (2012), 223–33.

[39] Aiming High for Disabled Children (AHDC) 2007 supports and delivers the aims of Every Child Matters and the Children's National Service Framework (NSF), supporting the need of families to lead ordinary lives by emphasizing three priority areas: access and empowerment, responsive services and timely support, and improved quality and capacity.

FRANCE – POLICY AND LEGISLATION TOWARD FAMILIES OF CHILDREN WITH DISABILITY

In Europe, France is known for having a progressive family policy and a special minister who is responsible for family issues.[40] Legislation reflects strong support of maternal employment and public childcare provisions aimed at reducing childcare costs for families.

In terms of disability policy, France is transitioning from social welfare to disability rights policy. Until 2005, disability policy in France was framed by the 1975 Orientation Law in Favor of Disabled People (*Loi d'Orientation en Faveur des Personnes Handicapées*).[41] The passage of the 2005 Act No. 2005–102, Equal Rights and Opportunities, Participation and Citizenship of Persons with Disabilities, marked a significant change in the equal rights of persons with disability. The following section highlights core general and specific benefits and provisions, while the second section analyzes the unique status of French family disability policy.

CORE GENERIC AND SPECIFIC BENEFITS AND PROVISIONS

Equal Rights and Opportunities, Participation and Citizenship of Persons with Disabilities (*Loi* No. 2005–102)

French disability equal rights legislation is known as *Loi No. 2005–102 du 11 février 2005 pour l'égalité des droits et des chances, la participation et la citoyenneté des personnes handicapées*. The law set out a new direction for disability rights policy in France and amended many existing provisions.[42] The general principle of this law is freedom of choice for

[40] See Jeanne Fagnani, "Family policy in France," in *International encyclopedia of social policy* (New York: Routledge, 2006), vol. 3, 501–506.

[41] *Loi No. 75–534 d'Orientation en Faveur des Personnes Handicapées* and *Loi No. 75–535 Relative aux Institutions Sociales et Médicosociales* completely changed the landscape and the political and social approach of disability in France. It reinforced a positive discrimination for disabled persons, giving benefits and income while stimulating and organizing service provision.

[42] See French government site, "Policy for the disabled in France," February 2006, updated in August 2007. Accessed 2/1/2011 at http://www.ambafrance-eau.org/IMG/disabled.pdf.

persons with disability and facilitation of their participation in all decisions concerning their own care. The legislation calls for a change in accessibility and compensation approach. Accessibility refers to physical, social, economic and cultural adaptations and accommodations; it enables inclusion in education, the labor market, housing, culture and leisure. The law offers new reform in structuring the delivery of disability services at the local level.[43] A *Commission des Droits et de l'Autonomie des Personnes Handicapées* (CDAPH) is responsible for assessing the needs and eligibility of persons with disability for a range of disability services, including social security, social services and education. Social security benefits for persons with disability are provided by the general social security authorities (the *Caisse Nationale des Allocations Familiales* or National Office for Family Allocations).

One important reform in the area of social services has been the introduction of a new scheme of *prestation de compensation du handicap* (PCH), which is a personalized cash payment intended to provide financial support linked to the loss of autonomy of disabled people. It comprises five separate elements: personal assistance, technical assistance, housing and transport, exceptional or specific expenses, and "animal assistance" (for example, when a person needs the assistance of a guide dog). Since 2008, it also applies to children.

FAMILY ALLOWANCES

Most of the government's family policy is carried out by the CNAF (*Caisse Nationale des Allocations Familiales*), a special division that covers more than 90 percent of all family allowance funds to recipients. The CNAF is regulated by the central government but delivered by the local authorities. Interestingly, in the 1980s more than 90 percent of the resources allocated to the family sector were provided by contributions paid by employers. Since the 1990s, the funding has shifted toward the tax system and state budget spending.

[43] A *Maison départementale des personnes handicapées* (MDPH) (Departmental Disability Center) was established in each *départment* (general council) under the responsibility of the *conseil general* of the *départment.*

The core provision under the Social Security Code is *Allocations Familiales*, which is considered supplementary income designed to offset some of the costs of raising children.[44] Therefore, this neither means-tested nor related-to-employment core cash benefit is paid to families with two children or more. Families with one child are entitled to a means-tested benefit if the child is less than three years old.[45] Benefits are paid for a dependent child until the age of sixteen when the period of compulsory schooling ends. There are differential allowances related to children's and family's conditions. A flat-rate allowance is payable to families with three or more dependent children whose child benefits are reduced when one or more of the children reaches the age of twenty (the age limit for child benefit). Family income supplement is a means-tested benefit payable to families with at least three children aged between three and twenty-one years. Family-support allowance is a non-means-tested allowance payable for any orphaned or half-orphaned child, any child not regarded as a legitimate child of either parent, or any child whose mother and/or father fail(s) to provide adequate support.

There are various benefits to offset the costs due to the arrival of a child and to help pay for the cost of childcare; they are grouped together under the early childhood benefit program. The latter, known as *Prestation d'Accueil du Jeune Enfant* (PAJE), was created in 2004 and offers a bonus payment at the time of birth or adoption dependent on the applicant's means. The bonus payment is made in the seventh month of pregnancy or at the time an adopted child moves into the home. This payment is intended to help the family cover the initial costs of the birth or adoption. A basic benefit payment is dependent on the applicant's means. The benefit payment is made every month for three years from the child's arrival in the home to help the family cover education costs. Working credit (*Complément de Libre Choix d'Activité*, known as CLCA) is intended for families in which one of the parents stops working or works less to look after his or her child. For families welcoming a firstborn, this benefit is paid for a maximum of six months. For other families, this benefit can be paid up until the month before the

[44] *Code De La Sécurité Sociale, art. L.512–1. Modifié par Loi No. 2006-1640 du 21 décembre 2006, Art. 130 JORF 22 décembre 2006.*

[45] See, for extended review, Jacques Commaille, Pierre Strobel and Michel Villac, *La politique de la famille* (Paris: La Découverte, 2002).

child's third birthday. Optional working credit (*Complément Optionnel de Libre Choix d'Activité*, known as COLCA) is for parents who have at least three children. Finally, care credit (*Complément de Libre Choix du Mode de Garde*, known as CMG) intends to help parents fund the services of a certified child minder or a home-based childcare provider. Dependent on the family's means, the CMG covers a part of the person's salary and all or part of his or her welfare contributions.

There are specific allowances that address families of children with disability and special needs. The non-means-tested Education Allowance for Disabled Child is paid to parents of a child with severe disability under twenty years of age and with a permanent disability rating of at least 80 percent, or between 50 percent and 80 percent if the child is in institutional care or receives care at home. While the allowance is non–means tested, those who are eligible for the allowance supplement have to undergo thorough assessment. The child's condition is classified by a Committee for the Rights and Self-dependency of Disabled Persons (CDAPH) in one of six categories, using a rating scale that assesses the special care needs and costs, the financial consequences arising from the disability and/or loss of income for a parent staying at home to look after the child, and the need for a paid carer. As an alternative to the supplement, parents can opt for the disability compensation benefit paid by the *Conseil Général*, which is intended to contribute toward the cost of the continuing care needs arising from the disability. The Daily Parental Attendance Allowance is an additional allowance aimed toward children with disability. This 2006 entitlement is paid to any person looking after a child younger than twenty who is suffering from a disease or severe handicap requiring constant assistance and attendance. To qualify, the beneficiary (primarily a parent) must be obliged to take time off work and be granted parent's attendance leave. A doctor's certificate attesting to the child's medical condition must be furnished to the medical board of the relevant Health Insurance Fund.

CHILDCARE

France is one of the leading countries in Europe in providing extensive public support for maternal employment. Childcare policies are subsidized and supported considerably by the state. The 1989 legislation set up the guidelines for nursery schools. Working mothers are offered a range of *crèche* types and childcare facilities for children aged three months to twenty-four months. The cost of childcare is income-related and administered under the Ministry of Health. The *écoles maternelles* (kindergartens) cover children from twenty-four month to five years and are publicly funded and administered under the Ministry of Education. They offer a basic free school-day program; the parent only has to pay for the supplements according to their income. However, most of the out-of-school care is provided by *centres de loisirs sans hébergement*[46] (recreation centers without accommodation), which charge fees that can be reduced.[47]

Interestingly, the French government also offers these services to children with disability; however, most of the centers are not committed to inclusion. The main source of family and child services in France is through the semipublic body, the *Caisse d'Allocations Familiales* (CAF). Social care delivery, along with social assistance, is delivered at the department level through the local *centres communaux d'action sociale* (communal social action centers).

EDUCATION

French education legislation enacted in 1989 guarantees everyone the right to education.[48] Children with disability are covered by separate legislation from 1975, known as the Act on Counseling for Disabled Persons.[49] This law calls for mainstreaming children with disability into regular classes. The 1989 legislation promotes educational integration,

[46] OECD Country Note, *Early childhood education and care policy in France*, Directorate for Education, OECD February 2004, http://www.oecd.org/education/school/34400146.pdf.

[47] See Jonathan Bradshaw and Naomi Finch, *A comparison of child benefit packages in 22 countries* (Leeds, Department for Work and Pensions Research Report, No. 174, Corporate Document Services, 2003).

[48] Guidance Law No. 89-486 of 10 July 1989 on Education set education as the nation's topmost priority. It amended and completed legislation on the educational system by reorganizing school timetables as well as educational cycles.

[49] Law No. 75-534 of 30 June 1975 – making training and career guidance for disabled children and adults a national obligation.

and Circular No. 99–187 of November 1999 reconfirms the right of every child to be integrated if the family requires it.[50]

The service delivery system is divided between *Service d'Éducation Spéciale et de Soins à Domicile* (special education and home care service) that handles children and teenagers with mental, motor and sensory disabilities and *Classes d'Intégration Scolaire* (school integration classes) geared toward integrating children with disability into regular classes. The concept is to facilitate a special class within an ordinary elementary or secondary school. Therefore, the general impression is that the French educational system leans toward collective rather than individual integration.[51]

HEALTH CARE

The French health-care system was established in 1945, and its coverage for its affiliates has undergone many changes since then. One of the major changes resulted in the expansion of health coverage to all legal residents under the law of universal coverage called *la couverture maladie universelle* (universal health coverage).[52] The unemployed and the poor are covered under universal health coverage. Funding is achieved through professional activity (being employed) and covered by *Sécurité Sociale* (social security).[53] The financing is supported by employers, employee contributions and personal income taxes. The working population has 20 percent of its gross salary deducted at source to fund the social security system, and employer and union federations jointly control the funds under the state's supervision, which involves an intricate collaboration between the various entities of the system. About 75 percent of the total health expenditures are covered by the public

[50] European Agency for Development in Special Needs Education (EADSNE), "Special needs education in Europe," 2003. Accessed 4/2/2010 at http://www.european-agency.org.

[51] European Agency for Special Needs and Inclusive Education, "Special needs education within the education system – France." Accessed 6/9/2012 at http://www.european-agency.org/country-information/france/national-overview/special-needs-education-within-the-education-system.

[52] Jean-Pierre Poullier and Simone Sander, "Rationing health care in France," *Health Policy* 50 (1999), 23–38.

[53] There are two additional funds for the self-employed and agricultural workers.

health insurance system. A part of the balance is paid directly by the patients and the other part by private health insurance companies that are engaged individually or in groups (*assurance complémentaire* or *mutuelle*, complementary insurance or mutual funds).[54]

Children younger than sixteen are covered by their parents' health insurance.[55] Children younger than six have to be evaluated and monitored periodically in the *centres de protection maternelle et infantile* (maternal and child welfare centers). After the age of six, children's health is monitored by school health services. *Centres de protection maternelle et infantile* provide specialist services for children younger than six with disability. Special diagnostic and treatment services are provided through schools.

FRENCH POLICIES TOWARD FAMILIES OF CHILDREN WITH DISABILITY: A DISCUSSION

France has a tradition of a strong family policy that has taken a dominant role in the social security system.[56] As a conservative corporatist state, it offers a solid social insurance system with implications for social care as well as health, involving employers, employees, and the state. Private health provision and private health insurance are growing within the health system. France was among the first countries to pay generous maternity and family allowances, to provide parental leave benefits and to offer affordable childcare.[57]

However, in recent years there has been an erosion in government commitment to familized policy. The main argument is that this policy is too costly economically and too unrealistic politically. The government is now tending to consider selective policies that support only

[54] Karine Chevreul et al., "France: health system review," *Health Systems in Transition* 12 (2010), 1–291.

[55] There are other age categories for children covered by their parents' health insurance: children under 17 if they are looking for work and registered at the National Employment Agency, under 18 if in an apprenticeship, and under 20 if they are students or are disabled.

[56] For additional reading, see Mark Kleinman, *A European welfare state? European Union social policy in context* (Houndmills, Basingstoke, Hampshire: Palgrave 2002).

[57] See Lewis, "Gender and the development of welfare regimes," 165.

households in need.[58] Since the early 80s, French governments have faced major challenges, including growing unemployment, a deficit in the social security system and changes in family structures, leading to a change from a universal family policies to a tailor-made family policy.[59] This was seen in the 1990s with the global expenditure on childcare, which moved from *crèches* toward cash benefits (cash-for-care system), resulting in a reduced number of *crèches* between the mid-90s and the mid-2000s.

Parallel to the gradual change from universal family policies to tailor made, France has been exposed to European policies that tend to be overwhelmingly selective and the general shift from the social welfare to the human rights approach. This has implications for policies affecting many populations, including children with disability and their families. The 2005 disability rights legislation set out a new direction, including the right to accessible accommodations and changes in compensation schemes toward individualized budgets and the development of tailor-made support services.[60]

Overall, child allowances are generous and universal but with growing modest special allowances such as the back-to-school allowance for low-income families, an adoption allowance and a single-parent allowance. The same applies to childcare policy, particularly for working parents of children younger than three.

Families of children with disability can receive supplementary allowances if their children have permanent disability. The application for such an allowance requires extensive professional assessment. For example, the Education Allowance for Disabled Child is paid to parents of child with a severe disability under twenty years of age and with a permanent disability rating of at least 80 percent. The same applies to the Daily Parental Attendance Allowance, an entitlement paid to any

[58] Claude Martin, "The reframing of family policy in France: Actors, ideas and instruments," *Journal of European Social Policy* 20 (2010), 410–21.

[59] Claude Martin, "The reframing of family policies in France: Process and actors," (paper distributed at the 7th ESPAnet Conference 2009, Session: nr. 21, "Explaining recent shifts in family policy"), 12.

[60] Mel Cousins & Associates, "Supports for families with a child with disability," (research report, November 9, 2012) 31–4. Accessed 1/9/2013 at http://www.welfare.ie/en/downloads/DCAReview-ResearchReport.pdf.

person looking after a child younger than twenty who is suffering from a disease or severe handicap requiring constant assistance and attendance. The qualification requires a doctor's certificate attesting to the child's medical condition furnished to the medical board of the relevant health insurance fund. Although France offers a progressive family policy for parents of children with disability, it appears that it is less advanced in offering inclusive education for such children with disability. Since the passage of the Equal Rights and Opportunities, Participation and Citizenship of Persons with Disabilities Act in 2005, there has been a gradual change toward integration in individual planning in French schools, but the impression is that it is still highly regulated and dependent on medical assessment.

SWEDEN – CORE POLICIES TOWARD FAMILIES OF CHILDREN WITH DISABILITY

Sweden is seen as a social democratic state offering comprehensive health care, social insurance and social protection provisions. Its policy is aimed at financial security and social rights guaranteed to all citizens, including children with disability and their families. The basis of this policy is a tax system in which all taxpayers contribute for the good of all according to capacity. Public services are almost totally financed by taxes. The user pays only a fraction of the costs (4% to 5%). The biggest share of the costs (about 82% to 85%) is covered by local taxes. National taxes cover the remaining costs of services and care.[61] The system is decentralized and consists of three levels of government: the parliament at the national level, county councils at the regional level and municipalities at the local level. There are 21 county councils (*Landsting*) and 289 municipalities. County councils and municipalities, which are run by elected bodies (known as municipal and county council assemblies), have their own decision-making powers.

[61] For additional reading, see Ann-Zofie Duvander, "Family policy in Sweden 2008," *Social Insurance Report* 15 (2008), Stockholm: Swedish Social Insurance Agency; Tommy Ferrarini and Ann-Zofie Duvander, "Earner-carer model at the crossroads: reforms and outcomes of Sweden's family policy in comparative perspective," *International Journal of Health Services* 40 (2010), 373–398.

The two pivotal legislations are the Health and Medical Services Act (1983) that provides health services for everyone, including rehabilitation and assistive devices for people with functional impairments, and the Social Services Act (1982). The latter stipulates that the municipalities have ultimate responsibility for ensuring that all residents in the municipality obtain the support and help they need. The municipalities have a special responsibility for people with physical, mental or intellectual functional impairments so that they are able to live in a way that corresponds to their needs and to play an active part in the community.

DISABILITY RIGHTS LEGISLATION AND NATIONAL ACTION PLANS FOR HUMAN RIGHTS

Sweden's disability rights policy is progressive; in 2008, the government ratified the CRPD and the Optional Protocol. Sweden has important national laws, policies and strategies concerning human rights of people with disability. In particular, there are four important acts prohibiting discrimination on the grounds of disability[62]: the Prohibition of Discrimination in Working Life of People with Disability Act (1999:132); the Equal Treatment of Students at Universities Act (2001:1286); the Prohibition of Discrimination Act (2003:307); and the Act on the Prohibition of Discrimination and Other Degrading Treatment of Children and Pupils (2006:67). The Act Concerning Support and Service for Persons with Certain Functional Impairments (1993:387) includes ten measures for increasing the welfare of some people with impairments.[63]

In addition, the Swedish government has adopted two national action plans for human rights, the first in 1999 and the second in 2006. The 1999 plan, called From Patient to Citizen, was extended until 2010; it called for a society with diversity as its basis, shaping and enabling all people with disability of all ages to participate fully in

[62] See information on Sweden Country Profile, as presented in 2009 by Academic Network of European Disability experts (ANED). Accessed 6/9/2013 at http://www.disability-europe.net/content/aned/media/Sweden%20-%20ANED%20country%20profile.pdf.

[63] The latter is discussed separately in the last section.

social life. In addition, it specified equality in living conditions for girls and boys and women and men with disability. Disability policy work is to be specifically geared to identifying and eliminating obstacles to full participation in society for people with disability; preventing and combating discrimination; and giving children, young people and adults with disability opportunities for achieving independence and self-determination. In 2006, the government presented the second national action plan for human rights (for the period 2006–2009), which was intended to provide guidelines and a structure for human rights work and, in this way, speed up the implementation of the recognized rights.

CHILDCARE

Childcare provision began in the early 1970s to facilitate parental work and ensure qualitative early education. It is provided by municipalities for children aged one to twelve so that parents can work or study. The childcare policy has been expanded over the years to include all children, unemployed parents or those on leave for other reasons.[64] Currently, parental contributions cover about 11 percent of the costs and are waived for families in economic difficulty. For families with more than one child, fees are capped at 3.2 percent and at 1 percent of the combined household income for the first, second and third child respectively.[65] From 1998, childcare has been regulated through the Swedish Educational Act of 1985. There are three types of childcare, among them preschools that are based on educational group activity; family day-care-home using a child minder to look after children in the parents' own home while parents work or study; or open preschool, a place for parents who are at home with their children or for child minders in family day care. In addition, there are

[64] Magnus Bygren and Ann-Zofie Duvander, "Parents' workplace situation and fathers' parental leave use," *Journal of Marriage and the Family* 68 (2006), 363–72.

[65] OECD, "Appendix E Country profiles: an overview of ECEC systems in the participating countries," in *Starting strong II: early childhood education and care* (2006) 408–13. Accessed 4/8/2013 at http://www.oecd.org/edu/school/37423778.pdf.

after-school childcare options for older children aged six to twelve, such as leisure-time centers, family day-care-home and open leisure-time centers.

Children with disability or special needs have a priority right to services and will be provided additional support, but they will be well integrated into the Swedish childcare system. All children in need of special support have written action plans set up in cooperation with the children, their parents and the professionals involved in their care.[66]

Health care

The Health and Medical Services Act sets out the respective responsibilities of county councils and municipalities for health and medical care.[67] The health-care system is fully government funded (about 70% through local taxation) and highly decentralized, organized and managed on three levels: national, regional and local. At the national level, the Ministry of Health and Social Affairs establishes principles and guidelines for care and sets the political agenda for health and medical care. In fact, most of the operation is managed regionally by twenty-one regional councils that determine priorities and allocations.[68] The system is universal and is supposed to cover all the health-care needs of children with disability. However, families of children with disability receive supplemental financial coverage through Care Allowance for Disabled Children and the Act concerning Support and Service to Persons with Certain Functional Impairments (*Lagen om stöd och service till vissa funktionshindrade*).[69]

[66] See (8§) in Skollag (2010:800). Accessed 6/9/2013 at http://www.riksdagen.se/sv/Dokument-Lagar/Lagar/Svenskforfattningssamling/Skollag-2010800_sfs-2010-800/ (Swedish).

[67] The Health and Medical Services Act 1982:763. See Sweden's Ministry of Health and Social Affairs. Accessed 6/9/2013 at http://www.ilo.org/dyn/travail/docs/1643/health%20a%20nd%20medical%20insurance%20act.pdf.

[68] Anna H. Glenngard et al., *Health systems in transition: Sweden*, WHO–Regional Office for Europe, 2005. Accessed 4/1/2014 at http://www.euro.who.int/__data/assets/pdf_file/0010/96409/E88669.pdf.

[69] These benefits are discussed in the next sections: "Benefits for all children and families" and "The right for personal assistance (Disability Reform of 1994)."

EDUCATION

Sweden's Education Act 1985 provides compulsory education from the ages of seven to sixteen.[70] The educational system is free of charge, and the state also covers incidental costs such as transportation, school meals, health care and educational aids. It is a decentralized system run by municipalities, and it encourages parental choice of school.[71] The law is based on the principle that schools must offer education to all children regardless of their background or socioeconomic situation.[72]

Integrative and special education

Children with disability are covered by the Education Act 1985; however, they are entitled to have an additional school year. Children who frequently miss school because of illness are entitled to be taught at the hospital or in their home. Sweden's inclusive education has changed over the years. In the early years, policymakers saw mainstreaming as an option for select children with disability. However, this has changed; all children with disability are entitled to study in regular schools, and those who need segregated settings are the exception.[73] Now, most of

[70] See the Education Act 1985. Children have the right to start school at age six if their parents want them to and if the municipality has the capacity. Preschool classes for six-year-olds are available free of charge for 525 hours per year.

[71] Sweden 1998: para 536. For further reading, see Maarit Jänterä-Jareborg, Anna Singer and Caroline Sörgjerd, *National report about parents' responsibilities in Sweden*, University of Uppsala, Sweden. Accessed 4/9/2013 at http://ceflonline.net/wp-content/uploads/Sweden-Parental-Responsibilities.pdf.

[72] The Swedish Education Law (1985:1100) states that all children and young people must have access to equal quality education irrespective of gender, geographical place of residence, and social and financial situations. Sweden has nine years of compulsory schooling from the age of seven, and education throughout the state school system is free of charge. Alongside the state school system are independent schools, open to all.

[73] Berhanu Girma, "Inclusive education in Sweden: responses, challenges and prospects," *International Journal of Special Education* 26 (2011), 128–48. Swedish social welfare/educational policy has traditionally been underpinned by a strong philosophy of universalism, equal entitlements of citizenship, comprehensiveness, and solidarity as an instrument to promote social inclusion and equality of resources. Within the past decades, however, Sweden has undergone a dramatic transformation. The changes are framed within neoliberal philosophies such as devolution, market solutions, competition, effectivity, and standardization, coupled with a proliferation of individual/parent choices for independent schools, all of which potentially work against the valuing of diversity, equity and inclusion.

the special schools (*specialskola*) are linked to regular elementary and secondary schools.

BENEFITS FOR ALL CHILDREN AND FAMILIES

Sweden has a diverse and extensive support system aimed at providing financial security to parents, contributing to their economic well-being and increasing their freedom of choice.[74] Swedish financial support to families is part of the Social Insurance Code, divided into three main areas: insurance, general allowances and means-/needs-tested allowances. The various types of family support are designed to meet specific needs (for example, the needs of parents living apart and parents of sick children or children with disability).[75]

INSURANCE BENEFITS

Insurance includes parental benefit, temporary parental benefit (*tillfällig föräldrapenning vid vård av barn*), pregnancy benefit, child pension and pension rights for childcare years. Parental benefit, paid for a total of 480 days per child, is the compensation parents receive to be able to stay at home with their children instead of working. Temporary parental benefit may also be paid in certain other cases (for example, when the child's regular caregiver is ill). The father of a newborn baby is entitled to ten days of temporary parental benefit, known as father days, in connection with the child's birth. There are other benefits such as the pregnancy benefit paid to women with physically demanding jobs who cannot carry out their duties toward the end of their pregnancy; child pension paid to parents who have lost their child; and pension rights for childcare years paid to a parent for the first four years of a child's life.

[74] Core social security legislation includes the following: General Child Benefit Act (*Lag om allmänna barnbidrag*) of 1947; Advance on Maintenance Payments Act (*Lag om underhllsstöd*) of 1996; Housing Allowance Act (*Lag om bostadsbidrag*) 1993; Social Insurance Act from January 1, 2002; Social Services Act 1982 (*Socialtjänstlagen*); and Act Concerning Compensation for Assistance (LASS) 1993.

[75] See government site on parental insurance and allowances to parents in Sweden. Accessed 3/4/2013 at http://www.government.se/sb/d/15473/a/183497.

GENERAL ALLOWANCES

There are two general allowances: child allowance (*barnbidrag*) and adoption allowance. Child allowance is tax free and paid to all families from the month following the child's birth up to the age of sixteen. A supplementary allowance for additional children is paid to families with two or more children. The adoption allowance contributes a fixed sum toward the costs of inter-country adoptions.

MEANS-TESTED ALLOWANCES

There are three core means-tested allowances: maintenance support, housing allowance and care allowance for disabled children. Maintenance support guarantees that children whose parents are living apart receive some support even when the parent who is required to pay maintenance support does not comply. It is paid to the parent with whom the child is living or directly to the child. The parent who is required to pay must reimburse costs paid from public funds for the maintenance support in full or in part. Housing allowance is provided to households with children living at home, and households with access rights to children can apply for housing allowance. The size of the allowance depends on housing costs, the size of the home, household income and number of children. Care allowance for disabled children is paid to a parent who looks after a child with disability or a parent with a sick child at home. To be eligible for care allowance, the child must need special supervision and care for at least six months or must have a disability or illness that entails substantial extra costs.

THE RIGHT TO PERSONAL ASSISTANCE (DISABILITY REFORM OF 1994)

Sweden is a pioneer in entitling persons with extensive disability to cash payments for the purchase of self-directed personal assistance services. The Act concerning Support and Service to Persons with Certain Functional Impairments (*Lagen om Stöd och Service till vissa funktionshindrade*) was passed in 1993; it is known as LSS or the Disability Reform of 1994 (its implementation year). The innovative legislation sets out rights for persons with considerable and permanent functional impairments, with ten measures for special support and service to provide good living conditions. Interestingly, the legislation refers to three specific impairment groups: (a) developmental impairments, autism or autism spectrum diagnoses; (b) intellectual impairments after brain damage in adulthood; and (c) major and permanent functional impairments that are not obviously age-related. It is evident that most of the children and adolescents who are covered by the law belong to the first category.

One of the measures constitutes the right to personal assistance as regulated by the Assistance Benefit Act (LASS). Personal assistance is considered to be the most important achievement of the disability reform, enabling eligible individuals to purchase personal assistance services from public and private entities, including for-profit companies, through a monthly sum from the National Social Insurance, which covers all costs of the services. The LSS applies to disabled people who need less than twenty hours of assistance a week; LASS applies to those in need of personal assistance in excess of twenty hours per week.

SWEDISH POLICIES TOWARD FAMILIES OF CHILDREN WITH DISABILITY: A DISCUSSION

Universalism and local autonomy

Sweden's implicit family policy is intertwined with labor market policy and social insurance, offering three core provisions: day-care centers and after-school services, parental insurance, and child allowance and other benefits.[76] Overall, family disability policy is consonant with this approach to universal coverage of children and adults with disability and their families. The comprehensive social insurance coverage includes child allowance, parental benefit, temporary parental benefit, pregnancy benefit, child pension and pension rights for childcare years.

[76] Duvander, "Family policy in Sweden 2008."

In addition, there are three universal pieces of legislation: the Social Services Act (1982), the Health and Medical Services Act (1983), and Sweden's Education Act 1985.

Interestingly, the government recognizes that the universal benefits cannot respond to all the needs of all families; therefore, it offers means-tested supplements such as maintenance support, housing allowance and care allowance for disabled children. The latter is a unique family-support policy for parents who look after a child with disability or have a sick child at home. However, the child must need special supervision and care for at least six months or must have a disability or illness that entails substantial extra costs.

Sweden offers a unique service delivery system; macro policy is determined at the national level, but most of the provisions are decentralized and operated by the 21 county councils and 289 municipalities, which raise local taxes. The fact that these municipalities are run by elected bodies allows them to have certain autonomy with respect to health and social services. There have been some power struggles between central and local governments, and since its election in 2006, the national conservative-led government has sought to exert more strategic authority over the officially independent twenty-one county councils.

THE DISABILITY REFORM AS A TURNING POINT

In the 1990s, Sweden experienced the worst economic slump since the 1930s, marked by mass unemployment, a serious budget deficit and drastic cuts and rule changes in income benefits and services. These negative changes began under a conservative-led coalition and continued under the Social Democrats. Rafael Lindquist observed decreased social insurance benefits and tightened entitlement criteria in what he called "deservingness ethics."[77] He believes that the government is offering selective social and civic rights instead of universal ones. However, critics tend to disagree with his approach, claiming that the

[77] Rafael Lindquist, "Swedish disability policy: from universal welfare to civil rights?" *European Journal of Social Security* 2 (2000), 399–418.

welfare state simply became unsustainable and its cost sent the budget deficit soaring.[78] They believe that Sweden's family disability policy is moving toward a more rational and less dependent approach.

The center of the debate is the Swedish Personal Assistance Act of 1994. Supporters view the legislation as extremely successful in empowering persons with disability and families, enabling them to live in the community in self-determination and dignity, with better choices than before. However, social democrats see the pitfalls, believing that the legislation is aimed at persons and families of children with severe and persistent functional difficulties in the activities of daily living. The concern is that this paradigm shift, from universal to selective cash payments, may deny benefits to the substantial number of persons with disability and the families of children with less severe functional difficulties.[79] However, from an international comparative approach, Sweden still looks like a family policy leader, with an impressive array of benefits to children with disability and families, though less so than in the past. Despite extensive cutbacks and restructuring in the 1990s, it appears that Sweden's welfare state has not been dismantled, though it has been and continues to be changed.

CONCLUSIONS

The chapter reviews and discusses three different European countries regarding family disability policy: the United Kingdom, France and Sweden. Based on Esping-Andersen's "Comparative macro-sociology of welfare states," the United Kingdom represents liberal and social democratic approaches of a welfare state, French policy is a mixture of liberal and conservative corporatist principles, while Sweden is a typical social democratic welfare state.[80] However, since the 1990s, the three countries, as well as other European countries, have undergone a

[78] Helen Lachs Ginsburg and Marguerite G. Rosenthal, "The ups and downs of the Swedish welfare state: general trends, benefits and caregiving," *New Politics* 11 (2006). Accessed 3/7/2013 at http://nova.wpunj.edu/newpolitics/issue41/Ginsburg41.htm.

[79] Peter Anderberg wrote Sweden's ANED country report on the implementation of policies supporting independent living for disabled people. All country reports were compiled by the Academic Network of European Disability experts (ANED) in May 2009.

[80] Esping-Andersen, *The three worlds of welfare.*

significant economic crisis that challenges their traditional policies, benefits and provisions paid to parents of children with disability.

The United Kingdom has a mixed family policy, with public campaigns aimed at improving universal coverage. In practice, entitlements and provisions continue to be selective, based on needs assessment and tedious with respect to procedure and handling. The aspiration to improve the system is reflected by ambitious plans such as the Aiming High for Disabled Children policy, which set new standards on information, transparency, participation, assessment and feedback, and promoting personal and individual budgets.[81] However, this endeavor is at an early stage and has to deal with resistance and obstacles from the current service delivery system. Children with disability and their families are still viewed as recipients of social services, and most of the provisions for children with disability are still based on needs assessment and means-tested policies and legislation. The CTC is a means-tested credit for parents on a low income, whether working or not, paid for each child, with additional amounts for a child who is registered as blind or receiving the DLA special provisions for children with disability and their families.

France is different from the United Kingdom, offering a solid family policy based on the principle of solidarity: the commitment is declared in the first article of the French Code of Social Security, the social insurance system incorporating employers and employees as well as the state. The country was among the first to pay maternity and family allowances and provide parental leave benefits and affordable childcare.[82]

However, the economic crisis has lessened government commitment to familized policy, allowing restructuring from universal family policies to tailor-made family policies.[83] This was seen in the 1990s in the global expenditure of childcare, which moved from *crèches* toward cash benefits (cash-for-care system). Parallel to the gradual change from universal family to tailor made, the French system of welfare has been characterized by a complex patchwork quilt of services, with efforts toward cost control. In addition, the country has been exposed

[81] Hilary Arksey and Caroline Glendinning, "Choice in the context of informal care-giving," *Health and Social Care in the Community* 15 (2007), 165–75.

[82] See Jane Lewis, "Gender and the development of welfare regimes," *Journal of European Social Policy* 2 (1995), 165.

[83] Ibid., 12.

to European policies that tend to be selective, and the shift has been made from the social welfare to the human rights approach. This has implications for policies affecting different populations, including children with disability and their families. The 2005 disability rights legislation set out a new direction, including the right to accessible accommodations and changes in compensation schemes toward individualized budgets and the development of tailor-made support services.[84]

Families of children with disability can receive supplemental allowances (the Education Allowance for Disabled Child and the Daily Parental Attendance Allowance). However, these allowances require medical regulation. Since the passage of the Equal Rights and Opportunities, Participation and Citizenship of Persons with Disabilities in 2005, there is a gradual change toward integration in individual planning in French schools, but the impression is that it is still dependent on medical assessment and is highly regulated.

Finally, in comparison to the United Kingdom and France, Sweden offers comprehensive social insurance coverage to families of young children. In addition, the government provides means-tested supplements for those with disabled children (maintenance support and housing and care allowance for disabled children).

However, as with the United Kingdom and France, Sweden has experienced a serious economic crisis followed by drastic cuts and rule changes in income benefits and services. The center of the debate is the Swedish Personal Assistance Act of 1994, viewed by supporters as extremely successful in empowering persons with disability and families.[85] Social democrats are concerned that this paradigm shift, from universal to selective cash payments, may deny benefits to the substantial number of persons with disability and families of children with disability with less severe functional difficulties. However, from an international perspective, compared to the United Kingdom, and to some degree France, Sweden still looks like a family policy leader, with an impressive array of benefits for children with disability and families, though less so than in the past.

[84] Cousin, "Supports for families with a child with a disability," 31–34.
[85] S. Berg, *Personal assistance in Sweden* (Stockholm: Independent Living Institute, 2003), http://www.independentliving.org/docs/wrfmono.pdf.

6 ASSESSMENT OF FAMILY DISABILITY POLICIES

Assessment of family policy includes descriptive data on recipients (children with disability and their families), government entitlements, the costs of government entitlements, access and utilization of government benefits and services, and the impact of certain entitlements or social rights on recipients. Unfortunately, there is scarce data on families of children with disability, entitlements and issues of access, utilization and impact. In terms of cross-country comparative data, there is more descriptive information about recipients and entitlements than access, utilization and impact. The exception is comparative data on families and child disability policies published by the Organisation for Economic Co-operation and Development (OECD).[1]

In general, the main reason for the lack of comparative studies is that family policy often overlaps with social, health and educational policies, which makes it difficult to set exclusive methods for evaluation and assessment. The border where family policy ends and health or educational policy begins (in particular parental components) is difficult to draw. This is also the case with tax benefits or health insurances that

[1] The OECD Family database was developed to provide cross-national indicators on family outcomes and family policies across the OECD countries, its enhanced engagement partners and EU member states. The database brings together information from various national and international databases, both within the OECD (see related OECD databases) and external organizations. The database currently (version December 2013) includes seventy indicators under four main dimensions: (i) structure of families; (ii) labor market position of families; (iii) public policies for families and children; and (iv) child outcomes. Each indicator typically presents the data on a particular issue as well as relevant definitions and methodology, comparability and data issues, information on sources and, where relevant, includes the raw data or descriptive information across countries. Accessed 6/9/2013 at www.oecd.org/social/family/database.

contain regulations related to family benefits. Maternity leave policies originate from work protection legislation, and parental leave policies interfere with employment protection legislation.

Until recently, most of the family policy studies were interested in looking for implementation issues, particularly in identifying those that are not properly implemented.[2] In recent years, there has been a transition from implementation-based to results-based approaches.[3] However, the latter has to take into account the socioeconomic context of each country or region in setting realistic family policy strategies that assure economic, social and demographic progress.[4]

SOCIODEMOGRAPHIC DATA

Two terms that are used interchangeably in family policy research are households and families. A household is classified as either a one-person household or a multi-person household, that is, a group of two or more persons living together who make common provision for food or other essentials for living.[5] The family within the household is defined as those members of the household who are related, to a specified degree, through blood, adoption or marriage. Given the complexity, it is important that information on relationship to the household head or reference person be properly processed.

The most important sociodemographic variable is the structure and type of family household. It is evident that western countries have

[2] For further reading, see Keith Mackay, "Helping countries build government monitoring and evaluations systems: World Bank contribution to evidence-based policymaking," Marco Segone (ed.), *Bridging the gap: the role of monitoring and evaluation in evidence-based policy making* (Geneva: UNICEF, The World Bank and the International Development Evaluation Association, 2008), 88–97.

[3] Whether and how the goals are achieved over time is assessed by Jody Zall Kusek and Ray C. Rist, "Ten steps to a results-based monitoring and evaluation system," in Segone, *Bridging the gap*, pp. 98–116.

[4] See Mihaela Robila, "Assessing family policies across the world: A focus on Eastern Europe" (paper for the United Nations Expert Group Meeting, "Assessing family policies: Confronting family poverty and social exclusion & ensuring work family balance" [New York: United Nations Division for Social Policy and Development, 2011]).

[5] UN Statistics Division, "Principles and recommendations for population and housing censuses." Accessed 8/1/2013 at http://unstats.un.org/unsd/demographic/sconcerns/fam/fammethods.htm.

moved toward more diversified and complex family structures. There is a significant increase in the number of one-parent families, stepfamilies, cohabiting couples, same-sex couples and children staying at home for longer periods. Sociodemographic information, which includes information about household size, shows that household size has decreased over the years. For example, the average household size in the United Kingdom fell from 2.6 persons per family to 2.4 in 2006, representing a decrease of 17 percent.[6] Fertility rate is an additional important variable associated with household size. There is a significant association between women having children later in life, reduced fertility rates and the shrinking household unit. Additional sociodemographic variables are related to the economy of the household unit, and particularly to family income and wealth, labor and consumption. It is clear, as in the case of the United Kingdom, that changes in family income and wealth differ markedly according to family structure, socioeconomic status and ethnicity. While the average disposable income of individual households has increased over time, wealth has also become more unequally distributed.[7] Poverty in families is probably the most central sociodemographic data and is the target of government social policy. The most common indicator in the United States is the federal poverty line,[8] while in other countries there are different measures. Poverty is often linked to parental education and unemployment, as in the case of the working poor. A recent report showed that the number of working

[6] The Department for Children, Schools and Families in the United Kingdom commissioned the Social Issues Research Centre at Oxford to provide an independent assessment of evidence relating to the impact of the commercial world on children's well-being. Their report, titled "Childhood and family life: sociodemographic changes," focuses on the engagement of families and children in the commercial world by taking a longitudinal approach to the changes and continuities in family life over the past half century. See, in particular, pp. 9–10. Accessed 8/2/2013 at http://dera.ioe.ac.uk/7413/12/Appendix-G_SIRC-report.pdf.

[7] Ibid., 20.

[8] Recently, the federal government introduced the new Supplemental Poverty Measure (SPM) when it comes to measuring families' fundamental needs (CCED 2013). This new measure calculates the financial resources it takes to live free of material deprivation – that is, the cost of food, clothing, shelter and utilities – by adjusting for average expenditures on these items (and accounting for geographic differences in housing costs), as opposed to simply adjusting for overall inflation. In addition, to calculate a poverty rate, the SPM reflects the resources available to households through government policies such as tax credits and in-kind public benefit programs that affect a family's income and, hence, their poverty status.

families is increasing, yet economic security remains out of reach. Between 2007 and 2011, the share of working families that are low-income – that is, below 200 percent of the official poverty threshold – increased annually and rose from 28 percent to 32 percent nationally.[9] Children in poor families have worse health and educational outcomes, are more likely to experience parental divorce and more often live in single-parent families compared to children growing up in more affluent families.[10]

There are other sociodemographic measures associated with family policy, including cost of housing, food, transportation, childcare, and other necessities such as clothing, personal care and housing supplies. Furthermore, some reports include information about local, state and federal tax paid by families and level of dependency on social assistance and social security benefits.

COMPARING FAMILY POLICIES

Overall, assessment of family policy differs in approach and focus; it depends on the researchers' interests and disciplines. Some approaches may also be designed to promote a particular policy model, and the selection of indicators may reflect this. In general, there are three methods of assessment and comparison of family policies: expenditures (cost), social rights or entitlements, and outcome. Assessment of expenditures or costs is probably the most common approach of data analysis

[9] The Working Poor Families Project (WPFP) is supported by the Annie E. Casey, Ford, Joyce and Kresge Foundations, a national initiative to strengthen state policies that can assist families striving to work their way into the middle class and achieve economic security. The brief data report by Brandon Roberts, Deborah Povich and Mark Mather entitled "Low-income working families: the growing economic gap" is based on new 2011 data from the US Census Bureau's American Community Survey, provides a snapshot of low-income working families in America and highlights the growing economic divide between working families at the top and bottom of the economic ladder. Accessed 8/2/2013 at http://www.workingpoorfamilies.org/wpcontent/uploads/2013/01/Winter-2012_2013-WPFP-Data-Brief.pdf.

[10] An interesting assessment of costs is reported by Mark Mather and Dia Adams in "The risk of negative child outcomes in low-income families," The Annie E. Casey Foundation Population Reference Bureau, April 2006. The report includes comparative assessment of the relative risks for children living in different types of families. Accessed 7/4/2012 at http://www.prb.org/pdf06/RiskNegOut_Families.pdf, p. 2.

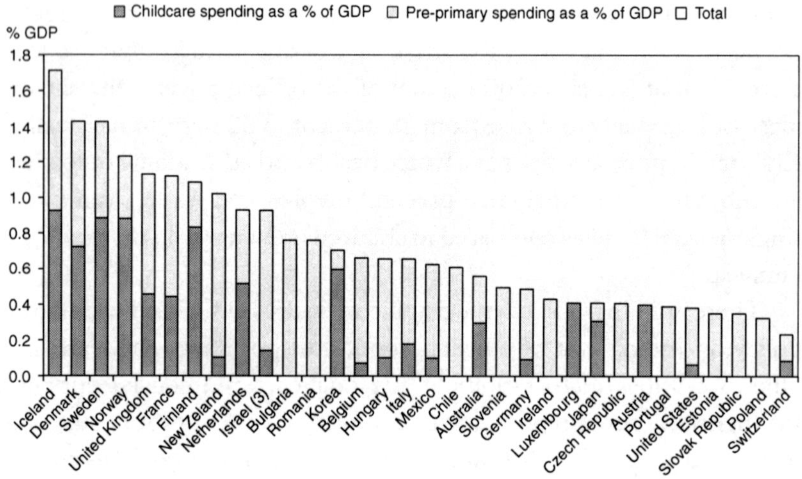

CHART 6.1 Public Expenditure on Childcare and Early Education Services as Percentage of GDP, 2009
Public spending on childcare including pre-primary education

used to gauge a given country's welfare effort or to compare it with others.[11]

Expenditures

Comparing expenditures on certain provisions is probably one of the most common measures used in policy analysis (see the histogram presenting public expenditures on childcare and early education services, as a percentage of GDP, 2009). It is usually expressed by the average annual cost in one of the international currencies or as a percentage of GDP. Chart 6.1 demonstrates 2009 public expenditures on either childcare or early education as a percentage of GDP.[12]

[11] See Herbert Obinger and Uwe Wagschal, "Social expenditures and revenues," Francis G. Castles et al. (eds.), *The Oxford handbook of the welfare state* (Oxford: Oxford University Press, 2010), 333–52. *The Oxford handbook of the welfare state,* the authoritative and definitive guide to the contemporary welfare state, is divided into eight sections. It opens with three chapters that evaluate the philosophical case for (and against) the welfare state. Surveys of the welfare state's history and of the approaches taken to its study are followed by four extended sections, running to some thirty-five chapters in all, which offer a comprehensive and in-depth survey of our current state of knowledge across the whole range of issues that the welfare state embraces.

[12] The OECD Family Database was developed to provide cross-national indicators on family outcomes and family policies across the OECD countries, its enhanced engagement partners and EU member states. The database brings together information from

The comparison shows that Nordic countries as well as Korea lead in terms of childcare spending. Interestingly, countries such as the United Kingdom and France have followed Nordic states on preprimary expenditure.

Social rights or entitlements

While the expenditures approach is used for comparing the overall policies of countries or states, the social rights perspective aims to compare specific benefits or entitlements. It is often used in comparing childcare, parental leave regulations and cash benefits among states or countries. This type of assessment often employs indicators, capturing in summarized form the content of legal regulations in a given country. Although constructing indicators longitudinally is not an easy task, in recent years there have been efforts by the OECD as well as other international organizations to offer this perspective.[13] An interesting illustration of comparing certain entitlements across countries was carried out by Center for Economic and Policy Research.[14] Its report reviews the national policies of twenty-one high-income economies as of June 2008. It focuses on two key aspects of parental leave policies: the level of support provided to parents and the degree to which leave policies promote an egalitarian distribution between mothers and fathers of the time devoted to childcare.[15]

various national and international databases, both within the OECD (see related OECD databases) and external organizations. The database currently (version December 2013) includes seventy indicators under four main dimensions: (i) structure of families; (ii) labor market position of families; (iii) public policies for families and children; and (iv) child outcomes. Each indicator typically presents the data on a particular issue as well as relevant definitions and methodology, comparability and data issues, information on sources and, where relevant, includes the raw data or descriptive information across countries. OECD Family Database, "PF3.1: Public spending on childcare and early education." Accessed 9/2/2013 at http://www.oecd.org/els/family/PF3.1%20Public%20spending%20on%20childcare%20and%20early%20education%20-%20290713.pdf.

13 OECD Family Database "CO1.9: Child disability," pp. 10–16 provides a cross-country comparison of entitlements. The comparative tables accessed 8/8/2013 at http://www.oecd.org/els/family/CO1%209%20Child%20disability%20FINAL.pdf.

14 Rebecca Ray, Janet Gornick and John Schmitt, "Who cares? Assessing generosity and gender equality in parental leave policy designs in 21 countries," *Journal of European Social Policy* 20 (2010), 196–216.

15 The table is presented by the Center for Economic and Policy Research, an independent, nonpartisan think tank that was established to promote democratic debate on the most important economic and social issues that affect people's lives. CEPR's advisory board

In terms of financial support, Sweden is the most generous of the countries examined, providing forty weeks of full-time-equivalent paid leave. The United States is one of only two countries that does not offer any paid parental leave. In terms of egalitarian distribution, the study demonstrates the use of the Gender Equality Index, measuring a country's parental leave policy on a fifteen-point scale, with fifteen points indicating full equality of workplace and caregiving benefits to men and women. Interestingly (see Table 6.1), among the twenty-one countries surveyed, Sweden earned the highest score (13 points); while the United States rates poorly on the time and money aspects of parental leave, it fares much better on gender equality.

It is evident that while each approach has its merits, the expenditure perspective reflects the payment of transfers at a highly aggregated level only when the social rights perspective provides information at the policy level, though it cannot take into account the actual take-up of transfers or services. Neither can provide information about the impact of a certain policy on families or households.

The outcome perspective allows for the actual assessment of the impact of family policies at the household level. The most common study is examining the impact of certain policies on family trends over time. An interesting example of this type of evaluation is presented by Angela Loci and Olivier Thévenon on the impact of family policy packages on fertility trends in developed countries.[16] Researchers from INED (*Institut National d'Études Démographiques*) in Paris examined the impact of different family policy settings on fertility using data from eighteen OECD countries spanning the years from 1982 to 2007. Using regression analysis, they found that each instrument of the family policy package (paid leave, childcare services and financial transfers) had a

includes Nobel laureates and economists Robert Solow and Joseph Stiglitz; Janet Gornick, professor at the CUNY Graduate Center and director of the Luxembourg Income Study; Richard Freeman, professor of economics at Harvard University; and Eileen Appelbaum, professor and director of the Center for Women and Work at Rutgers University. Accessed 6/9/2013 at http://www.cepr.net/index.php/press-releases/press-releases/european-countries-offer-more-parental-leave.

[16] An interesting example of impact research is in Angela Luci and Olivier Thévenon, *The impact of family policy packages on fertility trends in developed countries*, a combined report by INED (*Institut National d'Études Démographiques*) and OECD (Organisation for Economic Cooperation & Development Social Policy Division), March 2011. Accessed 11/11/2013 at http://paa2011.princeton.edu/papers/111793.

TABLE 6.1 *Parental leave league*
Generosity of paid leave[1] gender equality index[2]

Country	Rank	Weeks	Country	Rank	Score
Germany	1	47	Sweden	1	14
Sweden	1	47	Finland	2	12
Norway	3	44	Greece	2	12
Greece	4	34	Norway	2	12
Finland	5	32	Belgium	5	11
Canada	6	29	France	6	10
Japan	7	26	Italy	6	10
Italy	8	25	Portugal	6	10
France	9	22	Spain	6	10
Ireland	10	21	Germany	10	9
Denmark	11	20	US	10	9
Belgium	12	18	Denmark	12	8
Portugal	12	18	Netherlands	12	8
Spain	12	18	UK	12	8
Austria	15	16	Austria	15	7
Netherlands	15	16	Canada	15	7
New Zealand	17	14	Ireland	15	7
UK	18	13	New Zealand	18	6
Switzerland	19	11	Japan	19	5
Australia	20	0	Australia	20	1
US	20	0	Switzerland	21	0

Table notes:
[1] The generosity of paid leave is measured as full-time equivalent leave: the duration of paid leave multiplied by the portion of usual wages that parents receive during that time. For example, Switzerland offers 14 weeks of leave paid at 80 percent of usual wages or the equivalent of 11.2 (rounded to 11) weeks of full-time leave.
[2] The gender equality index is a scale from zero to fifteen. It incorporates the following factors: the portion of a couple's parental leave that is reserved for, or accessible to, fathers (accounting for 9 of the 15 points); the amount of fathers' wages that is replaced during leave available to them (accounting for 5 of the 15 points); and other incentives for fathers to participate in parental leave (plus or minus 1 point).

positive influence, suggesting that the addition of these supports for working parents in a continuum during early childhood is likely to facilitate parents' choice to have children.

Another illustration demonstrating the importance of outcome studies was released recently (2012) by Christina Gathmann and Björn Sass.[17]

[17] Christina Gathmann and Björn Sass, *Taxing childcare: effects on family labor supply and children* (Bonn: *Forschungsinstitut zur Zukunft der Arbeit* (Institute for the Study of Labor)), IZA DP No. 6440, March 2012. Accessed 2/11/2013 at http://ftp.iza.org/dp6440.pdf.

The researchers examined whether the reform in childcare in Thuringia, Germany, had an effect on childcare choices as well as on the elasticity of labor supply with respect to childcare costs. Using data from the German Socio-Economic Panel (GSOEP), the researchers analyzed about 3,000 households from this area and demonstrated that raising prices for public childcare reduced the demand for public day care in the general population. Declines in public day-care attendance were especially dramatic for children from low-skilled, single-parent and low-income families. Interestingly, the study showed that substantial substitution occurred away from informal care by relatives, friends or neighbors to childcare in the home by parents or other household members.

The criticism is that if societal outcomes cannot be detached from societal context and social demographic circumstances, it seems often arbitrary and irrelevant to compare outcome indicators without taking into consideration the social context.

COMMON MEASURES

There are common measures used in cross-national studies: composite indices, clustering by types of policies or provisions, and the representation of results in scorecards. Indices are considered handy tools that allow the collapse of a multitude of measures across countries into one dimension. The OECD-Family Policy Index was constructed in 2001 in view of the strong demand for cross-national indicators on the situation of families and children. The OECD index is probably one of the best-known in comparing family policies. A family database was developed to provide cross-national indicators on family outcomes and family policies across the OECD countries, its enhanced engagement partners and EU member states. The database brings together information from various national and international databases, both within the OECD and from external organizations. The database currently (version May 2014) includes seventy indicators under four main dimensions: (i) structure of families; (ii) labor market position of families; (iii) public policies for families and children; and (iv) child outcomes. Each indicator typically presents the data on a particular issue as well as relevant definitions and methodology, comparability and data issues, information on sources and, where relevant, includes the raw data or descriptive information across countries.

The clustering of typologies constitutes an approach of aggregation on the basis of ideological or other rationales. The most cited clustering is based on the work of Gøsta Esping-Andersen, demonstrating allocation of resources to families according to a given country's stance on capitalism.[18] A two-dimensional clustering approach was recently offered by Olivier Thévenon, showing how countries differ in the support they provide to working parents with young children and in their generosity of leave entitlements or cash transfers, and it distinguishes among five distinct groups of countries along geographical or cultural boundaries (Nordic, Anglo-Saxon, Southern European and Asian, Eastern European and Continental European).[19]

Finally, presenting subdimensions in scorecards does not fully aggregate indicators into one composite measure. There are approaches retaining a larger number of subdimensions but they collapse the information into qualitative categories.[20] Others use graphical tools to represent the information captured in a multitude of indicators in a form that is comparable across countries and indicators.[21] The latter translates a large range of indicators into standard deviations. These values are plotted on a common scale for all indicators and countries, which allows for a graphical assessment of a given country's family policy profile.

DATA SOURCES

Since the 1980s, most governments collect and publish family policy data in a standardized form. Expenditure data is found in the OECD databases (SOCX), Eurostat (ESSPROS), and ILO (Social Security

[18] Gøsta Esping-Andersen, *The three worlds of welfare capitalism* (Princeton, NJ: Princeton University Press, 1990).

[19] Olivier Thévenon, "Family policies in OECD countries: a comparative analysis," *Population and Development Review* 37 (2011), 57–87.

[20] See, for example, twofold categorization by UNICEF 2007. Accessed 4/1/2014 at http://www.unicef.org/evaldatabase/files/MICS.pdf.

[21] See Henning Lohmann et al., "Towards a framework for assessing family policies in the EU," OECD Social, Employment and Migration Working Papers, No. 88, OECD Publishing. Accessed 5/5/2013 at http://dx.doi.org/10.1787/223883627348.

Expenditure Database). However, in family policy it is not possible to differentiate between in-cash and in-kind transfers or to separate transfers by target group or specific program.

Social rights data are collected mainly by the scientific community or university-based centers. The most well-known data is the Social Citizenship Indicator Programme (SCIP) initiated by Walter Korpi and colleagues more than thirty years ago, covering eighteen industrialized countries over a long period of time (1930–2000). However, these indicators are not yet available in the public domain. Apart from SCIP there are no other initiatives with a broad scope that collect indicators on family policy from a social rights perspective.[22] One of the best investments in creating family policy databases is that undertaken by the OECD.[23] The database covers a wide area of topics from different empirical perspectives, combining information on family policy expenditure with a few social rights indicators and a larger number of outcome indicators. Some of the indicators are available in longitudinal perspective. However, information on changes across time is not included in a systematic manner. Most of the indicators are taken from other databases or publications, while a few indicators are available only on the OECD Family Database.

TYPES OF STUDIES ASSESSING FAMILY DISABILITY POLICIES

Research related to family disability policies is less prevalent and probably reflects scarce interest in cross-national comparison. Most of the

[22] There are additional resources that relate to single aspects of family policy. See, for example, Jonathan R. Bradshaw and Emese Mayhew, "Family benefit packages," in Jonathan Bradshaw and Aksel Hatland (eds.) *Social policy, family change and employment in comparative perspective* (Cheltenham: Edward Elgar, 2006), 97–117; John Bennett, "Early childhood services in OECD countries: review of the literature and current policy in early childhood field" (Innocenti Working Paper, Florence: UNICEF Innocenti Research Centre, 2008).

[23] See Willem Adema, Pauline Fron and Maxime Ladaique, "Is the European welfare state really more expensive? Indicators on social spending, 1980–2012; and a manual for the OECD Social Expenditure Database (SOCX)," OECD Social, Employment and Migration Working Papers, No. 124, OECD Publishing, 2011. Accessed 5/1/2013 at http://dx.doi.org/10.1787/5kg2d2d4pbf0-en.

studies try to establish common and standard disability measures for children's disability and characterize socioeconomic needs of their parents. In terms of policies, there are efforts made by the OECD and other international bodies to compare countries and states regarding selected entitlements or social rights, particularly with respect to their cost. The same applies to studies that assess the impact of certain policies on families of children with disability or assessing accessibility and utilization issues.

ASSESSMENT OF CHILDREN AND SOCIAL AND HOUSEHOLD CIRCUMSTANCES

Assessment of the prevalence of childhood disability and the circumstances and characteristics of children with disability is crucial to developing timely family policies and service provisions. There are certain standardized measures that are central for comparing children with disability and their families and family disability policies. The most common are type and severity of disability followed by age and gender variations. There is a growing effort in western countries to provide prevalence estimates for children with disability, but most countries, unfortunately, lack robust measures.[24] The source of the problem is inconsistency in collecting up-to-date data, in particular in low-income countries. The exceptions are international initiatives such as DISTAT (the Disability Statistics Database for Microcomputers established by United Nations Statistics Division) and a functional system offered by the Washington City Group (WG). These initiatives aim to improve disability statistics in low-income countries. Similar problems are reported by the OECD with respect to proportions of severity of disability among children with disability in different countries. The assumption is that underreporting of disability is more common when this kind of information is collected through a census and not through a

[24] See, for example, UNICEF, *Progress for children: A world fit for children, statistical review number 6*, New York: UNICEF, December 2007; Johanna H. van der Lee et al., "Definitions and measurement of chronic health conditions in childhood: a systematic review," *Journal of the American Medical Association* 297 (2007), 2741–51.

specialized survey, where disability benefits are not well developed or where disability is not well recognized.

There are more challenges in collecting standardized data about families of children with disability. Most of the data is based on secondary analysis of national censuses or household surveys, and it compares social and household circumstance, income and material deprivation between families with and without disability. For example, a secondary analysis of the UK Family Resources Survey (FRS) from 2004–2005 included, in addition, the number of dependent children in the family unit, housing tenure, income and material deprivation.[25] Most of the studies compare families of children with or without disability by family income. An illustration for this kind of study is the analysis "Caring for children with disability in Ohio: the impact on families," demonstrating circumstances for families caring for children with disability in that state.[26] The data demonstrates that families caring for children with disability have lower incomes than families that have similar characteristics but do not care for children with disability. Similarly, OECD family data provides household socioeconomic data including poverty rates by disability status.[27] It is interesting to learn the situation in the United States vis-à-vis other European countries. In the United States, the percentage of families of a child with disability living in poverty is the highest at 30.6 percent, but this is true also of those families without a child with disability at 19.5 percent (see Table 6.2). The percentage is substantially lower in France (10% compared to 8% for families of a child with disability). Interestingly, in countries such as Sweden and the United Kingdom, the percentage of families of a child with disability living in poverty is lower than in families of a child

[25] Department for Work and Pensions, "Households below average income statistics, 2004–5," (London: Department for Work and Pensions, 2006).

[26] UNICEF, *Progress for children*; Anthony Goudie et al., "Caring for children with disability in Ohio: the impact on families," (white paper prepared with a grant from the Ohio Developmental Disabilities Council, New York: 2007). Accessed 8/12/2012 at http://www.ddc.ohio.gov/pub/OHFamImpStudyWhitePaper-FINAL.pdf.

[27] Based on EUSILC European Commission Eurostat, "Directorate F: Social statistics and information society," *Unit F-3: Living conditions and social protection statistics*. Comparative EU intermediate quality report, Version 3, July 2011. Accessed 8/12/2012 at http://www.oecd.org/els/family/CO1%209%20Child%20disability%20FINAL.pdf.

TABLE 6.2 *Poverty rates by types of household, with/without a disabled member*

	Poverty rates (%) type of household		
Type of household	Without a disabled member	With a disabled member	Total
Austria	7.3	9.6	8.0
Belgium	11.7	8.7	11.3
Denmark	6.5	9.7	6.8
France	8.0	10.0	8.5
Germany	10.2	8.7	9.9
Netherland	6.1	7.2	6.3
Sweden	8.0	5.4	7.8
United Kingdom	13.0	9.5	12.5
United States	19.5	30.6	20.0

Source: OECD Secretariat's estimate based on EUSILC (2009) for European countries and LIS for the United States (2010).

without disability (Sweden 5.4% vs. 8.0%, and in the United Kingdom 9.5% vs. 13.0%).

COMPARATIVE ASSESSMENTS OF FAMILY POLICIES

Interestingly, there is a lack of studies that compare family policies or entitlements related to families of children with disability across countries. A possible reason, which was discussed earlier in the chapter, is that countries tend to use different definitions and assessment mechanisms for children with disability. Some countries use specific lists of impairments with the degree of severity required for benefit entitlement. Others use level of functioning or degree of care required for a child with a disability compared to that which is needed for a nondisabled child of the same age.[28] Another explanation is that countries use different social

[28] Ilene R. Zeitze, "Social insurance provisions for children with disability in selected industrialized countries," *Social Security Bulletin* 58 (1995), 32–48. Accessed 8/2/2013 at http://www.ssa.gov/policy/docs/ssb/v58n3/v58n3p32.pdf.

insurance programs related to an individual country's unique history, culture and economic conditions.

ACCESS, UTILIZATION AND IMPACT

In recent years, there have been scattered studies related to access and service utilization of children with disability and their families. Accessibility and utilization issues are often linked to financial as well as programmatic barriers.[29] Most of the research touches on families that live in poverty or are recipients of social welfare services because they are better known to public administrations. There are limited studies, primarily in the United Kingdom and the United States, that have examined certain entitlements or social rights of families of children with disability. These studies are often linked to poverty reduction or to families of children with autism, severe illness or disability.

ACCESS AND UTILIZATION

The basic assumption is that families caring for children with disability struggle with employment and financial challenges that substantially reduce their access and utilization of health and family care services. Accessibility and utilization are measured by surveys and secondary analysis of national or state data.

The 2008 Ohio Family Health Survey is a typical example of the role of financial challenges on accessibility and service utilization. The survey estimated that 78,771 families (52%) caring for children with disability have difficulty paying medical bills compared to one-third (32%) of families with children without disability.[30] Results from the *National Survey of Children with Special Health Care Needs* (NS-CSHCN 2005/06) demonstrate that 31 percent of Ohio families caring for children with disability experience financial hardship, indicating that

[29] Aaron J. Resch et al., "Giving parents a voice: a qualitative study of the challenges experienced by parents of children with disability," *Rehabilitation Psychology* 55 (2010), 139–50.

[30] Goudie et al., "Caring for children with disability in Ohio," 10–11.

the child's health care caused financial problems.[31] Financial hardship may be associated with having to change work schedules to meet the needs of the child. More than one-quarter (26%) have had family members cut back employment hours and nearly one-third (32%) of all families have had a family member stop working altogether to care for a child with disability.

A similar methodology to the Family Resources Survey was reported in the United Kingdom (2004/5) with 16,012 children aged zero to eighteen years.[32] The findings indicated that children with disability were more likely to live with low-income, deprivation, debt and poor housing. It is understandable that this has a significant impact on accessing and utilizing health care and educational services.

Accessibility is often associated with the financial strength of each state. A recent study used secondary data from the *2005 National Survey of Children with Special Health Care Needs* in combination with state characteristics to estimate the association among state residence, Medicaid reimbursement rate and problems accessing care for children with special health-care needs with and without autism.[33] Findings have shown significant variation among states in the relationship between having autism and problems accessing care. The state context in which families live impacts access to care for children with autism. Moreover, when families raising children with autism live in states with higher Medicaid reimbursement rates, they are less likely to experience problems accessing care.

In general, there is less information on actual access and utilization of services of children with ASDs. As states move toward managed care approaches for their Medicaid program, services information is critical. A recent study collected behavioral health service data for children with ASDs from a state Medicaid Managed Care (MMC) program and

[31] The U.S. Department of Health and Human Services, *The national survey of children with special health care needs chartbook 2005–2006*. Accessed 8/12/2012 at http://mchb.hrsa.gov/cshcn05/.

[32] Clare M. Blackburn, Nick J. Spencer and Janet M. Read, "Prevalence of childhood disability and the characteristics and circumstances of disabled children in the UK: Secondary analysis of the Family Resources Survey," *BMC Pediatrics* 10 (2010), 21. Accessed 8/12/2012 at http://www.biomedcentral.com/1471-2431/10/21.

[33] Kathleen C. Thomas et al., "Access to care for children with autism in the context of state Medicaid reimbursement," *Maternal & Child Health Journal* 16 (2012), 1636–44.

analyzed data from fiscal years 1995 through 2000.[34] Findings revealed that the number of children who received services over time increased significantly; however, the rate of service use was only one-tenth of what should be expected based on prevalence rates. The mean number of service days provided per child decreased significantly, about 40 percent, and the most prevalent forms of treatment changed. Day treatment vanished and medication and case management increased disproportionately to the number of children served.

IMPACT OF FAMILY POLICY STUDIES

The most advanced assessment is the examination of impact of certain social entitlement on children with disability and their families. There are qualitative and quantitative studies, both aimed at testing how recipients benefit from a specific provision or benefit. The qualitative approach is used in order to explore recipients' own perspective or receive their insightful thoughts about procedures and outcome. Quantitative research is carried out on a large scale, intending to see significant changes that have occurred in families of children with disability as a result of a specific policy. Most of these studies use secondary data and tend to track changes in household measures such as household income and employment rather than children's progress or well-being.

An example of qualitative assessment is the UK study that tested the additive value of the DLA.[35] This qualitative research study, based on semi-structured interviews with twenty families that have a child or children with disability, investigated the additional costs they incur and their experiences of applying for the DLA, which is intended to cover additional disability-related costs. Although this small study has reinforced previous research findings on families' needs and inadequate support systems, it enabled policymakers to understand in depth the impact that additional income (primarily the DLA and associated

[34] Lisa A. Ruble et al., "Access and service use by children with autism spectrum disorders in Medicaid Managed Care," *Journal of Autism and Developmental Disorders* 35 (2005), 3–13.

[35] Gabrielle Preston, "Helter skelter: families, disabled children and the benefit system," *CASEpaper* 92 (London School of Economics, Centre for Analysis of Social Exclusion, February 2005). Accessed 8/12/2012 at http://eprints.lse.ac.uk/6272/1/Helter_Skelter_Families,_disabled_children_and_the_benefit_system.pdf.

benefits) has on families' lives. How was the additional income spent? What were families' spending priorities? Did benefit income cover the extra costs of caring for a disabled child? What happened to families that did not claim (or were not awarded) the benefits to which their disabled children were entitled? What happened if the benefit was taken away? Interestingly, families reported that the DLA made a significant difference, not just for the child with disability but for the whole family. However, the fact that the DLA has been repeatedly down rated or withdrawn generated considerable fluctuations in income and high levels of stress and ill health. The report outlined issues that have to be addressed if the purpose of DLA entitlement is to reduce poverty amongst families of children with disability.

The most common analysis employs secondary data, trying to study the impact of certain entitlements by comparing surveys carried out in different periods. An interesting illustration is a study on the impact of child SSI enrollment on household outcomes. This analysis, taken from the survey of income and program participation between 1989 and 2005, found that the number of children receiving disability benefits from the SSI program in the United States increased from 0.26 million to 1.03 million.[36] The researchers utilized longitudinal data from the Survey of Income and Program Participation (SIPP) to estimate the effect of child SSI enrollment on total household income and the separate components of income, including earnings and transfers. The data suggested that child SSI enrollment had little effect, if any, on average household earnings. Similar secondary analysis of data demonstrated that the US federal government's program that provides cash benefits to low-income families with a disabled child has grown rapidly over the past twenty-five years. Unfortunately, this growth reflects changes in the implementation of the program rather than declines in children's health or family income.[37]

[36] Mark Duggan and Melissa Schettini Kearney, "The impact of child SSI enrollment on household outcomes: evidence from the survey of income and program participation" (NBER Working Paper No. 11568, August 2005). Accessed 9/1/2013 at http://www.brookings.edu/~/media/research/files/papers/2005/8/childrenfamilies%20kearney/200508 kearney.pdf.

[37] Richard V. Burkhauser and Mary C. Daly, "The changing role of disabled children benefits," *FRBSF Economic Letter* 25 (September 3, 2013). Richard V. Burkhauser is a professor of policy analysis at Cornell University; Mary C. Daly is a senior vice president

Policymakers are often interested in examining the possible impact of a new policy by testing the proposed policy on recipients. A good example is Baroness Grey-Thompson's inquiry into Disability and Universal Credit that examined whether this restructuring of support was likely to meet the government's objectives of simplifying the system, making work pay and supporting those with the greatest needs. The inquiry was carried out in a survey of around 1,400 parents of children with disability and their families. In particular, it addressed the potential impact of a cut in support of up to £28 per week for children who are receiving any rate of DLA apart from those on the higher rate of the care component (or who are registered as blind). One of the core findings was that the impact may be greatest for single parents caring for children with disability. More than three quarters of this group said they would need to cut back on food, and two-thirds said that they would get into debt; worryingly, as many as one in six said they might need to move their household if affected by the cut. The report provides key recommendations for changes to Universal Credit to ensure that it provides fair and progressive reform to support people with disability.

CONCLUSION

The chapter provides the methodology and measures of assessment of family policy in general and family disability policy in particular. There are four types of assessment, including recipients' profiles, government's entitlements and their costs, access and utilization, and impact of certain entitlements or social rights on recipients. There is scarce data on families of children with disability, entitlements and issues of access, utilization and impact. In terms of cross-country comparative data, there is more descriptive information about recipients and entitlements than access, utilization and impact studies.

and associate director of research in the Economic Research Department of the Federal Reserve Bank of San Francisco. They argue that the US disability system is failing, growing at an unsustainable pace for taxpayers and delivering relatively poor outcomes to those with disability. Accessed 1/2/2014 at http://www.frbsf.org/economic-research/publications/economic-letter/2013/september/disabled-children-family-benefits-ssi-supplemental-security-income/.

Research related to family disability policies depends on researchers' interests and their disciplines. Some approaches may also be designed to promote a particular policy model, and the selection of indicators may reflect this. Most of the studies try to establish common and standard disability measures for children's disability and characterize socioeconomic needs of their parents. In terms of policies, efforts have been made by the OECD, like other international bodies, to compare countries and states with respect to selected entitlements or social rights, particularly regarding their cost. The same applies to studies that assess the impact of certain policies on families of children with disability or assessing accessibility and utilization issues.

The most common comparison of cross-country family policies in the disability area is in entitlements or social rights. It is a narrative approach listing comparable programs, benefits, criteria for obtaining benefits or allowances. It provides insightful information demonstrating differences between the United States and European countries. Accessibility and utilization studies have merit as they tend to examine implementation of certain entitlements or provisions. The chapter provides examples primarily from the United States and the United Kingdom. Finally, the most advanced assessment is the examination of the impact of certain social entitlements on children with disability and their families. The chapter demonstrates qualitative and quantitative studies, primarily from the United Kingdom and the United States, aimed at testing how recipients benefit from a specific provision or benefit. The qualitative approach is used to explore recipients' own perspectives or to receive their insights about procedures and outcome. Quantitative research is carried out on a large scale and is intended to observe significant changes that have occurred in families of children with disability as a result of a specific policy. Most of these studies use secondary data and tend to track changes in household measures, such as household income and employment, rather than children's progress or well-being.

7 COMPARATIVE FAMILY POLICIES OF THE UNITED STATES AND EUROPEAN COUNTRIES

United States social policy is characterized by liberalism, strict work ethics, limited role of federal government and protection of the family as a private entity. Within this context, social policies affecting children with disability and their families focus primarily on modest in-kind benefits with means-tested cash benefits to some low-income families and differentiated tax benefits ranging from lower-middle to middle and upper-middle classes.[1]

A closer look at three representative European countries – Sweden, France and the United Kingdom – reveals two core models of policies toward families.[2] The first model, represented by Sweden and France, reflects generous policies with specific programs designed to achieve specified family goals. As a result of this, there is an extensive network of integrated, universal services for young children, with links to more specialized services for children who need extra care and protection. The second model, represented by the United Kingdom, lacks explicit policies regarding families and children, although it is possible to identify a set of uncoordinated family-related policies drawn from a wide range of policy areas. Parent and family-support services are patchy, uncoordinated and mainly targeted at the most disadvantaged sectors of the population.

These European countries can be looked at with respect to their view of the welfare state. The United Kingdom is perceived as a borderline

[1] Chapter 4 addresses US policies related to children with disability and their families.

[2] An interesting review of family support policies in Europe is presented by Sara Clavero, identifying two different approaches. France and Sweden reflect a parent-oriented approach and Britain and Ireland incremental and less committed ones. See Sara Clavero, "Parenting support: an international overview," School of Sociology and Social Policy, The Queen's University of Belfast, October, 2001. Accessed 1/3/2014 http://www.lenus.ie/hse/bitstream/10147/44896/1/6546.pdf.

case of liberal and conservative approaches of welfare state; France is considered to be based on conservative corporatist principles; and Sweden is perceived as a social democratic welfare state.[3] Policies in these states toward families of children with disability vary. The United Kingdom offers a mixed family policy based primarily on cash allowances (universal and means-tested) and tax benefits. Entitlements are based on functional assessments and determined by the severity of the child's medical condition or disability.

France offers a universal and solid family policy based on a social insurance system incorporating employers and employees as well as the state. There is a broad infrastructure of family care services and modest tax credit opportunities. Families of children with disability can apply for supplement allowances determined by medical and functional assessment.

Sweden offers comprehensive social insurance coverage, supported by strong childcare services, to parents of young children. Parents of children with disability can receive supplements on the basis of the child's needs assessment.

The chapter provides a comparative analysis of cash benefits, tax credits and deductions, and in-kind provisions of the United States, the United Kingdom, France and Sweden. These governments differ in their approaches to welfare, and this chapter provides an insightful look at the role of family policy in each country.

CONCEPTUAL DIFFERENCES

Chart 7.1 is a good reflection of the differences in family policies among countries. It reflects family benefits (tax breaks, services and cash) in OECD countries as a percentage of GDP 2009.[4]

[3] See Esping-Andersen's *Three worlds of welfare capitalism*, which presents a typology of eighteen organizations of OECD welfare states based upon three principles: decommodification (the extent to which an individual's welfare is reliant upon the market, particularly in terms of pensions, unemployment benefit and sickness insurance), social stratification (the role of welfare states in maintaining or breaking down social stratification) and the private-public mix (the relative roles of the state, the family, the voluntary sector and the market in welfare provision).

[4] The data is taken from OECD Social Expenditure Database, November 2012. Accessed 2/3/2014 at www.oecd.org/els/social/expenditure. The data includes only child payments and allowances, parental leave benefits, and childcare support.

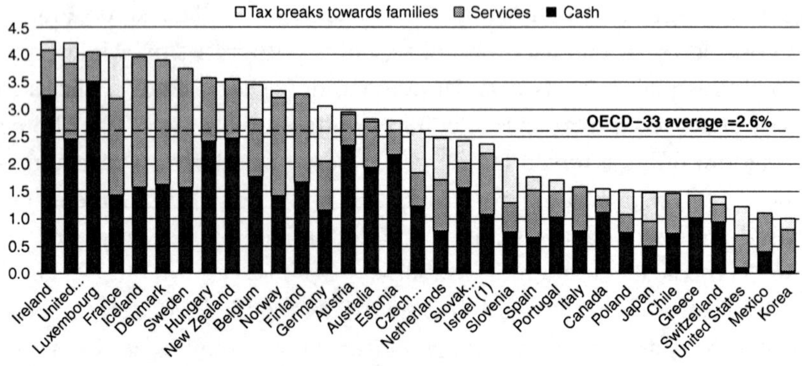

CHART 7.1 Family Benefits (Tax Breaks, Services and Cash) in OECD Countries as Percentage of GDP, 2009

The chart demonstrates the differences among countries with considerably high public spending on families (such as Ireland, the United Kingdom, Luxembourg, France, Iceland and Denmark), and those with lowest spending (such as United States, Mexico and Korea). Furthermore, it shows differences in type of public spending (cash, services and tax). Countries such as Ireland and Luxembourg primarily use cash benefits, whereas Sweden and Denmark use services. Chart 7.1 shows that Nordic countries with no tax credits compare to the United States, Japan and Germany, which incorporate them into their family policies.

COMPARISON OF CASH BENEFITS: UNITED STATES VERSUS UNITED KINGDOM

Based on Chart 7.1, it is evident that European countries such as the United Kingdom, France and Sweden demonstrate more generous family policies toward families of children with disability than does the United States. However, a closer look reveals that they vary in their approaches and reliance on cash benefits, tax breaks and infrastructure of services. The United Kingdom is well-known for reliance on cash benefits; France relies on cash benefits, services and tax breaks; and Sweden relies on cash benefits and services. The United States uses a selective approach, such as tax breaks and in-kind provisions, aimed at low-income families. An interesting comparison of family cash benefits, based on an OECD report (see Table 7.1), reveals the major differences among the United States, the United Kingdom and France.[5]

France, a country that provides an array of family care services, provides a limited monthly allowance to parents with education and health expenses for a child with disability (*Allocation d'éducation de l'enfant handicapé*); this amount may increase based on means testing and a child's health condition. Sweden, known for providing outstanding services for children with disability as well as family-support services, offers a decent childcare allowance, a monthly cash benefit available to parents of a child with disability. In addition, parents are entitled to the Attendance Allowance paid to those in need of personal assistance of more than twenty hours per week to cope with daily-life activities. Both benefits are non–means tested and are provided on the basis of medical and, particularly, functional assessment.

The United Kingdom is different from both France and Sweden. The government provides a non-means-tested allowance to children with disability (the DLA). In addition, families are entitled to the Carer's Allowance, paid to parents or other caregivers who spend at least thirty-five hours a week caring for someone with disability. Unlike Sweden, this allowance is modest and means tested. The United States pays cash benefits (SSI Payment Benefits for Children with Disability) only to families with low income; the amount varies among states.[6]

France and Sweden have different policies toward families of children with disability than the United Kingdom and the United States. Cash benefits serve as supplements to already comprehensive services available from early childhood. Both the United Kingdom and the United States are liberal states that use cash benefit systems; however,

[5] The sources used for constructing a comparable table of Family Cash Benefits for Children with a Chronic Illness or Disability is the OECD Tax and Benefits country notes and the following government websites: France, http://vosdroits.service-public.fr/; United Kingdom, http://www.child-disability.co.uk/; and the United States, http://www.ssa.gov/. Accessed 3/4/2014.

[6] For extensive review of the differences in policies toward families of children with disability, see Kay Tisdall and Allan F. Colver, *National contexts affecting the lives of disabled children in Denmark, France, Germany, Ireland, Italy, Sweden and UK, Volume 2* (Newcastle: University of Newcastle on Tyne Robinson Library, 2006). The report addresses factors relevant to the lives of disabled children which operate at national level in these seven European countries.

TABLE 7.1 *Comparison in cash benefits for France, Sweden, the UK, and the US*

Country	Program	Description	Maximum benefits in local currency	Upper age limit	Criteria	Income-tested	Observations
France	*Allocation d' éducation de l'enfant handicapé*	A financial allowance to help parents with the education and health expenses of a child with disability	Basic amount of €127.68 per month, which may increase with a supplement provided by the CDAPH	20	Eligibility is subject to the decision of the Commission of Rights and Autonomy of People with Disabilities (CDAPH), which decides on allocation of the allowance, supplements and duration of payment		The value of the allowance may increase with a supplement provided by the CDAPH, which varies according to a number of socioeconomic characteristics; it may also increase for caring expenses incurred due to the health of the child
Sweden	Childcare allowance	A monthly allowance available to parents with a disabled child to provide financial assistance	SEK 8,917 per month	19	The disabled or sick child needs special supervision and care for at least six months or if there are expenses related to his or her disability or illness	No	The amount varies according to the child's needs: full allowance (SEK 8,917 per month), three-quarters, half or a quarter of allowance (SEK 2,229 per month)
	Attendance allowance	A financial allowance provided to	SEK 282 per hour (in 2010)		Persons with a severe long-term	No	The amount varies according to need,

		disabled persons in need of personal assistance			disability who need personal assistance of more than twenty hours a week to cope with daily-life activities		ranging from SEK 252 to SEK 282 per hour
United Kingdom[7]	Disability Living Allowance (DLA)	A weekly allowance paid to parents/ guardians with children who have a disability or an illness	£131.5 per week	16	Disabled persons may need a medical certificate to determine the extent of their needs	No	
	Carer's Allowance	A financial weekly support for people who are looking after a sick or disabled person	£58.45 per week	None	Person needs to spend at least thirty-five hours a week caring for someone	Yes	
United States	SSI Payment Benefits for Children with Disability	Financial allowance to low-income families with a child with disability	Varies across states	No age limit	Eligibility is subject to meeting Social Security's definition of disability	Yes	SSI payments differ across states

[7] On March 5, 2013, the British government started replacing the Disability Living Allowance (DLA) with Personal Independence Payment (PIP) regulations. However, it is unknown what the government's plan is regarding DLA for children younger than sixteen. The government has said it wants to see how PIP works for sixteen- to sixty-four-year-olds before considering if children receiving DLA should move to PIP. Children will only move to PIP when the government can "demonstrate it provides a fairer, more objective and more transparent alternative to the current arrangements." The government has recognized that if it does move children to PIP, a specific assessment should be developed to ensure that the needs of disabled children are properly considered. The government has also ensured that children younger than sixteen will not be moved to PIP without public consultation, and any decisions made will be subject to parliamentary scrutiny. For further information, see the National Children's Bureau reaction to the delay to DLA reforms for children and adolescents younger than sixteen. It can be retrieved at http://www.edcm.org.uk/latest-news/2011/april-2011/4-april-11-dla-response.

there are many differences, including the type of population served, eligibility, array of cash benefits and their amount.

An insightful comparison can be made between two primary cash benefit programs for children with disability – the SSI in the United States and the DLA in the United Kingdom (see Table 7.2). The comparison focuses on their primary goals, eligibility, core provisions, coverage and impact on families of children with disability.

TABLE 7.2 *Comparison of US Supplemental Security Income (SSI) with UK Disability Living Allowance*

Disability Living Allowance (DLA) (UK)	Supplemental Security Income (SSI) (US)	Country comparison by:
A tax-free and non-means-tested benefit to help with the extra costs families may have for a child with disability.	Federal income supplement program operating in cooperation with the states, offering monthly allowance to low-income parents to afford the costs of their child's care at home.	**Primary goal**
Available for a child younger than sixteen who has difficulty walking and/or needs more care than a child of the same age. The DLA has been replaced by the Personal Independence Payment (PIP) for people aged sixteen to sixty-four.	Available for children up to age eighteen "with marked and severe functional limitations" whose family household income and resources fall within the eligibility limits.	**Eligibility**
The care rate component is between £21 and £79.15 a week, and the mobility component is between £21 and £55.25. Both depend on the level of help the child needs.	A minor child with severe disability can receive SSI benefits ($710/month in 2013) only if the parents meet the income and asset criteria.	**Core provision**
In 2011, about 335,000 children and youth under age sixteen were recipients of the DLA allowance. Interestingly, mobility	In 2012, 1.3 million children with disability received SSI, which represents fewer than 2 percent of all US children. Because of the stringent eligibility standards, fewer	**Coverage**

TABLE 7.2 *(cont.)*

Disability Living Allowance (DLA) (UK)	Supplemental Security Income (SSI) (US)	Country comparison by:
payments are considerably lower than care benefits.[8]	than 12 percent of US children with disability received SSI in 2012. In 2013, the maximum monthly benefit was $710, which was 56 percent below the federal poverty level for a family of three.	
Families report that the DLA makes a significant difference, not just for the disabled child but for the whole family. However, the DLA is repeatedly withdrawn, causing considerable fluctuations in income and high levels of stress and ill health.[9]	SSI benefits lifted more than 300,000 children with disability from below 50 percent of the poverty line to above that threshold.[10] However, there are concerns that it is restricted and forces redetermination of eligibility at the adult standard at age eighteen.	**Impact**

The SSI and the DLA for children have similar goals, that is, to provide cash benefits to support families with extra costs of caring for a child with disability. However, they differ in their approach; the SSI is means tested and aimed at low-income families to prevent their deterioration into poverty. The DLA is a universal cash benefit provided to all families of children with disability; however, one of its secondary goals is to reduce their dependence on welfare rolls.

8 "Disability Living Allowance reform: equality impact assessment," Department for Work and Pensions (DWP), May 2012. Accessed 4/1/2014 at https://www.gov.uk/government/uploads/system/uploads/attachment_data/file/220151/eia-dla-reform-wr2011.pdf.

9 Preston, "Helter skelter: families, disabled children and the benefit system."

10 CBPP analysis of the March 2010 "Current Population Survey and SSI income data," taken from the Urban Institute/HHS Transfer Income Model Version 3, downloaded from the TRIM3 project website, trim3.urban.org, on 12/10/12. This result is consistent with earlier statistics presented in Anne DeCesaro and Jeffrey Hemmeter, "Characteristics of noninstitutionalized DI and SSI program participants," Social Security Administration Research and Statistics Note No. 2008–02, Table 11. Accessed 1/3/2014 at http://www.socialsecurity.gov/policy/docs/rsnotes/rsn2008-02.html.

SSI's qualifying criteria for children raises difficult conceptual and practical issues. The two major criteria are low income and resources and the inability to achieve substantial gainful activity. Because the parents' income and resources are attributed to the child, the income and resources criteria are objective and can be well measured. However, defining childhood disability using the concept of substantial gainful activity has proven difficult. Until the Supreme Court decision in *Sullivan v. Zebley*, 493 US 521 (1990), the statute stipulated that children could be considered disabled if they suffered "from any medically determinable physical or mental impairment of comparable severity" to a condition that would qualify an adult for SSI.[11] The Social Security Administration determined whether a child met this criterion by comparing the child's disability to a list of about 100 mental or physical impairments. Children judged as having any of these impairments and who met the income and resources test were admitted to the program.[12] The monthly SSI benefit that is due is simply the federal benefit rate (FBR) reduced by the amount of any countable income, including in-kind support. In 2014, the official poverty standard was $11,490 for a non-elderly single person and $15,510 for a non-elderly couple.[13] The annualized FBR for that year – $8,657 for a single individual and $12,984 for a couple – was therefore less than even the poverty standard applied to elderly persons. Interestingly, the SSI for children assumes the same benefit for working-age adults and the elderly.

[11] The Zebley case centered on the inconsistency between eligibility determination of adults and children for SSI. The adult determination process has two steps to qualify for benefits. The first involves determining whether the applicant has several listed medical impairments or has an impairment that is equally restrictive for gaining employment. The second step allows an adult to qualify based on a functional assessment of his or her ability to engage in work given age, education and work experience. Until 1990, the child determination process only considered listed medical impairments and did not allow for any further functional assessment that would allow for unlisted comparable impairments. The court decision affirmed that a listings-only approach did not allow for children to qualify based on "comparable severity," that the existing child standard was stricter than the standard for adult disability cases, and that it was possible to do functional assessments of children based on their ability to perform age-appropriate activities. Accessed 1/4/2014 at http://supreme.justia.com/cases/federal/us/493/521/case.html.

[12] Ron Haskins, *The SSI program for children: time for change?*, Policy brief, The Future of Children, Spring 2012; *The full report on children with disabilities*, Janet Currie and Robert Kahn (eds.). Accessed 1/4/2014 at www.futureofchildren.org.

[13] See Federal Register, Vol. 79, No. 14, Wednesday, January 22, 2014, Notices, http://www.gpo.gov/fdsys/pkg/FR-2014-01-22/pdf/2014-01303.pdf.

The DLA, introduced in the United Kingdom in April 1992, presents a different approach; entitlement and award levels are based on proxies – care and mobility. It is definitely the greatest source of support for paying a child's disability bills, but it is not the only cash allowance available to families.[14] They also are entitled to apply for the Carer's Allowance, which is intended for people who provide regular and substantial care to a severely disabled person.[15] Unlike SSI, the only decision about whether to award the benefit is made on the basis of the severity of the child's care and mobility needs as a proxy for their extra costs. However, it seems that parental application and the process regarding a child's care needs and mobility difficulties is quite tedious. The form is very lengthy (43 pages) and requests detailed information on the impact that their child's impairment or health condition has on his or her ability to manage his or her care themselves and/or get around. In addition, the application has to be supported by detailed medical, psychological and functional evidence. However, more than 90 percent of those applying for the DLA receive an award. A claimant has one month following a decision to ask for it to be reconsidered or to make an appeal.[16] The current care rate component is between £21 and £79.15 a week and the mobility component is between £21 and £55.25. Both depend on the level of help the child needs.

There is no doubt that the UK welfare system is changing, demonstrating the government's demand to reform the DLA. In April 2013, the government replaced the DLA with PIP as part of a wider welfare reform. The change refers to people who were aged sixteen to sixty-four on April 8, 2013, or who reach the age of sixteen after that date. From October 2013, those older than sixteen whose existing award is coming to an end, or who report a change of circumstances, will be reassessed under the PIP system. This move raises concerns among parents of

[14] Social Security Contributions and Benefits Act 1992. Chapter 4. Accessed 1/3/2014 at http://www.legislation.gov.uk/ukpga/1992/4/pdfs/ukpga_19920004_en.pdf.

[15] The Carer's Allowance is a noncontributory benefit paid to people providing care for thirty-five hours or more per week to individuals who are receiving DLA (at the middle or highest rate for personal care).

[16] Mel Cousins & Associates, "*Supports for families with a child with a disability*," Research Report (November 9, 2012) 43–6, accessed 1/9/2013 at http://www.welfare.ie/en/downloads/DCAReview-ResearchReport.pdf.

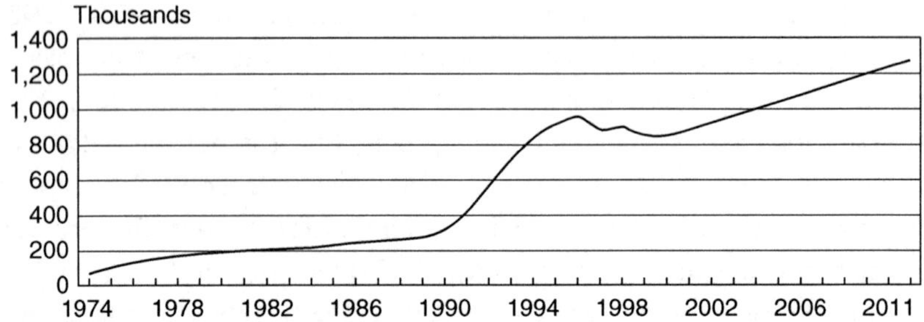

CHART 7.2 Number of Children under Age 18 Receiving SSI (1974–2011)

children with disability that it is a matter of time until the government will include them in the next reform.

COVERAGE AND IMPACT OF SSI AND DLA: A COMPARISON

The most important comparison between the SSI and the DLA is related to coverage and impact on families of children with disability. In terms of coverage, in 2012 the SSI provided monthly cash benefits to 1.3 million disabled children under the age of eighteen whose families have low incomes, about 1.7 percent of all children in the United States.[17] The rate has gone up gradually since its initiation in 1974, from about 71,000 disabled children to almost 1.3 million receiving aid in 2011 (see Chart 7.2).

Program growth increased most rapidly immediately following the 1990 Supreme Court decision in *Sullivan v. Zebley*, which greatly expanded disability eligibility criteria for children. Welfare reform in 1996 tightened eligibility standards and slightly reduced the rolls for one year.[18] One of the most interesting interpretations for the rising

[17] Social Security Administration, "SSI Monthly Statistics, October 2012," http://www.ssa.gov/policy/docs/statcomps/ssi_monthly/2012–10/index.html; Office of the Chief Actuary, *Annual report of the Supplemental Security Income Program*, May 2012, Table IV.B7, accessed 1/3/2014 at http://www.ssa.gov/OACT/ssir/SSI12/ssi2012.pdf.

[18] Richard V. Burkhauser and Mary C. Daly, "The changing role of disabled children benefits," sections entitled "Untangling caseload growth" and "Other factors driving program growth," *FRBSF Economic Letter* 25 (2013), accessed 3/3/2014 at http://www.frbsf.org/economic-research/publications/economic-letter/2013/september/disabled-children-family-benefits-ssi-supplemental-security-income/el2013-25.pdf.

number of SSI disabled children beneficiaries is the easing of eligibility standards and the interpretation of these standards by social welfare authorities.[19]

The demonstrated goal of the SSI program is to help families offset some of the additional costs of raising a child with disability, replace some of the parental income lost because of staying home to care for the child, and provide basic necessities such as food, clothing and shelter so they can raise their child at home rather than in an institution. The SSI provides a modest income supplement, and in most states it also provides automatic Medicaid eligibility.

However, in recent years there is growing criticism about the core mission of the program, particularly by conservative politicians who are interested in reducing federal spending and cutting the deficit. The main argument is that the typical SSI disabled children applicant family is headed by a low-income single mother who is also eligible for TANF. SSI disabled children benefits are larger than TANF benefits and lack the TANF work requirement. Thus, single mothers have an incentive to apply for SSI disabled children benefits.[20] The lack of sympathy toward the SSI is followed by sensational stories in the media characterizing SSI parents as predators determined to leech public money by exaggerating their children's impairments so that the children qualify for SSI.[21] It is therefore important to provide evidence-based reports about the impact of the SSI on children with disability and their families.

Research conducted by Mark Duggan and Melissa Schettini Kearney, using 1985–2004 household-level SIPP data, finds that child

[19] Richard V. Burkhauser and Mary C. Daly, *The declining work and welfare of people with disabilities: what went wrong and a strategy for change* (Washington, DC: American Enterprise Institute for Public Policy Research, 2011). In their critical book, the authors present the lessons from two recent policy initiatives – the reforms of US welfare policy and Dutch disability policy. Burkhauser and Daly call for fundamental changes in the way disability is insured and managed. In keeping with the Americans with Disabilities Act's philosophy of encouraging people with disabilities to remain in the workforce, the authors recommend changes in SSDI and SSI that make work, rather than benefits, the primary goal of federal disability policy.

[20] Burkhauser and Daly, *The changing role of disabled children benefits*, section on "Other factors driving program growth."

[21] Two examples of media coverage: Patricia Wen, "A coveted benefit: a failure to follow up," *Boston Globe*, December 13, 2010; Nicholas Kristof, "Profiting from a child's illiteracy," *New York Times*, December 7, 2012.

SSI participation increases total household income by an average of approximately $316 per month, or 20 percent. This is accomplished by a substantial increase in transfer income that is only partially offset by a reduction in other transfer income and earnings. To clarify, for every $100 in SSI income transferred to a family, total income increases by more than $72. The findings suggested that enrollment of a child in the program has little impact on the extensive margin of labor supply, but the pattern of coefficients over time and across various samples suggests that there might be an offset of conditional earnings in the order of 5 to 10 percent. While researchers usually consider an offset of earnings to be a negative consequence of transfer programs, to the extent that parents are reducing their earnings to stay home and provide care for a disabled child, any offset of earnings might actually be considered in line with the child SSI program goals.

The Center on Budget and Policy Priorities (CBPP) analysis found that SSI benefits lift more than 300,000 children with disability from below 50 percent of the poverty line to above that threshold.[22] In addition, the added income that the SSI provides, and its impact in lifting many children out of deep poverty, lasts over time. Poor children whose families receive a significant increase in income do better in school and work and earn more as adults.[23]

Compared to the US SSI, the UK DLA is a non-means-tested benefit that provides a cash contribution toward the extra costs of needs arising from an impairment or health condition. Overall, the numbers of people claiming the DLA increased between 2002–2003 and 2010–2011. A close look at Chart 7.3, with a focus on children and youth, demonstrates an increase in the numbers qualifying as *children or young teenagers*, particularly males in the age group of ten to fifteen.[24]

[22] See analysis of the March 2010 *Current Population Survey* and SSI income data from the Urban Institute/HHS Transfer Income Model Version 3. Accessed 12/10/12 from www.trim3.urban.org. This result is consistent with earlier statistics presented in Anne DeCesaro and Jeffrey Hemmeter, "Characteristics of noninstitutionalized DI and SSI program participants," Social Security Administration Research and Statistics Note No. 2008-02, Table 11. Accessed at http://www.socialsecurity.gov/policy/docs/rsnotes/rsn2008-02.html.

[23] Arloc Sherman, "Poverty in early childhood has long and harmful reach," Center on Budget and Policy Priorities, *Off the Charts* (blog), March 15, 2011. Accessed 1/3/2014 at http://www.offthechartsblog.org/poverty-in-early-childhood-has-long-and-harmful-reach/.

[24] Based on "Disability living allowance: growth in the number of claimants 2002/3–2010/11," Department for Work and Pensions (DWP), July 2011.

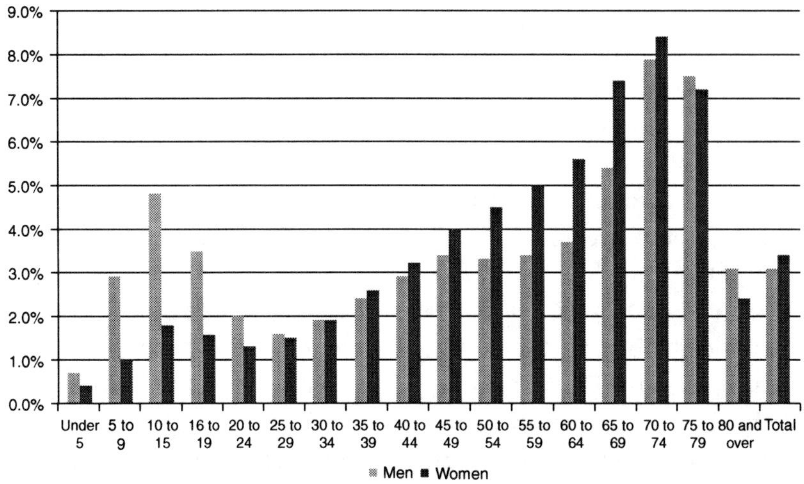

CHART 7.3 Increase in DLA Receipt, 1992/3 to 2010/11

Unlike SSI, which is aimed at low-income families, the DLA's primary goal is to assist families of children with disability with the extra cost of care.[25] It is based on quite detailed medical and functional assessment per se to reach the appropriate level of benefit.

A recent examination of DLA payments according to type of award (care or mobility) by claimant's age provides insights into each type. Mobility awards were more appealing and exceeded care awards. For example, there were 25,690 cases that obtained a higher rate of care compared to 125,676 cases receiving higher mobility rates. Interestingly, mobility awards stayed more or less stable over time, whereas care awards (higher rates) climbed from 25,690 (younger than five years of age) to its peak in the age group of five to younger than eleven (61,130 cases) and then decreased to 52,170 cases. The care awards at the middle rate went up from 25,870 cases under the age of five to 80,990 (five to younger than eleven), with the number climbing to 91,070 for eleven-year-olds to children younger than sixteen. Most of the recipients of care awards were concentrated in the high and middle rates, with marginal numbers in the lower care rates.

[25] Based on May 2013 calculation. See http://tabulation-%20ool.dwp.gov.uk/100pc/dla/tabtool_dla.html.

There is lack of evidence-based knowledge about the impacts of the DLA on recipients' care and mobility arrangements and their standard of living.[26] What is the main purpose of the DLA? Is it intended to assist families of children with disability with the cost of care or is it an income supplement? Most of the evidence is based on secondary data and qualitative research from the United Kingdom and Northern Ireland, providing modest but important insights about DLA.

An early qualitative study, "Helter skelter: families, disabled children and the benefit system," written by Gabrielle Preston in 2005, sheds light on the DLA as perceived by twenty families of children with disability who were awarded the DLA.[27] The DLA appears to assist parents with the extra cost of caring for their children with disability, but seems particularly important for low-income families that have been struggling for some years with disability-related costs without additional financial support. The DLA might simply bring family finances up to income support levels, which the government acknowledges are not sufficient to cover the extra costs of disability. The parents expressed concerns about lack of knowledge of other available benefits, such as the Carer's Allowance, and preferred that government (Department of Work and Pensions [DWP]) would be more responsive and less bureaucratic in processing their applications. Finally, they expected that government would be proactive in notifying them about their rights.

Using the Family Resources Survey data of 2006/7, Marina Monteith and others reported on the impact of the DLA and the AA on reduction of child poverty in Northern Ireland as compared to the United Kingdom.[28] They removed the DLA and the AA from household income and calculated the poverty rating for these children.

[26] Richard Berthoud, "The impact of disability benefits," Department for Work and Pensions (DWP), Working Paper No. 58. (2009).

[27] Gabrielle Preston, "Helter skelter: families, disabled children and the benefit system," *CASEpaper* 92 (London School of Economics, Centre for Analysis of Social Exclusion, February 2005). Accessed 4/1/2014 at http://eprints.lse.ac.uk/6272/1/Helter_Skelter_Families_disabled_children_and_the_benefit_system.pdf.

[28] Marina Monteith et al., "Taking a closer look: child poverty and disability," Northern Ireland Briefing, November 2009. Accessed 3/8/2013 at http://www.familyfund.org.uk/sites/default/files/Child%20poverty%20in%20Northern%20Ireland.pdf.

Interestingly, this method demonstrated that their removal affected overall child poverty rates in the United Kingdom to a great extent – with no change in Before Housing Cost figures – and the adjusted method showing a 1% increase in the conventional method after housing costs were taken out. However, in Northern Ireland, removal of the DLA and the AA from household income indicated a 2% increase in child poverty rates before housing costs were removed, and a 3% increase in the conventional method after housing costs were removed. It appears that the DLA combined with the AA has a marginal impact on poverty because it is basically aimed at reducing the additional cost of care. Therefore, their conclusion is that the DLA and the AA should not be included as income in analysis of poverty if the equivalence scales do not take into account the extra cost of caring for a disabled child or adult in the family.

However, a newer qualitative study examining the impact of the DLA on families of children with disability carried out by the DWP clarified parents' priorities regarding the DLA.[29] It is evident that they perceived the DLA primarily as a non-means-tested benefit to ease the burden of extra care for their children with severe disability rather than as an income supplement to families. It assisted them with their children's differential needs for care. The DLA's secondary goal was to help parents who had major extra responsibilities and tasks, to ease pressures on parents and enable them to do more for and with their child, and to compensate for additional costs and burdens on the whole family. Less widespread, but mentioned by some, was the child's DLA acting as income replacement for parents unable to do paid work because of the child's need for care, or the DLA providing extra money for parents who otherwise just did not have enough. Parents who had experienced recent major changes in personal circumstances, or who had fluctuating earnings, mentioned regularity and reliability of this income stream when they thought about the DLA.

[29] Anne Corden et al., *The impact of disability living allowance and attendance allowance: findings from exploratory qualitative research*, Department for Work and Pensions Research Report, No. 649, HMSO, Norwich, 2010. The findings relevant to the DLA for children are based on qualitative data taken from families of seven children aged two to nine years and eight aged ten to fifteen years.

THE CHALLENGES OF CASH BENEFIT POLICIES IN THE UNITED STATES AND THE UNITED KINGDOM

Sweden and France offer family-centered policies for households with disabled children. Although there are differences in the structure of social protection and infrastructure of services, both countries are solid in their commitment to families. There is consensus in both countries regarding family-support policies and the need to respond to differential needs of children with disability. While France faces modest cuts in child tax credit, Sweden is moving toward an even more progressive family policy emphasizing increased choice more than gender equality among all groups of parents.[30]

However, cash benefit policies geared toward families of children with disability are not taken for granted in the United States and the United Kingdom. The center of the debate in the United States is the SSI, which was discussed earlier in comparison to the DLA in the United Kingdom. Supporters of the SSI claim that the program for children is a critical lifeline for the nation's most vulnerable families – those who are both poor and raising children with disability.[31] Critics claim that the SSI's growth reflects changes in the implementation of the program rather than declines in children's health or family income, and that most children with disability do not become employed when they grow up.[32] The debate reflects the lack of consensus between conservatives and liberals about welfare programs and their outcome in reducing poverty in families.

Interestingly, the United Kingdom faces a similar debate regarding the 2012 Welfare Reform, a legislation that is considered the most

[30] See article by Eric Schulzke, "France's generous family policies put stress on taxpayers," *Deseret News*, National edition, Sunday, December 1, 2013. Accessed 1/3/2014 at http://www.deseretnews.com/article/865591634/Frances-generous-family-policies-put-stress-on-taxpayers.html?pg=all.

[31] Set of joint presentation slides based on a forthcoming working paper by Shawn Fremstad and Rebecca Vallas, "The children's Supplemental Security Income program: a review of recent research and trends" (Center for Economic and Policy Research, Washington, DC and Community Legal Services of Philadelphia, August 7, 2011). Accessed 3/2/2014 at http://www.cepr.net/documents/presentations/fremstad-childrens-SSI-presentation-8-9-11.pdf.

[32] Richard V. Burkhauser et al., "Disability benefit growth and disability reform in the U.S.: lessons from other OECD nations," Working Paper Series 2013–40, Federal Reserve Bank of San Francisco.

significant change in the past sixty years. At the center of the act is the introduction of the Universal Credit, which replaces much of the benefits and tax credits system for people both in and out of work. The change raises concerns by disability advocates about the status of current entitlements; parents of youth with disability are particularly concerned regarding the change from the DLA to PIP.[33,34]

TAX DEDUCTIONS AND TAX CREDITS: UNITED KINGDOM VERSUS UNITED STATES

Historically, countries have allowed tax exemptions or deductions for children. However, these were regressive, benefiting higher income families more than those with low incomes. In recent years, there has been increased use of the tax system, with specially targeted tax benefits providing income supports to families with children. The United States, France and the United Kingdom have enacted, and even expanded, existing tax credits to benefit families with children, often limiting them to working families. Sweden and most Nordic states tend toward universalism and significant regulation by government to increase social justice.

In general, child benefits are used for the same purposes as cash benefits; however, tax deductions and tax credits differ in their impact on family income. Tax allowances or deductions reduce taxable income before calculating tax obligations, while tax credits reduce tax liabilities and thus have the same value to all who pay income tax. However, unless these tax credits are refundable (as in the United States), meaning that those with incomes below the tax threshold receive a cash benefit, they are limited in value to more affluent families.

The United Kingdom and the United States differ in tax deductions and tax credits aimed at household taxpayers of children with disability. Interestingly, the United States offers cash supplements only to

[33] Department of Work and Pensions, "Simplifying the welfare system and making sure work pays." Accessed 3/27/2014 at https://www.gov.uk/government/policies/simplifying-the-welfare-system-and-making-sure-work-pays.

[34] UK Government, *Universal Credit Guide.* Accessed 6/2/2014 at https://www.gov.uk/universal-credit.

low-income families; others are channeled to claim tax deductions or tax credits. The United Kingdom takes a different approach: the primary cash benefit, the DLA, is non–means tested and based on a child's functioning. There are two tax credit supplements, which are viewed as supplements or boosters to families. The CTC and the WTC, administered by Her Majesty's Revenue and Customs, have nothing to do with the tax system or income. The CTC is paid for each child who is younger than sixteen (or younger than twenty if enrolled in education or in a training program). Parents of children with disability receive a higher amount, and those with severe disability receive an additional sum. The WTC is provided to working parents with low income and is based on the number of work hours. Here, also, there are particular elements paid for a child with disability or severe disability.

The United States offers taxpayers tax deductions and tax credit opportunities for having a dependent child with disability. In general, the tendency of the Internal Revenue Service (IRS) is to compensate families on the basis of their tax claims. At the bottom are parents receiving the SSI (and often Medicaid) for their child with disability, as they are scarcely qualified for tax deductions or tax credits. The most common tax credit is the Child or Dependent Care Credit relevant to taxpayers with children. The credit is nonrefundable, meaning that the credit amount is limited to the amount of taxes owed. There is special tax credit for working parents with low to moderate income. The Earned Income Tax Credit (EITC) is actually a tax subsidy that intends to increase the incentive to work by supplementing earnings from low-paid work and to reduce childhood poverty and the reliance on welfare programs.

The credit rises with earned income until it reaches a maximum (which varies by the number of qualified children); it then phases out as income rises further.[35] For 2013, the phaseouts begin at $17,530 for single filers and $22,870 for married filers; the average size of the credit is expected to be $2,828 for a family with children and $280 for a family without children. Critics complain that the EITC is too complex,

[35] For more information about EITC, see "Policy basics: the Earned Income Tax Credit," Center on Budget and Policy Priorities, updated February 1, 2013. Accessed 3/4/2014 at http://www.cbpp.org/cms/index.cfm?fa=view&id=2505.

forcing potential recipients to seek help filing their federal tax return: two-thirds of low-income parents get such assistance, typically from paid tax preparers.

The broadest deduction that compensates primarily high-income taxpayers is the one for medical expenses, covering amounts paid for diagnosis, cure, treatment, special diet, and even special education. For 2012 and prior years, medical expenses for most taxpayers were limited to an amount in excess of 7.5 percent of Adjusted Gross Income (AGI). For those subject to Alternative Minimum Tax, that limit was 10 percent.

Although there are substantial differences between the UK and the US tax systems with respect to families of children with disability, there has been a tendency in recent years to favor low- and middle-income families over higher income families.[36] A good example is the UK WTC and the US EITC. Both are in-work benefits that deal with the tradeoff between incentive and redistributive objectives. They provide means-tested transfers to low-income households with eligibility conditions on some employment requirements to avoid the harmful disincentive effects of the welfare trap.

SUPPLEMENT CASH BENEFITS AND TAX CREDIT IN PROGRESSIVE COUNTRIES: FRANCE AND SWEDEN

France and Sweden are considered family-centered countries that offer substantial social protection and cash benefit allowances. France uses tax credits marginally to compensate families, and Sweden even less. France, which has generous family-support services for working parents, offers supplements to families of children with disability, demonstrating receptiveness to parents' burden of care. The basic supplement is known as the *Allocation D'éducation de L'enfant Handicapé* (AEEH), a non-means-tested allowance paid to parents of a severely disabled child under twenty years of age. Interestingly, the amount of

[36] Gordon B. Dahl and Lance Lochner, "The impact of family income on child achievement: evidence from the Earned Income Tax Credit," *American Economic Review* 102 (2012), 1927–56.

the allowance is 32 percent of the monthly family benefit base (BMAF) (€127.68 per month in April 2012). There is an additional supplement for children with a disability with at least an 80 percent functional disability rate, with the amount varying according to their needs or degree of disability.[37] However, the number of applications from younger children is relatively low and the average age of a new claimant is seven years and five months. There do not appear to be any detailed evaluations of the AEEH. However, a report for the *École nationale d'administration* stated that the amount of the AEEH remained modest and could only cover a small part of the need for care (up to three hours per day).[38]

As an alternative to the supplement, parents can opt for the disability compensation benefit paid by the *Conseil Général*, which is intended to contribute toward the cost of the continuing care needs arising from the disability. The supplement may be paid concurrently with the "third element" of the compensation benefit, which is designed to help with home and vehicle conversion costs and transport costs. In addition to the non-means-tested supplements, families with disabled children are also eligible for special tax allowances.

In Sweden, the 2.1 percent of GDP that is spent on social protection and the 3.4 percent on family benefits alone probably provides better coverage than that in France.[39] The Swedish welfare state, supported by robust corporate arrangements between employer organizations and trade unions, is characterized by the principles of equality and universalism and has relatively strong redistributive effects. It is strongly service oriented with public spending for education, family and children above the EU average. Overall, families in Sweden benefit from a wide variety of support, among which are the universal benefits of family allowance, large family supplement, parent's cash

[37] In April 2012, the monthly amounts of the supplement were: first category, 24% of the BMAF (€95.76); second category, 65% of the BMAF (€259.35); third category, 92% of the BMAF (€367.08); fourth category, 142.57% of the BMAF (€568.85); fifth category, 182.21% of the BMAF (€727.02); sixth category, the amount of the constant attendance allowance (€1,082.43).

[38] École nationale d'administration, *La prise en charge des enfants handicapés en France* (ENA: Paris, 2006).

[39] Michael Förster and Gerlinde Verbi, "Money or kindergarten? Distributive effects of cash versus in-kind family transfers for young children: improve poverty, social policy and innovation" (Discussion Paper No. 13/04 May 2013). Accessed 1/12/2013 at http://webhost.ua.ac.be/csb/ImPRovE/Working%20Papers/ImPRovE%20WP%201304_1.pdf.

benefit and temporary parent's cash benefit paid for short periods of leave to look after a sick child. In addition, Swedish legislation gives the municipalities the right to introduce, finance and administer municipal childcare allowances. This allowance can be granted for children over the age of one but younger than three. To be entitled, parents must have taken at least 250 days of parent's cash benefit. The maximum amount of childcare allowance is SEK 3,000 (£280) per child and per month. The municipalities have been given the right to reduce the allowance if the child attends a publicly funded preschool establishment. The amount is reduced according to the amount of time the child spends in preschool. Therefore, the two special benefits aimed at parents of children with disability, childcare allowance (a monthly allowance available to parents with a disabled child to provide financial assistance) and attendance allowance (financial support provided to disabled persons in need of personal assistance), are just supplements to an extended social protection system. It is evident that tax credit or deduction is not a preferred instrument in Sweden, the exception being the gender equality bonus to improve the conditions for gender equality in both parental leave and participation in working life.

FAMILY CARE SERVICES: CROSS-COUNTRY COMPARISONS

One of the indications of family-support services is the status of childcare services. Table 7.3 presents a typology of childcare in the United States, the United Kingdom, France and Sweden.

In terms of infrastructure of childcare services, the United States and the United Kingdom are considered as following noninterventionist

TABLE 7.3 *Childcare typology in the US, the UK, France and Sweden*

	Country			
Type of care	US	UK	France	Sweden
Center-based	Private	Private	Public	Public
Preschool	Mixed	Mixed	Public	Public
School	Public	Public	Public	Public

family policies built on individualism and voluntarism in which the state is expected to play a lesser role than both the market and the family in supporting an individual's care. They differ greatly from France and Sweden regarding childcare programs for children. The latter demonstrate strong government commitment to families of young children, providing free public services.

Britain is often cited as an example of the liberal welfare state regime, which is built on individualism and voluntarism, in which the state is expected to play a lesser role than both the market and the family in supporting an individual's welfare and care.[40]

US childcare centers are predominantly private, similarly in the United Kingdom the majority of nurseries, child minders and playgroups are private. Interestingly, in the United States 40 percent of children aged three to four, and 70 percent of four- to five-year-olds are enrolled in educational programs, including pre-K, private kindergartens, Head Start and purchase-of-service. Head Start covers 11 percent of three- and four-year-olds. With school compulsory from the age of six, more than 80 percent of children from the age of five are enrolled in state-funded kindergartens (education auspices).

The UK preschool system is mixed, with only children aged three to four being entitled to 12.5 hours of free public education and reception class with primary school. In parallel, France and Sweden provide subsidized public childcare. France offers *crèches* and center-based *assistante maternalles* (childminders), and *écoles maternelles* for preschool. In Sweden, the *förskola* (preschool) and *familjedaghem* (family day care), particularly in rural areas, are provided for thirty hours per week. According to the Ministry of Social Welfare and Health, about 85 percent of the children aged one to five participate in public-funded childcare, most of them (79%) in *förskola*.[41]

All countries provide public education, with the United States a frontrunner in providing inclusive education for children with disability

[40] Anne H. Gauthier, "Family policies in industrialized countries: Is there convergence?" *Population* 57 (2002), 447–74.

[41] Jessica Löfvenholm, "PowerPoint presentation on Swedish family policy," Ministry of Health and Social Affairs, Social Insurance Division, Unit for Family Policy and Children's Rights and Committee of economy and cooperation between separated parents, 2006. Accessed 12/1/2013 at www.eurochild.org/../SE_%20Swedish%20Family %20Policy.ppt.

aged three to twenty-one. IDEA requires public schools to make available to all eligible children with disability a free, appropriate public education in the least restrictive environment suited to their individual needs. IDEA requires public school systems to develop appropriate Individualized Education Programs (IEPs) for each child with the specific special education and related services outlined in each IEP reflecting the individualized needs of each student. IDEA is a model for parental involvement and participation in the IEP. Subpart E, addressing Procedural Safeguards, is designed to protect the rights of parents and their child with a disability and, at the same time, give families and school systems several mechanisms by which to resolve their disputes.

The United Kingdom followed US legislation and initiated the National Service Framework for Children, Young People and Maternity Services and Aiming High for Disabled Children to promote partnerships working with parents via a system of regular meetings, joint writing of Family Service Plans, shared information, shared training and, where appropriate, regular support from a lead professional or key worker. Sure Start programs cooperate closely with families to ensure that services reflect family involvement and participation. Parents are represented in the management committees, and mechanisms are in place to ensure their regular evaluation of Sure Start services.

Sweden has a holistic approach to the child and family, making close cooperation between professionals and the family a priority. Families are involved in suggestions for action and intervention, and they are offered guidance and counseling.[42] France offers mainstreamed education for children with disability and special needs. According to the OECD study, the percentage of those studying in special education is below 1 percent of the total students, lower than in the United Kingdom, which is slightly above 1 percent.[43]

[42] The European Agency for Development in Special Needs Education (EADSNE) is an independent organization established by EU member countries to work collaboratively on the development of provision for learners with special educational needs. The agency published a report, *Early childhood intervention: Progress and developments 2005–2010* (2010). Accessed 5/1/2014 at http://www.european-agency.org/sites/default/files/early-childhood-intervention-progress-and-developments_ECI-report-EN.pdf.

[43] In 2012, Prof. Sheila Riddell, director of the Centre for Research in Education Inclusion and Diversity at the Moray House School of Education, University of Edinburgh, UK, published, with additional experts of the NESSE network of experts, a comparative report

RESPITE CARE: CROSS-COUNTRY COMPARISONS

One of the most important relief provisions for families is respite care ranging from one day to one week. This allows the parents to rest, be alone together, or concentrate on their other children. The leading country in this regard is Sweden, which in 1994 enacted the Act concerning Support and Service for Persons with Certain Functional Impairments (LSS). The law provides accessibility to respite care service as a legal right for families with children with disability, primarily aimed at giving parents and caregivers relief from care in daily life.

In France, respite services are under-supplied, although the cost of this service exceeds the value of the universal cash allowance. Similar schemes may entail having various organizations take care of the child during holidays or offer a variety of activities.[44]

The United Kingdom provides a respite care grant as a supplement paid by the Department of Social Protection to all carers who already have received Domiciliary Care Allowance, Carer's Allowance or Carer's Benefit, or are caring for someone who receives the AA. It is also payable to anyone providing full-time care to a person aged sixteen or older for at least six months.

The United States has a unique legislation, still in the initial stages, known as the Lifespan Respite Care Program. It was authorized by Congress in 2006 under Title XXIX of the Public Health Service Act (42 U.S.C 201).[45] Once implemented, Lifespan Respite Care Programs work to improve the delivery and quality of respite services available to families across the age and disability spectrum. Since 2009, Congress has appropriated approximately $2.5 million per year to

for the European Commission, *Education and disability/special needs: policies and practices in education, training and employment for students with disabilities and special needs in the EU.* Accessed 7/1/2014 at http://www.nesetweb.eu/sites/default/files/NESSE-disability-special-needs-report-2012.pdf.

44 "Better health, better lives: children and young people with intellectual disabilities and their families" (Background paper, World Health Organization (WHO) Europe, Bucharest, 2010). Accessed 2/30/2013 at http://www.euro.who.int/__data/assets/pdf_file/0003/126408/e94421.pdf.

45 Title 42—The public health and welfare's main goal is to amend the Public Health Service Act to establish a program to assist family caregivers in accessing affordable and high-quality respite care and for other purposes. Accessed 4/13/2014 at http://www.gpo.gov/fdsys/pkg/USCODE-2010-title42/pdf/USCODE-2010-title42-chap6A-subchapI.pdf.

implement Lifespan Respite Programs. As of 2012, competitive grants of up to $200,000 each were awarded to eligible agencies in thirty states and the District of Columbia. Eligible state agencies are those administering the state's program under the Older Americans Act of 1965; the state's program under Title XIX of the Social Security Act (Medicaid); or are designated by the governor to administer the state's program under this title. The eligible state agency must be an Aging and Disability Resource Center and work in collaboration with a public or private nonprofit statewide respite care coalition or organization. With these initial three-year grants, states have developed or built on respite infrastructures through a variety of approaches designed to enhance or improve access to and receipt of respite services. In 2012, seven of the original 2009 states received new grants to build on and expand the efforts begun during their previous three years of work.

CONCLUSION

The chapter analyzes US and European policies toward families of children with disability as reflected by comparative analysis of cash benefits, tax credits and deductions, and in-kind provisions of the United States, the United Kingdom, France and Sweden. The overall impression is that the United States provides modest family-support infrastructure, a strict cash benefits scheme aimed at low-income families, and tax credits and deduction opportunities for taxpayers. Sweden and France demonstrate generous policies and an extensive network of integrated, universal services for children, with links to more specialized services for those who need extra care and protection. The United Kingdom represents an intermediate level between the United States and France and Sweden, offering a mixed approach of means-tested and non-means-tested approaches to families of children with disability. However, parent- and family-support services are patchy, uncoordinated and mainly targeted at the most disadvantaged sectors of the population.

The chapter introduces an interesting comparison between two central cash benefits schemes, the US SSI and the UK DLA, providing insights into the substantial differences between the two countries. Both programs intend to assist with the extra cost of caring for children with disability. However, the SSI is means tested and geared toward low-income families, whereas the DLA is non–means tested and provided based on severity and mobility elements. Interestingly, both programs are being challenged for their increased cost and modest outcome, particularly by conservative scholars and politicians.

There are additional comparisons related to tax credits and deduction and in-kind provisions showing that Swedish and French policies rely on cash benefits and support services, particularly in the early years, and use tax credits and deductions marginally. UK policy is well-known for its cash benefit policy, offering moderate tax credits or deductions. US policy is limited to cash benefits provided to low-income families and modest infrastructure of services, tending to compensate primarily high-income taxpayers for medical expenses, covering amounts paid for diagnosis, cure, treatment, special diet and special education.

8 THE UN CONVENTION OF THE RIGHTS OF PERSONS WITH DISABILITIES (CRPD) AND FAMILY POLICIES

The CRPD is a pioneering legally binding international human rights document applying human rights to people with disability. On December 13, 2006, the United Nations General Assembly adopted the CRPD, which entered into force on May 3, 2008. The purpose of the CRPD is "to promote, protect and ensure the full and equal enjoyment of all human rights and fundamental freedoms by all persons with disabilities, and to promote respect for their inherent dignity."[1] Although this treaty is aimed at people with disability (PWD), it touches on the role of the family. Similar to the debate about the centrality of the family in social policy, the CRPD raises controversy regarding the role of the state in regulating family and, particularly, parents' rights. An additional dilemma is whether individuals' rights in the CRPD compete or complement families' rights. The common opinion raised by the Confederation of Family Organizations in the EU (COFACE) is that family members of children with disability provide the most immediate environment where they can develop their potential and enjoy a fulfilling life. Therefore, the rights of persons with disability are unavoidably linked with the quality of life of their families.[2] COFACE identifies

[1] The CRPD and its Optional Protocol was adopted on December 13, 2006, at the United Nations Headquarters in New York, and was opened for signature on March 30, 2007. Accessed 12/2/2012 at http://www.un.org/disabilities/convention/conventionfull.shtml.

[2] COFACE-Disability was founded by the Confederation of Family Organizations in the EU (COFACE) in 1998 in order to better represent the people with disability and their families. COFACE-Disability's mandate is to help people with disabilities achieve fulfillment throughout their entire lives, in particular within the family context. Its member organizations actively work together to see that a policy for family carers is mainstreamed across all EU policy spheres. COFACE-Disability advocates for families to be given a central place

this approach in Preamble (X), "Convinced that the family is the natural and fundamental group unit of society and is entitled to protection by society and the State, and that persons with disabilities and their family members should receive the necessary protection and assistance to enable families to contribute toward the full and equal enjoyment of the rights of persons with disabilities."[3]

An overview of the fifty articles reveals that five articles (8, 16, 22, 23, 28) make explicit reference to families, while eleven articles (5, 6, 7, 9, 12, 18, 19, 24, 25, 30, 33) implicitly require a mainstreaming of the family dimension in order to ensure effective implementation.

Article 8 – Awareness-raising – recognizes the importance of the family in this regard in Section 1a as follows:

a) To raise awareness throughout society, including at the family level, regarding persons with disabilities, and to foster respect for the rights and dignity of persons with disabilities.[4]

Article 16 – Freedom from exploitation, violence and abuse – is formulated sensitively with respect to families, calling for examining these negative expressions within the home (Section 1) and supporting families (Section 2), avoiding situations where the family or family members are the source of exploitation or abuse.

1. States Parties shall take all appropriate legislative, administrative, social, educational and other measures to protect persons with disabilities, both within and outside the home, from all forms of exploitation, violence and abuse, including their gender-based aspects.
2. States Parties shall also take all appropriate measures to prevent all forms of exploitation, violence and abuse by ensuring, inter alia, appropriate forms of gender- and age-sensitive assistance and

in policy on disability. Accessed 7/3/2013 at http://www.coface-eu.org/en/upload/15_Capacity_Building/Factsheet%20WG2%20UNCRPD%20en.pdf.

[3] United Nations Human Rights, "Convention on the rights of persons with disabilities. Listing all articles of the convention – the Preamble." Accessed 5/8/2013 at http://www.ohchr.org/EN/HRBodies/CRPD/Pages/ConventionRightsPersonsWithDisabilities.aspx#preamble.

[4] Hilde Haualand and Colin Allen, "Deaf people and human rights," World Federation of the Deaf and Swedish National Association of the Deaf, January 2009. The document compiled by the World Federation of the Deaf (WFD) and the Swedish National Association of the Deaf (SDR) contains information about the human rights situation of deaf people, including Article 8. Accessed 4/12/2013 at http://wfdeaf.org/human-rights/crpd/article-8-awareness-raising.

support for persons with disabilities and their families and caregivers, including through the provision of information and education on how to avoid, recognize and report instances of exploitation, violence and abuse. States Parties shall ensure that protection services are age-, gender- and disability-sensitive.[5]

Article 22 – Respect for privacy – calls in Section 1 to respect the family while maintaining the privacy of the person with disability. "1. No person with disabilities, regardless of place of residence or living arrangements, shall be subjected to arbitrary or unlawful interference with his or her privacy, family, home or correspondence or other types of communication or to unlawful attacks on his or her honour and reputation. Persons with disabilities have the right to the protection of the law against such interference or attacks."[6]

Article 23 – Respect for home and the family – is completely related to the family with respect to the right to marry and be parents (Sections 1–2) and the rights of children with disability (Sections 3–5), and particularly with respect to their well-being and care.

1. States Parties shall take effective and appropriate measures to eliminate discrimination against persons with disabilities in all matters relating to marriage, family, parenthood and relationships, on an equal basis with others, so as to ensure that:
   a) The right of all persons with disabilities who are of marriageable age to marry and to found a family on the basis of free and full consent of the intending spouses is recognized;
   b) The rights of persons with disabilities to decide freely and responsibly on the number and spacing of their children and to have access to age-appropriate information, reproductive and family planning education are recognized, and the means necessary to enable them to exercise these rights are provided;
   c) Persons with disabilities, including children, retain their fertility on an equal basis with others.
2. States Parties shall ensure the rights and responsibilities of persons with disabilities, with regard to guardianship, wardship, trusteeship, adoption of children or similar institutions, where these concepts

[5] "Convention on the Rights of Persons with Disabilities," Article 16. [6] Ibid., Article 22.

exist in national legislation; in all cases the best interests of the child shall be paramount. States Parties shall render appropriate assistance to persons with disabilities in the performance of their child-rearing responsibilities.

3. States Parties shall ensure that children with disability have equal rights with respect to family life. With a view to realizing these rights, and to prevent concealment, abandonment, neglect and segregation of children with disability, States Parties shall undertake to provide early and comprehensive information, services and support to children with disability and their families.
4. States Parties shall ensure that a child shall not be separated from his or her parents against their will, except when competent authorities subject to judicial review determine, in accordance with applicable law and procedures, that such separation is necessary for the best interests of the child. In no case shall a child be separated from parents on the basis of a disability of either the child or one or both of the parents.
5. States Parties shall, where the immediate family is unable to care for a child with disabilities, undertake every effort to provide alternative care within the wider family, and failing that, within the community in a family setting.[7]

Article 28 – Adequate standard of living and social protection – addresses the role of the state in providing adequate standards of living to families (Section 1) and assistance to those living in situations of poverty (Section 2c).

1. States Parties recognize the right of persons with disabilities to an adequate standard of living for themselves and their families, including adequate food, clothing and housing, and to the continuous improvement of living conditions, and shall take appropriate steps to safeguard and promote the realization of this right without discrimination on the basis of disability.
2. c).To ensure access by persons with disabilities and their families living in situations of poverty to assistance from the State with disability-related expenses, including adequate training, counseling, financial assistance and respite care.[8]

[7] Ibid., Article 23. [8] Ibid., Article 28.

Articles 5, 6, 7, 9, 12, 18, 19, 24, 25, 30 and 33 are relevant to families as beneficiaries of state policies.

Article 5 – Equality and nondiscrimination – refers to the state's role in ensuring these rights to all PWDs, including children with disability living within their families.

Article 6 – Women with disabilities – relates also to girls' rights living with their parents and siblings.

Article 7 – Children with disability – relates indirectly to their families and calls on the state to ensure that children's rights and well-being are protected within their natural environment, the family.

Article 9 – Accessibility – is general and refers also to PWDs living within their families or dependent on family members.

Article 12 – Equal recognition before the law.

Article 18 – Liberty of movement and nationality.

Article 19 – Living independently and being included in the community.

Article 24 – Education.

Article 25 – Health.

Article 30 – Participation in cultural life, recreation, leisure and sport – refers to all PWDs; the family is indirectly responsible for facilitating these rights, in particular for children and youth with disability who are legally dependent on parents.

Article 33 – National implementation and monitoring – is a general requirement by the states to move forward and endow these rights, including those related to families. There is no doubt that these articles challenged developing and developed nations over the role of family in the lives of persons with disability. In general, developing nations tended to see a greater role, with more responsibility and authority, while developed nations and NGOs viewed the family as secondary or separate, raising concerns that it might interfere with the PWD's independence and autonomy from the family.[9]

[9] However there are variations among developed countries. Countries with the highest fertility and lowest poverty rates are those where a high percentage of women perform paid work. In these countries, pro-family policies seem to strike a balance that is favorable to both women's employment and fertility. For this reason especially, work and family reconciliation policies are on the political agenda of a growing number of western countries. For further reading, see Olivier Thévenon, "Family policies in OECD countries: a comparative analysis," *Population and Development Review* 37 (2011) 64–6.

THE DEBATE ABOUT THE ROLE OF THE FAMILY IN THE CRPD

Although the CRPD recognizes the importance of the family in the life of persons with disability, there are concerns about possible conflict of interests between the rights of the person with disability and the family, and in particular between children and their parents.[10] Interestingly, these reservations have been raised by Japan as well as self-advocacy disability groups in the process of drafting the treaty. Japan expressed traditional values and concerns that families would overshadow and dominate the decision-making process at home. The United States was among the first countries that recognized the role of the family as the primary source of support for persons with disability. The US delegation accepted the idea that families have to receive support from the state and accepted the responsibility to promote rights of persons with disability. This approach received substantial support from several developing nations including Syria, Yemen, Qatar, the Philippines, India and Costa Rica.

There was overwhelming support to include families in the decision-making process at the state and local levels. This debate is best captured in the discussion about whether to include the family in Article 4 – General obligations. The International Disability and Development Consortium stance has been that states and local government must be obligated to both persons with disability and their families and representative organizations in shaping disability rights policy. However, states expressed different views about the role of families in this regard. India and Israel, for example, argued that families should be stakeholders in all planning and policy discussions. Many delegations, including Jordan, Costa Rica, New Zealand, Kenya, Trinidad and Tobago, Inclusion International and Venezuela, offered similar views. Japan has been consistent in opposing the family reference, stating that care should be exercised when incorporating the family into consultation because family can negatively impact people with disability. Norway, China and Jamaica raised similar concerns about including family in Article 4, and

[10] This language came largely from a U.S. amendment to Article 23 – Respect for Family – but was deemed more appropriate and relevant for the entire CRPD treaty.

preferred that this article would exclude families. Ultimately, the reference to families did not carry enough support and was deleted from the CRPD.

The debate regarding the Preamble, culminating in the discussions over Article 19 – Living independently and being included in the community – has been between developing and western countries. Israel argued that independent living and family involvement and support are not mutually exclusive, and that there are situations where PWD need family support and involvement to be able to live separately. New Zealand supported PWD autonomy and integration into the community, while India and Mexico supported some independent lifestyle choices for PWD within cultural norms. The debate was also among NGOs and advocacy groups, demonstrating the diversity of ideas concerning Article 19. On the one hand, the Canadian Association for Community Living (CACL) called for interdependency, facilitating PWD who could not live independently to be supported by their families. On the other hand, Disabled Peoples' International (DPI) advocated for the "explicit expression to the principle of autonomy" of Article 19's choice of residence. It is evident that most developing nations supported the middle way and supported the idea that PWD could be pushed to extreme ideas about autonomy when the majority of the nondisabled society and culture lived in large family arrangements.

THE CONSENSUS ABOUT THE ROLE OF THE FAMILY IN THE CRPD

Aside from the debate related to the Preamble and Article 4 about the role of the family in the convention, there was consensus that the family would be included in several sections of the convention. Article 23 reflects respect for home and family. Its provisions include the following[11]:

> States Parties shall take *effective and appropriate measures* to eliminate discrimination against persons with disabilities in all matters

[11] "Convention on the Rights of Persons with Disabilities," Article 23.

> relating to marriage, family, parenthood and relationships, on an equal basis with others.
>
> States Parties shall ensure the rights and responsibilities of persons with disabilities with regard to guardianship, wardship, trusteeship, adoption of children or similar institutions, where these concepts exist in national legislation; in all cases the best interests of the child shall be paramount. *States parties shall render appropriate assistance to persons with disabilities in the performance of their child-rearing responsibilities.*
>
> States Parties shall ensure that a child shall not be separated from his or her parents against their will, except when competent authorities subject to judicial review determine, in accordance with applicable law and procedures, that such separation is necessary for the best interests of the child. *In no case shall a child be separated from parents on the basis of disability of either the child or one or both of the parents.*

Surprisingly, the family was not included in Article 24 (Education) and Article 25 (Health), although traditionally it is mentioned in most of the education and health policies of OECD countries.

The need to provide adequate standards of living and social protection to persons with disability and their families is the focus of Article 28.[12]

1. States Parties recognize the right of persons with disabilities to an adequate standard of living for themselves and their *families*, including adequate food, clothing and housing, and to the continuous improvement of living conditions, and shall take appropriate steps to safeguard and promote the realization of this right without discrimination on the basis of disability.
2. States Parties recognize the right of persons with disabilities to social protection and to the enjoyment of that right without discrimination on the basis of disability, and shall take appropriate steps to safeguard and promote the realization of this right, including measures:
   a) To ensure equal access by persons with disabilities to clean water services, and to ensure access to appropriate and affordable services, devices and other assistance for disability-related needs;

[12] Ibid., Article 28.

b) To ensure access by persons with disabilities, in particular women and girls with disabilities and older persons with disabilities, to social protection programs and poverty reduction programs;
c) To ensure access by persons with disabilities and their *families living in situations of poverty* to assistance from the State with disability-related expenses, including adequate training, counselling, financial assistance and respite care;
d) To ensure access by persons with disabilities to public housing programs;
e) To ensure equal access by persons with disabilities to retirement benefits and programs.

This article is a pivotal component of any social protection policy and therefore has been interpreted differently by western and developing countries. The stance of countries such as India and the Philippines was that the families should be the center of Article 28 in combating poverty. According to their view, state services and funds should be available to the families as well as the disabled to encourage family support and care and to maintain a minimum standard of living and social protection for the entire family. Kenya elaborated that in most developing countries social security depended on the family, and so the protections and support of the state should be extended to the family alongside people with disability. The implication is that in many instances the impoverished family would suffer a lower standard of living because of the dedication of family resources toward the care of the disabled family member.

While there was overwhelming support for these arguments, some western nations and groups argued that the role of the family should be limited in state subsidies for disabled persons. While Japan was consistent in eliminating the role of the family from the convention, advocating that the focus of this article should be solely on people with disability and not on families, the International Disability Caucus (IDC) voiced concerns that state funding for families might result in families exploiting people with disability to receive state resources.[13]

[13] Although Japan is considered traditionalist with respect to social welfare provisions, there have been incremental changes since the early 1990s toward family policy legislation, particularly parental leave legislation and childcare infrastructure. For further reading,

This debate reflects not only the common discussion around family-centered policies but also about the role of family and the need for promoting autonomy and independence of PWD. Interestingly, most of the delegations supported maintaining the role of the family in state support and protection.

A delicate issue that was in the background of the CRPD was the abuse and exploitation of PWD by their families. Concern about the vulnerability in guardianship arrangements of children with disability was raised by the National Association of Community Legal Centers. Similarly, People with Disability Australia argued for stronger adult PWD autonomy in decision-making arrangements, citing a 2004 Australian consultation report that showed significant exploitation, abuse and neglect by family members. Family members might exploit financial resources, fail to perform beneficial medical procedures and allow unnecessary restrictive interventions such as non-therapeutic sterilizations. The IDC raised its concern that in Article 23 the family would use involuntary institutionalization and sterilization of children and adult PWD. The fact that the convention omits explicit reference to possible cases reflects the general approach to families. Instead, the treaty handled abuse and exploitation indirectly in Article 8 (Awareness raising), administering general protections as well as prevention and oversight measures for all forms of abuse and exploitation of PWD in Article 16, and protecting PWD and family rights in Article 23.

THE CRPD MEETS NATIONAL FAMILY POLICIES

The real challenge of the CRPD is not in its confirmation or ratification but in the steps of implementation in each state. The overall impression is that this task is expected to vary internationally on the basis of prevailing national disability legislation, policies and existing socioeconomic conditions. States are required to apply it according to explicit articles that express family matters: Preamble (x); Article 16, Freedom from exploitation, violence and abuse; Article 23(4), Respect for home and the family; and Article 28(1), 2(c), Adequate standard of living

see Hiroshi Kojima, "Religion and attitudes toward family policies in Japan, South Korea and Singapore," *Waseda Studies in Social Sciences* 12 (2011), 23–48.

and social protection. It is obvious already from reading Paragraph (x) of the Preamble that persons with disability have the same equal rights as the family.[14] However, it seems that the primary obligation is responding to the rights of persons with disability, while the family is considered a facilitator or proxy.[15] In implementation, countries will need to change prevailing images portraying persons with disability as burdens on the family.[16]

FINDING THE GAPS: THE CRPD MEETS CURRENT POLICIES AND LEGISLATION

United States

The debate about ratifying the CRPD in Congress raised concerns that the treaty could supersede federal, state and local laws.[17] Some are concerned that US ratification may give governments, and not US parents, the right to make educational and treatment-related decisions for their disabled children. Others, including the Obama administration, hold that existing federal, state and local laws protect parental rights. Interestingly, conservative parents groups targeted Article 7(2), which states, "In all actions concerning children with disability, the best interests of the child shall be a primary consideration," thinking that it demonstrates government ruling over parents' treatment- or education-related decisions for their children. For example, homeschooling advocates are concerned that the committee could declare homeschooling inconsistent with the best interests of the child, thereby undermining the right of parents to educate their children as they see

[14] See Rosemary Kayess and Phillip French, "Out of darkness into light? Introducing the Convention on the Rights of Persons with Disabilities," *Human Rights Law Review* 8 (2008), 25–6.

[15] The states' obligation is specified in Article 8(1)(a), Awareness-raising; Article 23(5), Respect for home and the family; and Article 28(1), 2(c), Adequate standard of living and social protection.

[16] See earlier section, "The debate about the role of the family in the CRPD."

[17] Luisa Blanchfield, Cynthia Brougher and James V. DeBergh, "The United Nations Convention on the Rights of Persons with Disabilities: issues in the US ratification debate," Congressional Research Service, March 2013.

fit.[18] On the other hand, supporters of the Convention, including the Obama administration, contend that existing federal, state and local laws provide adequate protection for parents to do what they believe is in the best interests of their children.

In a comprehensive paper, the National Council on Disability (NCD) compared the degree to which current US law is consistent with the CRPD.[19] The analysis of explicit and implicit articles related to family policy demonstrates the capability of implementation but also the gaps between US disability laws and the Convention.

Article 8 (Awareness raising) is a good example of the differences between US policy and the Convention. Federal government avoids regulating or mandating the media industry in creating positive imagery of people with disability or changing attitudes toward them or their families. The main argument is that the First Amendment rights relating to freedom of expression protect media outlets from being forced to broadcast particular content. This is also the case with the Individuals with Disabilities in Education Act; although it requires public schools to accommodate and integrate children with disability in public education, it does not affirmatively mandate the breakdown of social stigma relating to children with disability.

Article 16 (Freedom from exploitation, violence, and abuse) demonstrates a similar approach, claiming that the antidiscrimination law is the primary response to exploitation, violence and abuse against people with disability and their caregiving families. However, it seems that people with disability continue to be exploited or abused and that the antidiscrimination law has not been interpreted to fully prevent it, with the main obstacle appearing to be reliance on negative rights and private enforcement mechanisms. Article 16 overlooks cases where the

[18] See, for example, Michael P. Farris's response, "The UN Convention on the Rights of Persons with Disabilities: a danger to homeschool families." Accessed 5/29/2012 at http://www.hslda.org/docs/news/2012/201205250.asp.

[19] The National Council on Disability (NCD) published on May 12, 2008, a paper, titled "Finding the gaps: a comparative analysis of disability laws in the United States to the United Nations Convention on the Rights of Persons with Disabilities (CRPD), National Council on Disability." The purpose of paper was to clarify how the CRPD, if ratified by the United States, might impact US disability laws by examining the degree to which US law has been consistent with the CRPD. Accessed 2/8/2013 at http://www.ncd.gov/raw media_repository/bbae6ede_8719_48b8_b40f_33938b9a2189?document.pdf.

exploitation or abuse is perpetrated by a parent or other members of the family.

Regarding Article 22 (Respect for privacy), the ADA protection of confidentiality of medical records is one of the few per se violations of the act. Therefore, the applicable US laws on these issues appear to be administered evenhandedly, although not with any particular protections for disability.

One of the explicit articles related to family policy is probably Article 23 (Respect for home and the family). In general, state courts tend to underestimate the abilities of parents of children with disability in determining custody disputes, even in cases citing the "best interests of the child."[20] Many states do not consider parental termination proceedings to be "programs, services or activities" for the purposes of Title II of the ADA, thereby removing these proceedings from ADA protection and opening the door for disability discrimination based on stereotypes. It appears that the CRPD properly enforced US law in particular to court decisions that undermine parenting of people with disability.

The most challenging is probably Article 28 (Adequate standard of living and social protection). The ADA and the Rehabilitation Act refer to the provision of government services, including equal access to social assistance, clean water, assistive devices, public housing and retirement benefits, as long as the provision of such services does not require major change to state programs providing any of those services. However, in terms of income support schemes for children with disability and their families, the primary legislation (SSI Payment Benefits for Children with Disability) covers only low-income families, based on eligibility criteria. Other families of children with disability may benefit from tax benefits or recognized tax expenditures.

Among the most interesting implicit articles relevant to family law and policy are Article 7 (Children with disability) and Article 12 (Equal recognition before the law). The Rights of Children (Article 7) is more under the province of the states than the federal government. So, while there are laws protecting people with disability generally, and children

[20] See, for example, Susan Kerr, "The application of the Americans with Disabilities Act to the termination of the parental rights of individuals with mental disabilities," *Journal of Contemporary Health Law and Policy* 16 (2000), 402.

with disability in the school setting, there are no specific antidiscrimination laws aiming at the protection of children with disability more globally.

The ADA, the Rehabilitation Act, as well as general Constitutional principles generally prohibit discrimination against persons with disability in the provision of government services. However, the legal capacity of people with disability (Article 12) is generally under the province of state laws.

One of the historical court decisions that refers to legal capacity was the *Buck v. Bell* decision of May 2, 1927[21] in which the US Supreme Court upheld a Virginia statute that provided for the eugenic sterilization of people considered genetically unfit. The court's decision, delivered by Oliver Wendell Holmes, Jr., included the infamous phrase, "Three generations of imbeciles are enough." Upholding Virginia's sterilization statute provided the green light for similar laws in thirty states, under which an estimated 65,000 Americans were sterilized without their consent or the consent of a family member. Although Indiana passed the first eugenic sterilization statute in 1907, this and other early laws were legally flawed and did not meet the challenge of state court tests. To remedy this situation, Harry Laughlin of the Eugenics Record Office (ERO) at Cold Spring Harbor designed a model eugenic law that was reviewed by legal experts. The Virginia statute of 1924 was closely based on this model. The plaintiffs of the case, Carrie Buck and her mother Emma, had been committed to the Virginia Colony for Epileptics and Feebleminded in Lynchburg, Virginia. Carrie and Emma were both judged to be "feebleminded" and promiscuous, primarily because they had both borne children out of wedlock. Carrie's child, Vivian, was judged to be "feebleminded" at seven months of age. Hence, three generations of "imbeciles" became the "perfect" family for Virginia officials to use as a test case in favor of the eugenic sterilization law enacted in 1924. On the eve of the Virginia legal contest, the ERO dispatched its field worker, Dr. Arthur Estabrook, to provide expert testimony. After some cursory examination, Estabrook testified that the seven-month-old Vivian "showed backwardness." The superintendent

[21] *Buck vs. Bell* Supreme Court Decision, May 2, 1927. Accessed 3/7/2013 at http://www.eugenicsarchive.org/html/eugenics/static/images/260.html.

of the Virginia Colony, Dr. Albert Priddy, testified that members of the Buck family "belong to the shiftless, ignorant, and worthless class of anti-social whites of the South." Upon reviewing the case, the Supreme Court concurred "that Carrie Buck is the probable potential parent of socially inadequate offspring, likewise afflicted, that she may be sexually sterilized without detriment to her general health and that her welfare and that of society will be promoted by her sterilization."

Buck vs. Bell was flawed in many ways. "Feeblemindedness" is no longer used in medical terminology; it was clearly a catchall term that had virtually no clinical meaning. It is impossible to judge whether or not Carrie was "feebleminded" by the standards of her time, but she was not patently promiscuous. According to Carrie, Vivian's conception was the result of Carrie's rape by the nephew of her foster parents. She, probably like many unwed mothers of that time, was institutionalized to prevent further shame to the family. Just as clearly, Vivian was no imbecile. Vivian's first grade report card from the Venable School in Charlottesville showed that this daughter of a supposed social degenerate got straight As in deportment (conduct) and even made the honor roll in April 1931. She died a year later of complications following a bout of the measles. Although in 1942 the Supreme Court struck down a law allowing the involuntary sterilization of criminals, it never reversed the general concept of eugenic sterilization. It was only in 2001 that the Virginia General Assembly acknowledged that the sterilization law was based on faulty science and expressed its "profound regret over the Commonwealth's role in the eugenics movement in this country and over the damage done in the name of eugenics."

This case raises concern that persons with disability in the United States are still not accorded their full rights of legal capacity, although the ADA and Rehabilitation Acts have had the beneficial effect of extending disability antidiscrimination principles to these issues. However, more rigorous enforcement by the federal government could better ensure the implementation of these fundamental rights.

The United Kingdom

An overview of articles related to the family reveals that most of them comply with UK legislation. The only reservation that was discussed through the ratification of the Convention referred to Article 12. This was because the existing social security benefit appointee system lacked appropriate safeguards in the arrangements to enable the appointment of a person to collect and claim benefits on behalf of someone else. However, a review and a pilot demonstrate that Article 12.4 responds to these concerns.[22]

A detailed review of possible gaps between implicit articles that cover family issues reveals the following:

The UK government, it seems, supports raising awareness of the rights of people with disability and their families (Article 8) across society as a whole as an essential step toward achieving equality. A survey carried out in 2009 has shown positive signs of progress as 72 percent of the general population was aware of the DDA.[23]

Regarding Article 16 – Freedom from exploitation, violence and abuse – it seems that all people are legally protected from exploitation, violence and abuse. United Kingdom policies on hate crime, health and social care build on this by ensuring that additional safeguards are in place to protect disabled people. People with disability and families that need health or social care support want reassurance that such support is effectively regulated and that their rights will be respected. The government is committed to ensuring that safeguards are in place so that disabled people can have confidence in the system through the operation of effective regulation systems. The same applies to Article 22 – Respect to privacy – as people with disability have the same right to privacy as anyone else and are covered by Article 8 of the ECHR, the Data Protection Act (DPA) 1998, the Confidentiality Code of Practice

[22] Her Majesty's Government, Office of Disability Issues, *UK initial report on the UN Convention on the Rights of Persons with Disabilities*. The report describes how the Convention on the Rights of Persons with Disabilities (the Convention) is being implemented in the United Kingdom. Accessed 5/1/2014 at http://odi.dwp.gov.uk/docs/disabled-people-and-legislation/uk-initial-report.pdf.

[23] Office of National Statistics (ONS), *Life opportunities survey (LOS) Interim Report 9*, December 2010, was the first major social survey in Great Britain to explore disability in terms of social barriers to participation, rather than only measuring disability in terms of impairments or health conditions. In addition, the findings estimated people with rights according to the Disability Discrimination Act 1995 (DDA), *Opinions (Omnibus) survey*. Accessed 7/8/2013 at http://www.ons.gov.uk/ons/about-ons/surveys/a-z-of-surveys/opinions-survey/index.html (last accessed 26/10/2011).

and common law duty of confidentiality that applies to health-care practitioners.

Article 23 – Respect for home and the family – is fully supported by current policies, enabling people with disability to enjoy the same opportunities for family life as anyone else, and it provides a range of support for parents and children to help ensure this. The United Kingdom recognizes that the parents, families and carers of young disabled people can face challenging circumstances and may need coordinated and extra support to help ensure their well-being and that of the young person. This support is provided in a variety of ways. Across the United Kingdom, the government is providing £20 million for additional respite care for carers of severely disabled children. Up to £30 million funding was made available in 2010/2011 to support local projects developing children's palliative care services.[24] The underlying assumption is that all children, including disabled children, are best looked after by their families, unless there is reasonable cause to believe that the child is suffering, or is likely to suffer, from significant harm. The Children Act 1989 requires local authorities to meet the differing needs of children in their care and to put in place a comprehensive and regularly reviewed care plan for each child. The Care Planning, Placement and Case Review (England) 2010 Regulations, underpinned by the Children and Young Persons Act 2008, has streamlined and strengthened guidance and requirements.

Finally, Article 28 – Adequate standard of living and social protection – reflects, more than other articles, UK family-support legislation and policies. Unfortunately, regarding the social protection provisions, there are twice as many people with disability living in persistent poverty compared to nondisabled adults.[25] It appears that the DLA and the attendance allowance providing cash contribution toward disability-related extra costs are not sufficient. Although the UK government is committed to tackling poverty and has enacted the Child Poverty Act 2010, which enshrines in legislation a commitment to eradicate child

[24] Her Majesty's Government, Office of Disability Issues, *UK initial report on the UN Convention on the Rights of Persons with Disabilities*, pp. 67–8.

[25] *British household panel survey* 2005–08. Persistent poverty is defined as spending three or more years out of any four-year period in a household with below 60 percent of median household income.

poverty by 2020, children living in families with a disabled adult and children living in families with a disabled child are included among the groups disproportionately more likely to be in poverty and affected by socioeconomic disadvantage.

European countries

The EU ratified the CRPD on December 23, 2010, just weeks after the EC published the European Disability Strategy 2010–2020, which sets out a detailed program of action to empower people with disability so that they can enjoy their rights and benefit fully from participating in society and in the European economy. Although the CRPD introduces legal safeguards to overcome discrimination against persons with disability and their families, there are still gaps in implementation among European countries.

Among the core obstacles are uneven implementation of the treaty by states, uneven reach of nondiscrimination laws, lack of accessibility, outdated legal capacity systems, institutionalization that prevails in a few states without recognizing the right to live in the community, and lack of adequate standard of living and social protection.[26]

An interesting brief recommendation written by COFACE in line with the plan of European Disability Strategy 2010–2020 addressed core family policy goals:[27]

- Ensure accessibility to goods, services – including public services – and assistive devices for people with disability and their families.
- Ensure an adequate standard of living for all persons with disability and their families.
- Promote autonomy of living and inclusion in the society for all (including persons with disability and their families) and support Member States' efforts toward deinstitutionalization.

[26] *Study on challenges and good practices in the implementation of the UN Convention on the Rights of Persons with Disabilities* (VC/2008/1214), Final report for the DG Employment, Social Affairs and Equal Opportunities of the European Commission. Accessed 6/9/2013 at http://www.sabancivakfi.org/files/html/hakkimizda/konsorsiyum/executive_summary.pdf.

[27] European Commission, European Disability Strategy 2010–2020, "A renewed commitment to a barrier-free Europe," Brussels, 11/15/2010.

- Enable family carers to better balance their work and family responsibilities, in the framework of the Strategy for Equality between Women and Men 2010–2015; ensure recognition of skills and promote training of family carers.
- Take the special needs of children with disability and their families into account in the EU Strategy on the Rights of the Child, in order to prevent all forms of mistreatment or violence and promote inclusive education for students with disability.
- Ensure better access to health-care systems and that persons with disability and their families are informed about their rights by promoting information and awareness-raising campaigns.
- Address problems of mobility within the EU for persons with disability and their families and ensure their full participation in cultural life, recreation, leisure and sport.
- Legislate further on nondiscrimination, including discrimination by association.
- Make best use of EU funding instruments for accessibility and nondiscrimination for persons with disability and their families.
- Integrate the family dimension of disability among the indicators and statistics used for monitoring the situation of persons with disability with reference to key Europe 2020 targets.

However, one of the most important challenges of the EU is how to transform the principles of the CRPD into practice. Gerard Quinn and Suzanne Doyle of the National University of Ireland at Galway called for adequate use of EU Structural Funds:

> The current debate about the need to radically amend the Regulations governing the EU Structural Funds to ensure compliance with the CRPD is rightly seen as a major test of EU commitment to the convention. Those who advocate for a radical change from the past argue that, at a minimum, the Funds should no longer be used (as they once were) to build new institutions to warehouse people with disabilities and that new innovative ways of transitioning people to community living should be found using the Funds as a spur.[28]

[28] Gerard Quinn and Suzanne Doyle, "Taking the UN Convention on the Rights of Persons with Disabilities seriously: the past and future of the EU Structural Funds as a tool to

CONCLUSION

The CRPD is definitely the most important treaty concerning rights of people with disability in the twenty-first century. Although the Convention targets individuals' rights, it relates to families as an immediate environment but not as a separate entity. Therefore, there is an interesting debate over whether the CRPD is a favorable treaty that supports family rights or is just a supplement to members with disability in the family. Interestingly, the debate parallels the discussion about the centrality of family policy in most of the developed countries and those between conservatives and liberals regarding the role of the state in providing rights and services.

The most interesting debate has been around ratification of the Convention in the United States; conservative advocacy groups raised concerns that US ratification may give governments, and not US parents, the right to make educational and treatment-related decisions for their disabled children. On the other hand, the Obama administration defuses these concerns, stating that current US legislation supports parents' rights and there will not be any major change. At the center of the debate is Article 7(2) concerning the debate about protecting the best interests of the child with disability, the parent or the state, and the fear of homeschooling advocates that the Convention will undermine their parental right to educate their children.

Compared to the United States, where the debate is conceptual and relates to the conflict between domestic and international values, it seems that the CRPD fits into UK policies and current legislation, including family explicit articles. The only reservation that has been discussed through the ratification of the Convention was regarding Article 12, because the existing social security benefit appointee system lacked appropriate safeguards in the arrangements to enable the appointment of a person to collect and claim benefits on behalf of someone else. However, a further review denied these concerns, and safeguards have been put in place to prevent such incidents. The debate in the United Kingdom is about the ability of government, in light of the

achieve community living," Centre for Disability Law & Policy, National University of Ireland Galway, 2012, p. 2.

current legislation and Article 28 of the Convention, to reduce poverty in families of children with disability.

Similar to the United Kingdom, the EU also ratified the CRPD just weeks after the EC published the European Disability Strategy 2010–2020, which sets out a detailed program of action to empower people with disability so that they can enjoy their rights and benefit fully from participating in society and in the European economy. The concerns in Europe include uneven implementation of the treaty by states, the uneven reach of nondiscrimination laws, lack of accessibility, outdated legal capacity systems, institutionalization that prevails in a few states without recognizing the right to live in the community, and lack of adequate standard of living and social protection. Therefore, the most important challenge is how to transform the principles of the CRPD into practice.

9 CLOSING REMARKS

The book introduces and analyzes national and international comparative policies toward families and households of children with disability. The main conclusion is that there is lack of consensus among scholars and researchers regarding the definition, nature and scope of family policy. The book has therefore adopted a pragmatic scientific comparative approach to analyze the differences in concurrent policies between the United States and three different models of European countries (Sweden, France and the United Kingdom). In these closing remarks, I want to share with the reader central themes that reflect my insights and a future projection of family policy and disability. The first theme is an effort to provide the reader with my thoughts about the conceptual base of family policy in general and toward households of children with disability in particular. The second theme identifies the gaps between family needs as demonstrated in surveys of households and contemporary family policies. The third theme provides insights into the differences between the United States and three European policies toward families of children with disability and within European countries. The fourth theme discusses the place of the family in the CRPD, examining whether the treaty supports family rights or does so just as a supplement to members with disability in the family. Finally, the chapter projects the future of family policy toward families of children with disability in times of economic crisis, and the concern that it may increase the disparities that already exist among strong and weak economies.

THE STATUS OF FAMILY POLICY

Although the family attracts a lot of rhetoric in the public domain, family policy is not widely recognized or commonly used by policymakers or the public. In terms of social science, it has not achieved the status of a subdivision in public or social policy.[1] However, the impression is that researchers and policymakers are much more aware of its limitations. One of the weaknesses is that family policy has been conceptualized not only as an expected outcome but also as a prospective or valid tool for achieving social and tax policies.

It is difficult to define family policy in a world that is torn between individualism and communitarianism (familism) approaches. Are family policies considered as such if they affect families explicitly? What is the status of policies that are just relevant to families (implicit) but not planned to act upon the family unit? Interestingly, there is lack of consensus about the definition and boundaries of family policy, and the debate is between academic and pragmatic views.[2] If the definition is explicit, family policy is restricted to France; however, if it allows implicit policies, the definition corresponds to most of western countries; the Nordic states, such as Sweden, reflect a generous model, with the rest ranging between modest to moderate ones.

Implicit policies can address the needs of a family member and indirectly the family as such. A good example is housing policies that respond to the needs of children with disability but indirectly serve the family as a whole. There are policies that use the family household as an instrument to compensate for a disabled or sick child. This practice is common in tax policies, allowing family households to deduct medical expenditures of children with special needs.

It is evident that most of the family policies in the disability area are implicit because they compensate and support families that care for a child or member with disability. Furthermore, most of these policies recognize the family as the primary provider of care or as an instrument

[1] Karen Bogenschneider and Thomas J. Corbett, "Family policy: becoming a field of inquiry and subfield of social policy," *Journal of Marriage and Family* 72 (2010), 783–803.

[2] For further reading, see foreword by Theodora Ooms in Karen Bogenschneider, *Family policy matters: how policymaking affects families and what professionals can do*, 3rd ed. (New York: Routledge, 2014).

used to deliver cash benefits or tax deductions. However, there are differences between countries with explicit childcare family policies and those with implicit ones. In countries with explicit policies, provisions for families of children with disability are often generous, whereas in countries that adopt implicit family policies they are modest and often marginal.

In order to understand the essence of family policies in general and in the disability area in particular, it is important to adopt a comparative approach, allowing the study of countries' commitment and spending on families of children, including those with disability. An interesting typology that distinguishes among four types of policies has been offered by Daly: (a) pro-natalist and pro-family orientation countries, such as France and Belgium, linking together fertility, family and national interest; (b) countries with minor intervention in families, mainly through income transfers, such as West Germany; (c) countries in favor of redistribution and social justice such as Sweden; and (d) countries whose policies intended to reduce poverty in families, such as the United Kingdom and the United States.[3]

Following Daly's typology, as well as others, the recommendation is to gain better understanding of family policies by studying US and selected European family policies. The overall conclusion is that European policies reflect greater commitment to families than does the United States. Insights regarding the comparison between US and European policies, as well as among European countries, are discussed in these concluding comments.

THE GAP BETWEEN FAMILY NEEDS AND FAMILY POLICY

The most striking observation is the gap between evidence-based needs reported by families of children with disability and current family policies. The overall impression is that these needs attract the attention of practitioners as well as parents' advocacy groups but not policymakers.

[3] Mary Daly, "What adult worker model? A critical look at recent social policy reform in Europe from a gender and family perspective," *Social Politics* 18 (2011), 1–3.

The discrepancy is probably related to the fact that policies tend to be generic whereas family needs are specific and differential. These policies are also related to the type of social welfare policies in each country. There are definite differences between countries that offer universal and care policies (such as Sweden and France) and incremental and means-tested policies (such as the United States). Regardless of the country's policy, it seems that policies are often based on a child's medical or functional testing and assessment of family level of income and economic resources. It is clear that policies cannot respond to families of children with specific or rare disability, such as those with ASD or multiple disabilities.

Families' most evident burden is financial, and in particular the direct and indirect costs of caring for a disabled or sick child. Even if there is willingness on the part of local authorities to respond to a family's excessive costs, it is often impossible to measure the indirect monetary costs and out-of-pocket expenditures on health care; clinical, behavioral or educational services; and transportation. It is even more complicated to estimate reductions in parents' ability to sustain paid employment or the cost of unavailability of adequate childcare. These estimates vary from one country to another and are greatly dependent on explicit and implicit policies.

It is recommended that governments carry out periodic household surveys on families' needs, examining parents' complaints about inadequate and inaccessible services. Surveys, such as the national survey on families of offspring with ID/DD prepared for the ARC by the University of Minnesota, demonstrate that the number of family caregivers reporting unmet needs exceeds 40 percent.[4] The survey finds that the most met needs are education and to some degree childcare and respite, whereas the unmet needs are primarily medical, financial, housing and transportation.

Policymakers have to be responsive to families of children with ASD. These families report lack of information about available services, how

[4] 2010 *FINDS National Survey*, "Family and individual needs for disability supports," prepared for The Arc by the University of Minnesota, Research and Training, Center on Community Living, May 2011, 9–10.

to handle their children's difficult behaviors or how to teach them skills.[5] Similarly, families of children with mental health disorders experience greater economic burdens of care than those with other special health-care needs.[6] Parents often need to serve as case managers for their child and struggle for access and better coordination of services. However, the most significant challenges are experienced by families of children with CMC. They are in need of intensive hospital or community-based service requirements, rely on technology and home care, risk frequent and prolonged hospitalizations and have an ongoing need for care coordination.[7]

U.S. AND EUROPEAN POLICIES TOWARD FAMILIES OF CHILDREN WITH DISABILITY

Although comparative research in family policy is the preferred method of assessment, there is scarce data on families of children with disability, entitlements and issues of access, utilization and impact. In terms of cross-country comparative data, there is more descriptive information about recipients and entitlements than about access, utilization and impact studies. The challenge is to compare US to European policies toward families of children with disability and within European countries.

The comparative analysis reveals that the United States espouses a liberal policy, characterized by marginal government regulation of individuals, and particularly families, and respecting family values and privacy. The provision for families of children with disability is means tested, and modest cash benefits are provided to low-income families. There is debate between liberals and conservatives about government spending, the latter criticizing the growing spending on SSI, claiming that it has increased dependency. The compensation to taxpayers of

[5] See Warren Mansell and Kathleen Morris, "A survey of parents' reactions to the diagnosis of an autistic spectrum disorder by a local service: access to information and use of services," *Autism* 8 (2004), 387–407.

[6] See, for example, Susan H. Busch and Colleen L. Barry, "Mental health disorders in childhood: assessing the burden on families," *Health Affairs* 26 (2007), 1088–95.

[7] Ragendu Srivastava, Bryan L. Stone and Nancy A. Murphy,, "Hospitalist care of the medically complex child," *Pediatric Clinics of North America* 52 (2005), 1165–87.

children with disability is given through the tax system in the form of tax credits and allowed deductions. Interestingly, US tax policy has been changed from individual to household-based, using the family as an effective tool for tax credits and deductions.

In parallel, Sweden, France and the United Kingdom demonstrate two core models of policies toward families. Sweden and France are considered as having explicit family policies demonstrating universal services for young children, with additional provisions aimed toward children with disability. The United Kingdom has a set of uncoordinated family-related policies mainly targeted at the most disadvantaged and most severely affected population. The most insightful understanding of differences within these European countries is through their commitment to the idea of the welfare state. The United Kingdom adopts a liberal and conservative approach to the welfare state, France bases its policies on conservative corporatist principles, and Sweden on the social democratic welfare state.[8] The United Kingdom therefore offers mixed family policy based primarily on cash allowances (universal and means-tested) and tax benefits. Entitlements are based on functional assessments and determined by the severity of the child's medical condition or disability. The French model is universal, providing solid social insurance and infrastructure of childcare services. Families of children with disability can apply for supplemental allowances determined by the child's medical and functional assessment. Finally, Sweden has probably the most comprehensive social insurance coverage for families of young children, supporting home-based family care services. As in France, parents of children with disability can receive supplements on the basis of a child's needs assessment. However, it seems that the global economic crisis, and its impact on the EU, has shaken these progressive countries. There are government efforts, particularly in the United Kingdom and France, to reduce benefits and provisions to families in general, including those with disabled children.

In order to gain insight into the differences between countries, the book provides a detailed comparison between two central cash benefits schemes, the US SSI and the UK DLA. These programs are cash

[8] See Esping-Andersen, *Three worlds of welfare capitalism*, 9–33.

benefits provisions intended to assist families with the extra cost of caring for their children with disability. The SSI is means tested and geared toward low-income families, whereas the DLA is non–means tested and provides assistance based on severity and mobility elements. Interestingly, both are being challenged for their increased spending, particularly by conservative politicians. Swedish and French policies are based on cash benefits and family-support services, particularly during the child's early years. United Kingdom policy, which is based on a cash benefit policy, offers moderate tax credits or deductions. Interestingly, the United States, which offers cash benefits only to low-income families, is quite generous to taxpayers, allowing them to deduct medical expenses, including the cost of special diets and special education.

FAMILY ARTICLES OF THE CRPD AND FAMILY POLICY

The CRPD is considered to be the most important treaty concerning rights of people with disability in the twenty-first century and a roadmap for promoting social rights. Although the Convention primarily focuses on individuals' rights, it refers partially to families, but not as a separate entity. The general impression is that the CRPD is torn between supporting family rights and facilitating families in caring for family members with disability. The debate reflects the tension that we have noticed in the United States and the United Kingdom about explicit and implicit family policies.

It is not surprising that the ratification process in the United States has been the center of debate between conservatives and liberals about government's right to make decisions instead of families. The argument revolves around Article 7(2) concerning whether the state has the authority to interfere in family and parental responsibility toward children with disability, a concern expressed by homeschooling advocates that the Convention will undermine their parental right to educate their children. Compared to the United States, the EU ratified the CRPD just weeks after the EC published the European Disability Strategy 2010–2020. The concern in Europe is about uneven implementation of the treaty by states, the uneven reach of nondiscrimination laws, lack of accessibility, outdated legal capacity systems, institutionalization that prevails in a few states without recognizing the right to live in the community, and lack of adequate standard of living and social protection. The most important challenge, therefore, is how to transform the principles of the CRPD into practice.

THE FUTURE OF FAMILY POLICY AND DISABILITY IN TIMES OF ECONOMIC CRISIS

The economic crisis has deeply affected many public policy areas through cuts in public spending, presenting a real risk to family policies, even in the leading European countries and the United States.[9] The overall impression is that most OECD countries have avoided direct cuts to family benefits; however, the projection is that the economic crisis can have a negative direct and indirect impact on family-support programs. A recent report by Gauthier demonstrated that some countries have already implemented measures that have reduced the level of support for families by reducing the duration of payments, reducing the actual amount of benefits for some children, and making the benefits taxable.[10] There is a concern that this pattern will continue and increase the disparities that already exist among strong and weak economies in Europe.[11] There is also concern about the future of the SSI in the United States. The program that pays benefits to low-income US families of children with disability is being criticized for its increased spending. The main argument is that the program allows too many children with mild impairments to qualify for the SSI,

[9] N. Van Mechelen and J. Bradshaw, "Child poverty as a government priority: child benefit packages for working families, 1992–2009," Ive Marx and Kenneth Nelson (eds.), *Minimum income protection in flux* (New York: Palgrave Macmillan, 2013).

[10] Anne H. Gauthier, "The impact of the economic crisis on family policies in the European Union," European Commission, Directorate-General Employment, Social Affairs & Inclusion, 2010. Accessed 29/3/2014 at http://europa.eu/epic/docs/final_revised.pdf.

[11] See "The impact of the economic crisis on children: lessons from the past experiences and future policies," proceedings of the ChildONEurope Seminar on the Impact of the Economic Crisis on Children, Florence, Istitutodegli Innocenti. Accessed 29/3/2014 at http://www.childoneurope.org/issues/publications/COE%204_Impact.pdf ChildONEurope 2011.

and opponents are arguing for reform, paying benefits directly to children with severe impairments rather than providing families with cash.[12] This call is currently being rejected by the Obama administration, but the fact that Social Security is in deficit and under attack may bring change in the near future.

[12] Ron Haskins, *The SSI program for children: time for change?*, Policy brief, The Future of Children, Spring 2012.

INDEX

Accommodations, 52, 68, 69n8, 71, 74, 75n14, 76, 77, 91, 109, 112, 115, 127; private, 104; public, 62, 73, 74, 86–87, 87n31
Act Concerning Compensation for Assistance (LASS) (Sweden), 121n74
Act Concerning Support and Service for Persons with Certain Functional Impairments (Disability Reform of 1994) (LSS) (Sweden), 117, 119, 119n69, 122–123, 172
Act on Counseling for Disabled Persons (France), 112, 112n49
Act on the Prohibition of Discrimination and Other Degrading Treatment of Children and Pupils (Sweden)
ADA. *See* Americans with Disabilities Act (ADA) of 1990
Adams, Dia, 131n10
Additional Maternity Leave, 23. *See also* Maternity Leave, Ordinary Maternity Leave
ADHD (1997–2008), 37 (table)
Administration of Children and Families of the Department of Health and Human Services (United States), 68
Adoption and Children Act (UK), 94
Advance on Maintenance Payments Act (Sweden), 121n74
Affordable Care Act (ACA) of 2010 (United States), 82
Aid for Families with Dependent Children with Temporary Assistance for Needy Families (TANF) (United States), 70–71
Aiming High for Disabled Children (AHDC) (UK), 4, 102, 107, 107n39, 126, 171
Aiming high for disabled children: better support for families, 102
Allin, Sara, 42, 44
Allocations Familiales (France), 110
Allowances, adoption, 133; attendance, 151, 168n37, 169, 191; carer's, 5, 31, 32, 32n69, 119, 122, 123, 124, 127, 151, 157n15, 162, 172; cash, 149, 157, 167, 172, 201; child, 10, 14, 30, 111, 115, 122, 123, 127, 151, 169; disability, 99, 99n17; family, 14, 20, 26, 27–28, 33, 109–111, 114, 126, 151, 168; France, 26, 27–28, 29, 109–111, 151; general, 4n8, 121, 122; guardians, 24n52, 25; home care, 29; housing, 4, 14, 31, 104, 121n74; jobseekers, 26; means-tested, 27, 121, 122; Sweden, 4n8, 29, 30, 31, 32, 121, 122, 123, 124; tax, 165, 168; United Kingdom, 99, 99n17, 104, 151, 154–155 (table), 169; United States, 151, 154–155 (table)
American Community Survey (U.S. Census Bureau), 131n9
Americans with Disabilities Act (ADA) of 1990 (United States), 3, 69n8, 73–76, 76n17, 84, 86–87, 90, 187, 188, 189; 159n19; implications for children with disabilities and their parents, 74–75; Title I: Employment, 74; Title II: Public services, 74, 187; Title III: Public accommodations and commercial facilities, 74, 87, 87n31; Title IV: Telecommunications, 74; Title V: Miscellaneous, 74

Americans with Disabilities Act Amendments Act (ADAAA) of 2008 (United States), 69n8, 75–77, 84–85
America's Children in Brief: Key National Indicators of Well Being 2012, 35–36n4
Appelbaum, Eileen, 134n15
ARC (United States), 48, 56
Arlington Central School District v. Murphy, 89
Assistive Technology Act of 2004 (United States), 83
Autism, 36, 37 (table), 39, 56, 72, 83, 123, 142, 143
Autism Spectrum Disorder (ASD), 47, 54–55, 143

Balanced Budget Act of 1997 (United States), 65
Baydar, Nazli, 46
Benefits, 4, 10, 12, 26, 42, 44, 92, 128, 133; caregiving, 134; cash, 3, 5, 10, 15, 20, 22, 62, 77, 78, 89, 90, 115, 126, 133, 145, 149, 150, 151, 151n5, 152–153 (table), 154, 155, 165, 173, 174, 198, 200, 201–202; disability, 140, 145; employment-related, 12; entitlement, 83, 83n25, 84, 84n26; family, 129, 149, 150 (chart), 168, 203; France, 26, 27, 28, 92, 108, 108n41, 109, 110, 114, 115, 151, 201; in-kind, 3, 10, 19, 21, 62, 89, 148; means-tested, 23, 26, 28, 84, 90, 107, 124; parental leave, 26, 114, 126, 149n4; paternity, 30; pregnancy, 121; retirement, 183, 187; Social Security, 131; Sweden, 30, 121, 123, 124, 125, 127, 148, 149, 150, 168, 169; survivor's, 21; tax, 3, 20, 21, 62, 83, 84, 107, 128, 147, 148, 187, 201; United Kingdom, 92, 99, 107, 126, 143, 145, 147, 148, 149, 154–155 (table), 162, 165, 167, 190, 194, 201; United States, 53, 62, 68, 70, 71, 77–79, 83, 84, 85, 89, 145, 147, 148, 149, 151, 154–155 (table), 156, 158, 159, 159n19, 160, 167, 203, 204
Blindness (1997–2008), 37 (table)
Bogenschneider, Karen, 13, 17, 18
Brown, Hilary K., 55
Buck, Carrie, 188, 189
Buck, Emma, 188, 189
Buck, Vivian, 188, 189
Burkhauser, Richard V., 145–146n37, 159n19
Bush, George H. W., 73, 73n13
Bush, George W., 18, 63n3, 65

Caisse d'Allocations Familiales (CAF) (France), 112
Caisse Nationale des Allocations Familiales (National Office for Family Allocations) (CNAF) (France), 109
Capital expenditures, 64, 90
Care Allowance for Disabled Children (Sweden), 119
Carers (Equal Opportunities) Act 2004 (UK), 101, 101n22
Carers (Recognition and Services) Act 1995 (UK), 100, 100n19
Carers and Disabled Children Act 2000 (UK), 100, 100n20
Catbert (character from cartoon strip *Dilbert*), 75n14
Center for Economic and Policy Research (United States), 133, 133n15, 164n31
Center on Budget and Policy Priorities (CBPP) (United States), 160
Centers for Disease Control and Prevention (CDC) (United States), 37 (table), 81
Centres de loisirs sans hébergement (France), 112
Centres de protection maternelle et infantile (maternal and child welfare centers) (France), 114
Cerebral palsy (CP), 37 (table); 53–54; definition, 54
Child Benefit and Guardian's Allowance (UK), 24n52
Child Poverty Action Group (UK), 104
Child Tax Credit (CTC) (United States), 20, 103
Child Trends Data Bank, 35n3
Childcare Act 2006 (UK), 96, 106
Childcare and Early Education Services, Public Expenditure on (chart), 132
Childcare, 12n16, 49–50; France, 111–112, 169 (table); Sweden, 31, 118–119, 152 (table), 169 (table); spending as a percentage of GDP, 132 (chart); typology of, 169 (table); Thuringia, Germany, 136; United Kingdom, 25–26, 169 (table); United States, 169 (table)
Childhood and family life: sociodemographic changes (UK), 130n6

Childhood disabilities, cost of to families, 43n27, n30
Children Act 1989 (UK), 94n5, 191; Part III, 94, 106
Children Act 2004 (UK), 95
Children and Families Bill 2003 (UK), 97, 97n13
Children with Special Health Care Needs (CSHCN) (UK), 79
Children's Health Act of 2000 (United States), 81
Children's Health Insurance Program (CHIP) (United States), 65–66, 79n23
Children's Health Insurance Program Reauthorization Act of 2009 (United States), 66
Children's National Service Framework (NSF) (United States), 107n39
Children's plan: building brighter futures (UK) 96, 96n10; goals of, 97
Choice for parents, the best start for children: a ten-year strategy for childcare (UK), 96, 96n9
Chronic Illness and Medical Complexities (CMC), 57–58
Chronically Sick and Disabled Persons Act of 1970 (UK), 98, 98n15, 99
CLASP (Center for Law and Social Policy) (United States), 68–69n7
Classes d'Intégration Scolaire (school integration classes) (France), 113
Clearinghouse on International Developments in Child, Youth, and Family Policies (Columbia University, New York), 18–19, 18n39
Climbie, Victoris, 95, 95n8
Cohen, Eyal, 57
Combating Autism Act of 2006 (United States), 83
Combating Autism Reauthorization Act of 2011 (United States), 83
Commission des Droits et de l'Autonomie des Personnes Handicapées (CDAPH) (France), 109
Committee for the Rights and Self-dependency of Disabled Persons (CDAPH) (France), 111
Complément de Libre Choix d'Activité (Working credit) (France), 110–111
Complément de Libre Choix du Mode de Garde (Care credit) (CMG) (France), 111
Complément Optionnel de Libre Choix d'Activité (Optional working credit) (COLCA) (France), 111
Compulsory education, France, 28, 110, 112n48; Sweden, 120, 120n72; United Kingdom, 93; United States, 19, 101, 170
Condition of Education (United States), 73n12
Confederation of Family Organizations in the European Union, 175, 175–176n2
Corbett, Thomas, 18
Council on Contemporary Families (United States), 26n55
CRPD (United Nations), 2, 6, 7, 105, 105n33, 117, 175–195; articles, 176–179; consensus about the role of the family, 181–184; debate about the role of the family, 180–181; European countries and, 192–193; national family policies, 184–185; United Kingdom and, 192; United States and, 185–189
Current Population Survey (March 2010), 160n22

Daily Parental Attendance Allowance (France), 111, 115, 127
Daly, Mary, 15, 105, 145–146n37, 159n19, 198
Deficit Reduction Act (United States), 80, 81
Department for Children, Schools and Families (UK), 130n6
Dependency tax exemptions, 63, 65, 90
Developmental Disabilities Assistance and Bill of Rights Act (DD Act) (United States, 71–72; Title I, 72
Developmental disabilities in US children, 37 (table)
Dia, David A., 40, 131n10
Disability Act 2001 (UK), 101–102
Disability Discrimination Act (DDA) (UK), 101–102, 101n24, 107, 190n23
Disability in the United Kingdom 2011: Facts and figures, 36n6
Disability Living Allowance (DLA) (UK), 99, 99n17, 153 (table); compared to United States SSI, 154–155 (table), 158–161, 161 (chart)
Disability Living Allowance, Highest Rate Care Component of (UK), 104
Disability, definition, 44, 69n8, 75, 76, 79, 80, 85, 141, 156; media images of, 34n2

Disabled Persons (Services, Consultation and Representation) Act 1986 (UK), 99, 99n16
DISTAT (Disability Statistics Database), 139
Down syndrome, 39, 56, 87, 104
Doyle, Suzanne, 40
Duggan, Mark, 159–160
Duvdevany, Ilana, 59n81

Early childhood education and care (ECEC) (United States), 20
Early Head Start (United States), 68
Early Periodic Screening, Diagnosis and Treatment (EPSDT), 79
Earned Income Tax Credit (EITC) (United States), 20, 65, 65n4, 166
Écoles maternelles (France), 112, 170
Education Allowance for Disabled Child (France), 111, 115, 127
Education for All Handicapped Children Act of 1975 (United States), 3
Educational decision making, parents rights to participate in, 3, 62, 87–88, 90
Elementary and Secondary Education Act (ESEA) (United States), 67
Employment Act 2002 (UK), 98n14
Entitlement programs, 84
Equal Rights and Opportunities, Participation and Citizenship of Persons with Disabilities (France), 108–109, 116
Equal Treatment of Students at Universities Act (Sweden), 117
Equality Act 2010 (EA) (UK), 103
Esping-Andersen, Gøsta, 92, 92n1, 93 (table)
Estabrook, Arthur, 188
Ester Seals Poster Child with Polio, 46
European Agency for Development in Special Needs Education (EADSNE), 171
Eurostat (ESSPROS), 137
Every Child Matters, 95, 95n7, 96, 102, 107n39; as compared to the United States Department of Education strategy, No Child is Left Behind, 106n37
Every Disabled Child Matters (EDCM) (UK), 51

Fair Housing Act of 1968 (United States), 69–70, 69n9
Fair Housing Amendments Act (FHAA) (United States), 70
Families, 8–10; functional approach definition, 9; structural approach definition, 8–9
Family allowances, 10, 14, 109; France, 114, United States, 20
Family and Childcare Trust, 26n54
Family and Individual Needs for Disability Supports (FINDS), 56, 61n86
Family and Medical Leave Act of 1993 (United States), 19–20, 66–67, 66n6
Family Change and Family Policy, 22n43
Family Educational Rights and Privacy Act (FERPA) (United States), 69
Family leave, 19–20
Family Opportunity Act of 2006 (FOA) (United States), 80, 86
Family policy, assessment of, 128–147; children and social household circumstances, 139–141; common measures, 136–137; comparison of, 131–136, 141–142; conceptual base, 8–33; data sources, 137–138; definition, 1, 11, 14, 196, 197; dimensions of 12–14; France, 26–29; sociodemographic data, 129–131; studies of, 138–139, 142–146; Sweden, 29–32; typologies of, 14–15; United Kingdom, 22–26; United States, 16–19
Family Resources Survey (ERS) (UK), 140, 143, 162
Family to Family Health Information Centers (F2F HICs) (United States), 80
Fatherhood Institute (UK), 40n20
Federal Education Rights and Privacy Act (FERPA) (United States), 69
Federal Interagency Forum and Family Statistics (United States), 35–36n4
Federal poverty level (FPL) (United States), 36, 52, 68, 86, 130, 155 (chart). *See also*, Poverty.
Finch, Naomi, 22–23n46
Flora, Peter, 22n43
Food Stamp Program (United States), 70
France, allowances, 26, 27–28, 29, 109–111; benefits, 26, 27, 28, 92, 108, 108n41, 109, 110, 114, 115, 151, 167–168, 201; childcare, 111–112, 169 (table); education, 112–113; health care, 113–114; maternity leave, 27; parental leave, 27; policy and legislation, 108–116; respite care, 172; tax credits, 167–168, 173–174

Freeman, Richard, 134n15
Friedrich, Wanda L., 39
Friedrich, William N., 39
From Patient to Citizen (Sweden), 117–118

Gathmann, Christina, 135–136
Gender equality bonus (Sweden), 29, 32, 32n69, 169
Gender Equality Index, 134, 135 (table)
General Child Benefit Act of 1947 (Sweden), 121n74
Gilbert, Neil, 14, 16
Globalization and families: accelerated systemic social change, 10n8
Globalization, 10n8
Gornick, Janet, 133n14
Gould, Elise, 58
Grey-Thompson, Baroness, 146
Guardian's Allowance (UK), 24, 25

Halfon, Neal, 34
Head Start (United States), 68, 86, 170
Health and Medical Services Act (Sweden), 4n8, 117, 119, 119n67, 124
Health and Social Care Act 2001, Section 57 (UK), 100
Health and Social Services and Social Security Adjudications Act 1983 (United States), 101
Health Care and Education Reconciliation Act of 2010 (United States), 82
Health Care Reform Law (United States), 82
Health insurance (France), 114, 114n55
Health Resources and Services Administration (United States), 81
Hearing loss (1997–2008), 37 (table)
Helter skelter: families, disabled children and the benefit system, 162
Henneck, Rachel, 26n55
Her Majesty's Revenue and Customs (HMRC) (UK), 24, 103, 160
High Income Child Benefit (UK), 24
Holmes, Oliver Wendell, Jr., 188
Home and Community-Based Services Waiver (HCBS) (United States), 79
Home Care Allowance (Sweden), 29, 32, 32n69
Home care allowance 2008, 32n69
Housing allowances, 1, 4, 31, 122; United Kingdom, 104; Sweden, 124
Housing Benefit (HB) (UK), 104, 107
Housing entitlements, 93

ILO (Social Security Expendable Database), 137–138
Impact of disability living allowances and attendance allowance findings from exploratory qualitative research, 163n29
Individualized Education Program (IEP), 71, 88, 171
Individualized Family Service Plan (IFSP), 73
Individuals with Disabilities Education Act (IDEA) (United States), 3, 68, 69n8, 72, 73, 84, 88, 89, 90, 171; Part B: Assistance for Education of All Children with Disability, 72; Part C: Infants and Toddlers with Disabilities, 72–73
Inkelas, Moria, 47
Institut National d'Études Démographiques (INED) (France), 134
Institute for Public Policy Research (IPPR) 2007: Disability 2020 (UK), 36n7
Intellectual disability (1997–2008), 37 (table)
Intellectual disability and developmental disability (ID/DD), 48, 49, 55–56

Joseph Rowntree Foundation (JRF), 51

Kahn, Alfred J., 1, 22n43
Kamerman, Sheila B., 1, 11, 22, 22n43
Kaufmann, Franz X., 15
Kim, Sue E., 47
Korpi, Walter, 138
Kouao, Marie Therese, 95n8

Laming, William Herbert (Lord), 95, 95n8
Land, Hilary, 22
Larimer v. IBM, 75n14, 87, 87n32, 90n40
Laughlin, Harry, 188
Learning disability (1997–2008), 37 (table)
Lewis, Jane, 22–23
Lifespan Respite Care Act of 2006 (United States), 82
Lindquist, Rafael, 124
Local Housing Allowance (LHA) (UK), 104
Loci, Angela, 134
Lukemeyer, Anna, 47

Maison départementale des personnes handicapées (MDPH) (France), 109n43
Manning, Carl, 95n8
Marital relations, 39–40, 60

Maternal and Child Health Bureau (MCHB) (United States), 79, 80
Maternity leave, 16n31, 129; France, 27; United Kingdom, 23; United States, 19. *See also* Additional Maternity Leave, Ordinary Maternity Leave.
Mather, Mark, 131n9, n10
McManus, Margaret A., 47
Medicaid (United States), 3, 65, 79–80, 81, 82, 86, 90, 143, 159, 166, 173
Medicaid Managed Care (MMC) (United States), 143–144
Medical expenses, 47, 58, 63–64, 167, 174, 202
Mental health disorders (Mental illness), 34, 36, 38, 58, 200
Mental retardation, 37 (table), 59n81, 72
Meyers, Marcia K., 47
Miller, George, 76n16
Moen, Phyllis, 11
Monteith, Marina, 162, 163
Murphy v. United Parcel Service, Inc., 76n17

National Center on Birth Defects and Developmental Disabilities (United States), 81
National contexts affecting the lives of disabled children in Denmark, France, Germany, Ireland, Italy, Sweden and UK, Volume 2, 151n6
National Dissemination Center for Children with Disability (NICHCY) (United States), 41
National Health Service (NHS) (United States), 93
National Institutes of Health (United States), 81
National Lifespan Respite Resource Center (United States), 82
National Service Framework for Children, Young People and Maternity Services and Aiming High for Disabled Children (UK), 171
National Survey of America's Families (1999) (United States), 43
National Survey of Children with Special Health Care Needs (NS-CSHCN) (2001) (United States), 43, 142
Neely-Barnes, Susan L., 40
Newachek, Paul W., 47
No Child Left Behind Act (NCLB) (United States), 67, 87–88, 106n37
Nutrition, 70

Obama, Barack, 6, 18, 47, 66, 185, 186, 194, 204
OECD, 5, 128, 128n1, 133, 136, 137, 138, 139, 140, 141, 147, 149, 149n3, 150, 151, 164, 171, 182, 203
OECD Family Database, 132–133n12, n13, 138
OECD Social Expenditure Database, 138n23, 149n4
OECD-Family Policy Index, 136
Office for Standards in Education, Children's Services and Skills (OFSTED) (UK), 25, 25n53
Office of Head Start (United States), 68
Ohio Family Health Survey (2008) (United States), 142–143
Ooms, Theodora, 9
Ordinary Maternity Leave, 23, 23n51; *See also* Maternity leave, Additional Maternity Leave
Ordinary Paternity Leave, 23, 23n51
Organisation for Economic Co-operation and Development. *See* OECD
Orientation Law in Favor of Disabled People (Loi d'Orientation en Faveur des Personnes Handicapées) (France), 108, 108n41
Oxford handbook of the welfare state, 132n11

Parental involvement, 85, 171, definition, 88n33
Parental leave, 10, 23, 98, 129, 133, 134, 135 (table); France, 26, 27, 114, 126, 135 (table); Japan, 183n13; Sweden, 30, 32, 169
Parental responsibility, 94, 100, 202; definition, 94
Parish, Susan L., 43, 44
Patient Protection and Affordable Care Act (2010) (United States), 65, 82
People with traumatic brain injuries (PATBI), 81
Persistent poverty, definition, 191n25
Personal Independence Payment (PIP) (UK), 99, 99n18, 153–154 (table)
Personal Independence Payment, Enhanced Daily Living Component of (UK), 104

Personal Responsibility and Work Opportunity Reconciliation Act of 1996. *See* Welfare Reform Act
Policy Institute for Family Impact Seminar (United States), 14n24
Poverty, 16, 18, 21, 22, 68, 76, 86, 103, 104, 130n8, 131, 140, 141 (table), 142, 145, 155, 156, 160, 163, 164, 178, 179n9, 183, 191, 191n25, 195, 198; child, 96, 106, 162–163, 166, 191–192. *See also,* Federal poverty line.
Povich, Deborah, 131n9
Prestation d'Accueil du Je (France), 110
Prestation de compensation du handicap (PCH) (France), 109
Preston, Gabrielle, 162
Priddy, Albert, 189
Prohibition of Discrimination Act (Sweden), 117
Prohibition of Discrimination and Other Degrading Treatment of Children and Pupils Sweden, 117
Prohibition of Discrimination in Working Life of People with Disability Act (Sweden), 117
Projects of National Significance (United States), 72
Protection and Advocacy (P&A) Systems, 72, 81
Public Health Service Act, Title XXIX (United States), 82, 172, 172n45

Quinn, Gerard, 193

Reconciliation Act of 2010 (United States), 66, 66n5
Rehabilitation Act of 1973 (Section 504) (United States), 69, 69n8, 71, 75
Relative aux Institutions Sociales et Médicosociales (France), 108n41
Removing Barriers to Achievement, 102, 102n25
Respite care, 49, 49–51, 54, 55, 56, 57, 59, 80, 82; cross-country comparisons of, 172–173, 178, 183, 191; definition, 50; France, 172, United Kingdom, 172, United States, 172–173
Richard Gorry v. (1) Wiltshire Council (2) Secretary of State for Work and Pensions, 104, 104n30
Riddell, Sheila, 171–172n43
Rimmerman, Arie, 59n81
Roberts, Brandon, 131n9

Sass, Björn, 135
Schaffer v. Weast, 88
Schettini Kearney, Melissa, 159–160
Schorr, Alvin L., 11
Sécurité Sociale (France), 113, 113n53
Seizures (1997–2008) (table), 37
Service d'Éducation Spéciale et de Soins à Domicile (Special education and home care service) (France), 113
Smeeding, Timothy M., 47
Social Citizenship Indicator Programme (SCIP) (Sweden), 138
Social Insurance Act, (Sweden), 121n74
Social Insurance in Sweden, 30n66
Social Security Act (United States), Title V, 80–81; Title XVI, 77; Title XIX, 79, 79n22, 173; Title XXI, 65
Social Security System, France, 28, 113, 114, 115; UK, 93
Social Services Act 1982 (Sweden), 4n8, 117, 121n74, 124
Solow, Robert, 134n15
Special Educational Needs (SEN) (UK), 98, 101, 102n25
Special Educational Needs and Disability Act 2001 (United States), 102
Special needs, definition, 79
SSI (United States), 3, 5, 21, 68, 77–79, 85, 90, 145, 151, 153 (table), 154, 156, 156n11, 157, 158 (graph), 164, 166, 173, 174, 187, 200, 201, 202, 203;
compared to UK Disability Living Allowance, 154–155 (table), 158–161
Stabile, Mark, 42
State Children's Health Insurance Program (SCHIP) (United States), 65
State Councils on Developmental Disabilities (United States), 72
Statutory Maternity Leave (UK), 23, 23n49
Steiner, Gilbert, 14
Stiglitz, Joseph, 134n15
Still in the shadows with their future uncertain on family and individual needs for disability support (United States), 56n71
Strach, Patricia, 9
Student financial aid, 12n16
Stuttering (1997–2008) (table), 37
Sullivan v. Zebley, 156, 156n11, 158

Supplemental Nutrition Assistance Program (SNAP) (United States), 70
Supplemental Poverty Measure (SPM) (United States), 130n8
Supplemental Security Income (United States). *See* SSI
Sure Start Maternity Grant (UK), 23, 23n50
Survey of Income and Program Partisipation (SIPP), 145
Sutton v. United Airlines, Inc., 75n15, 76n17
Sweden, benefits, 30, 121, 123, 124, 125, 127, 148, 149, 150, 168, 169; childcare, 31, 118–119, 152 (table), 169 (table); compulsory education, 120, 120n72; gender equality bonus, 29, 32, 32n69, 169; home care allowance, 29, 32, 32n6; home allowances, 124; parental leave, 30, 32, 169; tax credits, 168–169
Swedish Educational Act of 1985 (Swedish Education Law), 118, 120, 120n72
Swedish Personal Assistance Act, 125, 127

Tax credits, 5, 15, 20, 22, 23; France, 167–168, 173–174; Sweden, 168–169; United Kingdom, 25, 103–104, 166, 167; United States, 20, 65, 65n4, 103, 166; United States as compared to the UK, 165–167
Tax deductions for domestic service work (Sweden), 31n68
Tax Equity and Fiscal Responsibility Act (TEFRA) of 1982 (United States), 80
Tax versus means-tested entitlements, 83–86
Temporary Assistance for Needy Families (TANF) (United States), 21, 68, 70
Thévenon, Oliver, 134, 137
Three worlds of welfare capitalisam, 149
Toyota Motor Manufacturing v. Williams, 75n15
Tramatic brain injuries (PATBI), 81
Transportation, 36n6, 42, 48, 49, 50, 53, 56, 61, 64, 74, 79, 98, 120, 131, 199
Trask, Bahira Sherif, 10n8
Tsimicalis, Argerie, 47

United Kingdom, 22–26; benefits, 92, 99, 107, 126, 143, 145, 147, 148, 149, 154–155 (table), 162, 165, 167 190, 194, 201; childcare, 25–26, 169 (table); compared to the United States, 150–167; compulsory education, 93; CRPD and, 192; guardian's allowance, 24, 25; housing allowances, 124; maternity leave, 23; policy and legislation toward families of children with disability; 93–104; tax credits, 25, 103–104. 166, 167
United Nations Convention of the Rights of Persons with Disabilities. *See* CRPD
United States, allowances, 151, 154–155 (table); benefits, 53, 62, 68, 70, 71, 77–79, 83, 84, 85, 89, 145, 147, 148, 149, 151, 154–155 (table), 156, 158, 159, 159n19, 160, 167, 203, 204; childcare, 169 (table); compared to the United Kingdom, 150–167; CRPD and, 185–189; disability policies and laws, 71–83; education, 67–69; family leave in, 19–20, 134; family policy in, 16–19; health, 67; housing, 69–70; maternity leave, 19; nutrition, 70–71; tax credits, 20, 65, 65n4, 103, 166
United States Supreme Court, 75, 76–77, 76n17, 88, 156, 158, 188, 188n21, 189
University Centers for Excellence in Developmental Disabilities (United States), 72
Urban Institute-Brookings Institution Tax Policy Center (United States), 84
US Department of Labor, Wage and Hour Division, 67

Washington v. Illinois Department of Revenue, 75n14, 87, 87n32, 90n40
Welfare reform, 70–71, 157, 158
Welfare Reform Act (UK), 71
Welfare Reform Act 2012 (UK), 99, 164–165
Working Families Tax Act of 2004 (United States), 63, 63n3
Working parents, recognized rights of, 62, 86–87, 90
Working Poor Families Project (WPFP) (United States), 131n9
Working Tax Credit (WTC) (UK), 25, 166, 167

Van Voorhis, Rebecca A., 16

Yankelovich, Daniel, 16

Lightning Source UK Ltd.
Milton Keynes UK
UKOW04n2315300115

245435UK00002B/18/P

9 781107 049178